Judith Stone and Felicity Taylor

The Parent's Schoolbook

Penguin Books

Penguin Books Ltd,
Harmondsworth, Middlesex, England
Penguin Books,
625 Madison Avenue, New York, New York 10022, U.S.A.
Penguin Books Australia Ltd,
Ringwood, Victoria, Australia
Penguin Books Canada Ltd,
41 Steelcase Road West, Markham, Ontario, Canada
Penguin Books (N.Z.) Ltd,
182–190 Wairau Road, Auckland 10, New Zealand

First published 1976
Copyright © Judith Stone and Felicity Taylor, 1976

Made and printed in Great Britain by
Cox & Wyman Ltd, London, Reading and Fakenham
Set in Monotype Times

Pelican Books
The Parent's Schoolbook

Judith Stone and Felicity Taylor between them have experience of every type of school either as pupils, teachers, parents or governors. Graduates of St Hilda's College, Oxford, they read different subjects and were not there at the same time. After she left Oxford, Mrs Stone trained as a Froebel teacher and taught for a time at a primary school in Paddington. Mrs Taylor worked in the training department of the British Iron and Steel Federation.

They met on the committee of the Camden Campaign for the Advancement of State Education. Mrs Stone is a member of the government committee of inquiry into school governors. Their first joint publication was a parent's guide to the ILEA's scheme for transferring children to secondary schools, produced for CASE committee. Since then they have been regular contributors to *Where* magazine and have also written on educational topics for a number of newspapers including the *Sunday Times* and the *Observer*.

To our families, but for
whom this book would never
have been written and without
whom it would have been
written in half the time

Contents

Introduction

The Parent's Schoolbook does not tell parents how to bring up their children and it does not tell teachers how to teach them.

Everyone wants the best possible education system. Teachers, education officers and politicians are all equipped with the means to fight for what they want: unions, political parties, professional knowledge and expertise, legal advice, money and resources. But what about the $8\frac{1}{2}$ million ordinary children in state schools and their parents? They have no union, no resources and little knowledge and expertise about how the system works. Yet parents have a unique contribution to make because they are looking at the system with a unique perspective. For a politician the horizon is the date of the next election which may be three or five years away. For an administrator the horizon may be the next budget or planning schedule. But parents have a much more stringent time-scale. If they have to wait two or three years their child has missed out on some vital part of infant schooling; a four-year wait and junior schooling is lost; another five-year programme postponed and the child has left school altogether.

More than forty years ago. R. H. Tawney wrote:

> The capital fact about English educational policy is that it has been made by men, few, if any, of whom themselves attended the schools principally affected by it, or would dream of allowing their children to attend them. In such circumstances it is not surprising that they should grudge expenditure upon it . . . As a society sows, so in the long run it reaps. If its schools are sordid will its life be generous? . . . What a wise parent would desire for his own children, that a nation, in so far as it is wise, must desire for all children.

If the people who are responsible for educational policy do not send their children to the schools principally affected by it, then the people whose children *do* go to those schools must be given a voice in policy-making. Then the views, experience, energy and goodwill of all those parents, all wanting the best education for their

children, could provide the steam-power to drive the state education system forward, instead of condensing into a cold shower of
apathy and antipathy as it so often does now. This is a reference
book for parents, like ourselves, of children in state schools in
England and Wales.

We started writing for parents about the education system in
1971. Since then we have had the chance to talk to parents throughout the country to find out what they want to know. The Americans
invented the expression 'passing the buck' but parents find that
the art has been perfected in the English educational system. All
the people involved – the headteacher, the governors, the local
education authority, the Department of Education and Science –
can quite truthfully say, whatever they are asked, 'It's not entirely
up to me.' But the buck must stop somewhere and the problem for
parents is to find out where. *The Parent's Schoolbook* sets out to
tell them.

Part One explains the legal framework within which decisions
are made; where the power and responsibility rests for everything
from **Admissions** to **Work experience**. Seventy-six major topics are
covered. We have tried to identify them by the generic name most
people will recognize. So each genus will have many species. For
instance, **Admissions** discusses Admission to Primary School, Admission to Secondary School and Registration. The sub-heading
Admission to Secondary School includes, in turn, Selection: the
Eleven-Plus and Non-selective Systems. **Choice of school** includes,
among other topics, Zoning and Appeals. Never assume a topic is
not covered because it is not listed in the Contents; it is essential
to make good use of the Index if you are looking for a minor
species.

Part One concentrates on telling you where and why decisions
are made; Part Two tells you how these decision-making organizations work so that you know what you are up against in trying
to get things changed. It also suggests techniques for mobilizing
the resources needed to put things right when they have gone
wrong.

Our own experience has suggested the questions but the answers
have come from the most authoritative sources we could find. In
particular, we have made heavy demands on the patience and ex-

pertise of the officers of the Department of Education and Science, the Inner London Education Authority and the National Union of Teachers. Although we are indebted to them they are not responsible for our interpretation of their opinions. Time and again they have told us that education law is a minefield strewn with uncertainties, gaps and conflicts. Court cases clarify the law, but of the twenty or so to which we have referred, most are to do with a child being hurt on purpose (by corporal punishment) or by mistake (through negligence). Few parents are prepared to make their child the focus of a court case for the sake of a principle. One friendly DES officer told us 'We have to rely on the "best guess" our legal advisors can arrive at.' So, where no clear interpretation of the law has been made in the courts, we have asked the experts for their 'best guess' and then given you our own.

Judith Stone and Felicity Taylor
February 1976

We have used 'he' as an abbreviation for 'he or she'. Other abbreviations used throughout the book are:

ACE Advisory Centre for Education
DES Department of Education and Science
DHSS Department of Health and Social Security
HMI Her Majesty's Inspector
HMSO Her Majesty's Stationery Office
LEA Local Education Authority
ILEA Inner London Education Authority
NAS National Association of Schoolmasters
NUT National Union of Teachers
TES *Times Educational Supplement*

Some of the examples in the text refer to LEAs by the names by which they were known before the reorganization of local government.

Admissions

Do parents choose schools or do schools choose children? The question does not matter unless there are not enough places in a school for all the people who want to go there. And then the answer becomes clear: whoever is responsible for admissions to the school chooses the pupils for the school. Parents can choose only whether to say 'yes' or 'no' to the place which is offered to their child.

The section on **Choice of school** discusses parents' rights in getting a place at any particular school, and how to appeal when a child does not get the place the parents want.

The LEA decides on the procedure for admitting children to county schools, including the age at which children may start at any type of school. Headteachers may be consulted and routine admissions may be delegated to them, but control always remains with the LEA. The heads of Inner London county secondary schools used to select their own pupils within guidelines laid down by the authority. In 1972, the ILEA decided that in future their Divisional Officers would allocate children to secondary school. Although the heads felt particularly bitter about this (partly because heads of voluntary secondary schools continued to interview and select their own pupils) they were unable to prevent the authority from taking back the function which had previously been delegated to them.

The Model Articles for voluntary schools suggest that the governors should be responsible for the admission of pupils. If a voluntary school has reached an agreement with the LEA as to how to organize their admissions, then the school must act in accordance with the agreement. According to *County and Voluntary Schools** this agreement may cover such things as zoning so as to define the areas to be served by aided schools of each denomination or, in the case of a selective school, provisions by which the

* Alexander, W., and Barraclough, F., Councils and Education Press Ltd, 4th edn, 1967.

LEA can be satisfied about the educational standards of the pupils to be admitted. In practice, if the governors and the LEA fail to agree on any arrangements, the DES has said that they would support the governors' right to retain full control over admissions, provided that their arrangements were regarded by the Secretary of State as reasonable. Admissions are probably done by the head-teacher, but he is always answerable to the governors. The right of voluntary schools to select their own pupils is often incorporated in the articles of government because it appeared eminently reason-able for church schools to insist on having pupils belonging to their own sect. It was not predicted, however, that non-denominational charitable foundations, as well as church schools, would use these rights to continue to select pupils by academic attainment when the LEA was committed to ending the eleven-plus.

Admissions to Primary School

The headteachers of primary or first schools are nearly always in charge of admissions. Admission lists are often prepared in the early spring for the large intake of children in September.

If the LEA permits, the headteacher may decide to plan ahead for admissions by keeping a waiting list, including the names of babies a few months old. Parents should not take it for granted that they are automatically guaranteed a place just because their child's name was once put on the waiting list or that a new head will feel that he has to honour any promises made by his predecessors.

A child who is five in March is legally entitled to a place for the summer term in April (see **Compulsory school age**). Parents can insist on being given a place then, but they cannot insist on a par-ticular school. They may have to face the prospect of going to another school in order to start in the summer term instead of waiting till September when the child will be five and a half for a place at the school they really want.

ADMISSIONS TO JUNIOR AND MIDDLE SCHOOL

Most infant and junior schools are linked in some way. In many cases they are combined with one headteacher in charge of the whole primary school age range. Some schools share the same building but have different headteachers in charge of the infants and juniors. However the different departments are organized, any child who enters the infants automatically has a place reserved for them in the juniors and it is assumed that they will move on from one to the other. This also applies to areas where there is a system of first and middle schools. If a parent wants to 'opt out' when everyone is moving on, their child will normally be able to transfer to a different junior or middle school which has room for them.

Admissions to Secondary School

In areas where there are still schools which select pupils by ability, children have to go through some kind of selection procedure. So much is certain. But the clear divide between primary education and its methods and organization and secondary education with a more formal curriculum has been blurred by the introduction of a bewildering variety of schemes for organizing secondary schools. There are middle schools which may cater for 8 to 12 year olds in one area, 9 to 13 or 10 to 14 year olds in others; intermediate or lower secondary schools from 11 to 13 years with upper schools for 14 years upwards; lower secondary from 11 to 16 combined with sixth form colleges for 16+. The names and the age ranges vary and the procedures for entry vary even more. However, it seems likely that at least half the children in the country still move on to secondary school when they are eleven and, in spite of all the publicity for parents angry because the system denies them the school place they wanted, two thirds of all comprehensive schools acquire their new pupils each year as a matter of routine from feeder schools or from the children living in the school's catchment area.

A Bill was introduced into the House of Commons in the 1975–6 parliamentary session which said that 'Local Authorities shall in the exercise and performance of their powers and duties relating to secondary education have regard to the general principle that such education is to be provided only in schools where the arrangements for the admission of pupils are not based wholly or partly on selection by reference to ability or aptitude.'

SELECTION: THE ELEVEN-PLUS

Some authorities still carry out the old eleven-plus examination throughout their area or in some parts of it. The name 'eleven-plus' refers to the age of the children when they start at secondary school, not their age when they sit the exam several months earlier. Children take an exam based on intelligence tests and this is usually combined with a headteacher's report. The 'top' children are offered places at selective schools. A survey carried out by *The Times Educational Supplement* in March 1975 estimated that 25 per cent of children in England and Wales were still sitting eleven-plus exams.

New forms of eleven-plus, disguised under a less emotive name, have evolved in areas where some schools are called comprehensive even though local grammar and secondary moderns coexist with them. They often masquerade as 'guided parental choice'.

NON-SELECTIVE SYSTEMS

Even in a fully comprehensive system there still has to be a method of getting thousands of children into secondary schools. LEAs have devised a variety of ways of doing this.

Feeder schools. In this system several primary schools are linked to one middle or secondary school and virtually all the pupils automatically move on together in the same way as they usually progress from infant to junior school or from first to middle school.

Catchment areas. The authority draws a catchment area around each school – sometimes an extraordinary shape on the map – and allocates all the children in each area to a particular school.

Guided parental choice. The primary school head or the authority suggest to parents which school would be the most suitable, then parents make their choice. Children will usually be tested during the course of ordinary school work and will also be assessed and graded by headteachers. Although this kind of scheme has the merit of taking a child's whole school career into account, it lacks the objectivity of the externally administered eleven-plus exam, and it is open to abuse, or the suspicion of abuse. After competitive selection 'guided parental choice' offers more scope for conflict between the authority and parents who have been refused a place at their first choice of school than any of the other systems. At least with a catchment area they know where they live and which school their child can attend.

In Inner London there is a guided choice system. This is what London parents have to take into account when they exercise this choice: children are graded into three bands of ability by the primary school head and places at comprehensive schools are allocated in order to achieve a 'balance of ability', that is to say, a fair share of children from each band for each school. Siblings get priority; then, within the scope of the quota for each band, places are allocated according to geographical nearness to the school. Keeping groups of primary schoolchildren together and special medical and social reasons are also taken into account. What this means in practice is that parents have to make a whole lot of assumptions about the likelihood of getting a place at the school they prefer – assumptions related to the popularity of the school, whether it is more popular for boys than girls, how many brothers and sisters of older children will take up places, whether it is likely to be oversubscribed in their child's ability band and whether they live near enough to be sure of a place. With so many qualifications guided parental choice is in fact no choice, it is at best the expression of a preference – a right that can lead to bitterness and disappointment if the preference is not satisfied.

Registration

When can parents be sure of their child's place at a school? A child does not legally become a pupil of a school until his name is entered in the Admissions Register. All schools, including independent schools, are required by law to keep proper registers. The governors of the school are held legally responsible for making sure that registers are accurately kept and HMIs and LEA officers have the right to inspect them. Any person who fails to comply with the Registration Regulations can be fined up to £10.

The register is filled in on the first day of the first term. Parents are asked to take along their child's birth certificate to confirm his age (see **Compulsory school age**).

Parents who have been relying on getting a place at a school and have been refused at the last minute have to appeal by the methods set out under **Choice of school**. Once the child has been registered as a pupil of the school it is in a different situation. When the name of a child of compulsory school age is safely on the register, the school can exclude him only under the conditions set out by DES regulations (see **Suspension, Expulsion**).

Attendance

Practically every phrase in Section 36 of the 1944 Education Act has needed a Chief Justice to interpret precisely what it means. The only point which has not had to be clarified is that it is the parent's responsibility to make sure that a child is educated. The complete text sounds straightforward enough: 'It shall be the duty of the parent of every child of compulsory school age to cause him to receive efficient full-time education suitable to his age ability and aptitude either by regular attendance at school or otherwise.' But that leaves wide open the questions: What is full-time education? What is attendance at school? What is 'otherwise'? The answers to these questions have had to be found in the law courts.

What is a School?

A school is any institution providing primary or secondary education. It may be maintained by an LEA on a county or voluntary basis; an independent school; a direct grant school. The laws concerning attendance at school apply to every kind of school.

What is a Full-time Education?

A child is not having a full-time education within the terms of the Education Act unless he arrives in school by the time the register is called and stays there all day. In 1961 the father of a boy who was repeatedly marked absent was taken to court charged with failing to see that his son had a full-time education. At the Appeal, Chief Justice Parker said 'even if this boy had regularly arrived only a minute or two late . . . there would be a failure to attend regularly within the meaning of the Act' (Hinchley v. Rankin).

Strictly speaking, it is breaking the law to take a child out of school for as little as one hour a week for private lessons. Parents can opt out of school altogether (if they provide an alternative education) but they cannot pick and choose from what the school provides. Although the case which established this was heard in 1927, the legal principle stated then by the Chief Justice still applies:

It was never intended that a child attending the school might be withdrawn for this or that hour to attend the lesson thought by the parent to be more useful or possibly in the long run more remunerative. The time-table and discipline of the school could be reduced to chaos if that were permissible (Osborne v. Martin).

British children start full-time schooling younger than in almost any other country. For some five-year-olds – particularly those who have not been to a nursery school or play-group – a whole day at school can be too much to cope with at first. Some infant head-teachers find that more flexible arrangements – such as working a half day – help the children to settle in better. This is theoretically illegal for children who are over compulsory school age, but most LEAs turn a blind eye.

What is Attendance at School?

In legal terms a parent has not caused his child to receive an education by presenting him at the school gate. He has not fulfilled his duty unless he is sure that the child will be allowed in to lessons. A parent is legally responsible when his child is refused admission by the school as long as the school is acting reasonably in the eyes of the law. In 1922 a twelve-year-old girl refused to have a compulsory medical inspection and the school would not let her in until she agreed to have it. She made a number of attempts to come back into school. In due course her father appeared in court. His defence was that he *had* sent her to school and it was the school which was responsible for not letting her go to lessons. He lost his case because he knew that she would not be allowed in when he sent her to school without having the medical (Fox v. Burgess).

Schools which make rules about pupils' clothes or hair may refuse to allow children into school who are not dressed in the approved style or because their hair is too long or, ironically, too short (see **Uniform**).

What is a Good Excuse for a Child being off School?

Parents are not breaking the law every time their child misses a day's school as long as they have either been given permission by someone with authority to give it or can produce one of the reasons allowed by Section 39 of the 1944 Education Act. These are the excuses allowed by the Act:

SICKNESS

No one expects a child to go to school if he is ill or infectious. Parents are normally asked to send a note giving the reason when a child has been off school. A doctor's certificate is not required by law and the DES have said they would not support any school or LEA which tried to make it compulsory for pupils.

'UNAVOIDABLE CAUSE'

Although the Education Act concedes that it is legitimate for a child to miss school for 'any unavoidable cause', very few causes for staying off school are literally unavoidable. Most schools will accept a cause which is merely reasonable, such as a family celebration, as long as it does not happen too often. When a child has missed a significant amount of school, 'reasonable' is not good enough – the law requires the cause to be unavoidable *in relation to the child*. In other words, an unavoidable cause which really affects the family and not the child will not do unless it is an emergency. In 1949 Mrs Hannah Howells was taken to court because her fourteen-year-old daughter had missed 225 out of 390 school sessions. Mrs Howells was in very poor health and had had a chronic heart condition for several years. Her daughter was the only person able to do household duties for the family. Although the court was sympathetic and described the case as 'distressing', their conclusion was that 'the alleged "unavoidable cause" in the present case was one which really affected the mother and not the child' (Jenkins v. Howells).

Long before that in 1919 it was decided that children should not miss school to look after younger brothers and sisters at home while the parents were at work. Families can suffer from stress and hardship because older children who could help out have to go to school. But this is the consequence of recognizing the principle that every child, however difficult their home circumstances, should have the same right to education.

RELIGIOUS OBSERVANCE

Children are allowed to stay at home on any days 'exclusively set apart for religious observance' by their church. Jewish and Roman Catholic children can do quite well out of this, but school holidays are already planned around the Church of England religious festivals, so the only extra holiday Anglicans can claim is Ascension Day.

TRANSPORT

Under certain circumstances the LEA has a legal obligation to provide transport for children to get to school (see **Transport**). If the LEA fails in its duty a parent cannot be prosecuted because the child is not in school.

Sometimes the journey is so difficult that it is impracticable for a child to get to and fro each day. In that case it is up to the LEA to find somewhere for the child to live in suitable 'digs' near by or to board at the school itself. If they fail to make proper arrangements the parent will not be legally responsible for the fact that a child is not going to school.

CLEANLINESS

If a child has been excluded from school because he has nits or some other form of infestation, provided the parents have applied to the LEA to make arrangements for cleansing they cannot be prosecuted for keeping the child at home, however long they have to wait for an appointment (see **Health**).

ENTERTAINMENT LICENCE

Children of compulsory school age cannot have time off school to take part regularly and professionally in plays, films, TV shows or other entertainments unless they have a licence from the LEA. A licence is not necessary for the occasional charity show or the school play. The licence will specify the times when a child may be absent from school and will not be granted unless the LEA is satisfied that proper arrangements are being made for the child's education and welfare. HMSO publishes *The Law on Performances by Children* which is a guide to all the national regulations which have to be observed. The LEA may make additional regulations of its own.

What is 'Otherwise'?

When the Education Act stipulates 'efficient full-time education' in Section 36, it says that this can be achieved 'either by regular attendance at school or otherwise'. Parents must decide which method they are going to adopt – school or otherwise – and be consistent.

No one disputes a parent's right to educate their child at home either themselves or by employing a teacher, provided that they can demonstrate that the education is 'efficient'. The local education authority will want some kind of proof – samples of work, lists of books which have been read – as well as evidence that the teaching is systematically organized. The most famous case on this issue is that of Mrs Joy Baker whose dispute over her children's teaching dragged on for ten years before she finally won. The point in dispute was not her right to opt out of school but whether or not the education she was giving her children was efficient. She refused to provide the LEA with the kind of evidence they wanted about her teaching scheme for the children.

Children's Rights Workshop produce 'Education otherwise than at School – notes for parents' (duplicated).*

* Available from 73 Balfour Street, London SE17.

Attendance Orders

The LEA has to make sure that parents carry out their duty to see that their children are educated. A child who is a registered pupil at a school but fails to attend for long periods at a time or frequently misses odd days or sessions is dealt with as a truant (see **Truancy**).

Some children do not get as far as being registered as pupils with any school. The Education Act lays down a detailed procedure to be followed, if the child does not appear to be getting a satisfactory education in any other way.

Chart 1 summarizes the differences between the procedure which would be followed where the child was registered at a school and was failing to attend and where the child was not registered at a school at all. Chart 2 sets out the procedures involved in the issue of School Attendance Orders.

A Child who is not Registered at a School

These procedures would be used differently by parents according to their reason for keeping the child away from school. Their reason might be:

wanting to educate the child at home;

wanting the child to go to a particular school, where he has been refused a place;

refusing to send the child to the school where the LEA has given him a place except 'over my dead body';

holding the view that all education is a waste of time.

1. THE PARENT WHO WANTS TO EDUCATE HIS CHILD AT HOME

The legal right of parents to make this choice has been explained above. This parent will not be involved in Attendance Order proceedings unless he has failed to convince the LEA that he is giving his child a satisfactory education at home. Stage 2 on Chart 2 – the issuing of a notice to parents – shows that the LEA is not satisfied with the child's education. A parent in this situation would not respond to either statutory notice and in due course will find him-

CHART 1

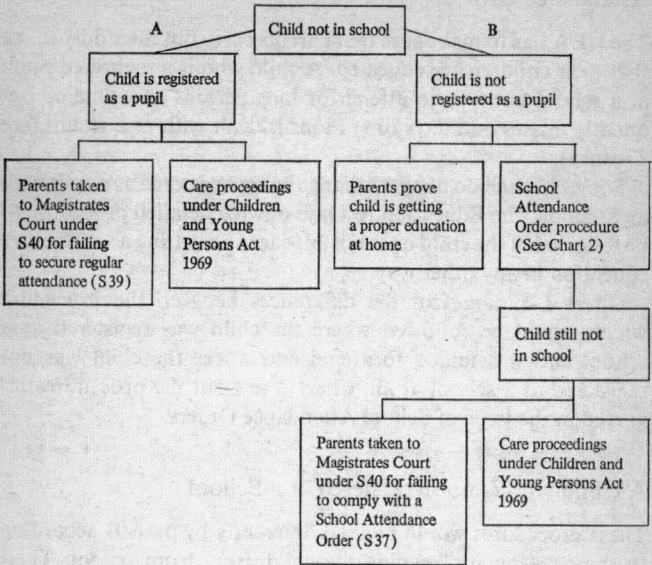

A — Child not in school — **B**

- Child is registered as a pupil (A)
  - Parents taken to Magistrates Court under S 40 for failing to secure regular attendance (S 39)
  - Care proceedings under Children and Young Persons Act 1969

- Child is not registered as a pupil (B)
  - Parents prove child is getting a proper education at home
  - School Attendance Order procedure (See Chart 2)
    - Child still not in school
      - Parents taken to Magistrates Court under S 40 for failing to comply with a School Attendance Order (S 37)
      - Care proceedings under Children and Young Persons Act 1969

CHART 2

School Attendance Order Procedure (SAO)

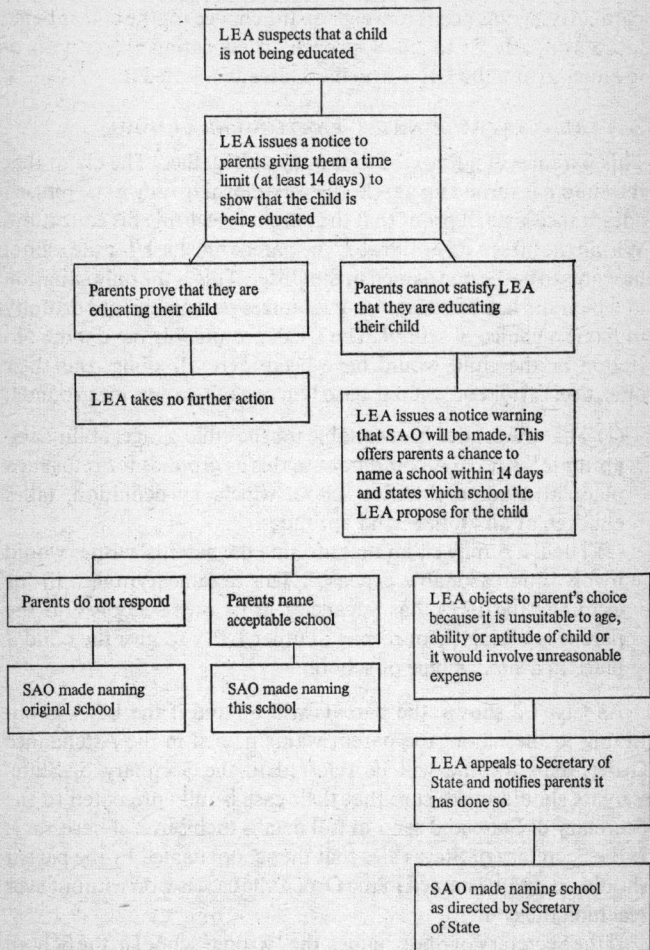

LEA suspects that a child is not being educated

LEA issues a notice to parents giving them a time limit (at least 14 days) to show that the child is being educated

Parents prove that they are educating their child

LEA takes no further action

Parents cannot satisfy LEA that they are educating their child

LEA issues a notice warning that SAO will be made. This offers parents a chance to name a school within 14 days and states which school the LEA propose for the child

Parents do not respond

SAO made naming original school

Parents name acceptable school

SAO made naming this school

LEA objects to parent's choice because it is unsuitable to age, ability or aptitude of child or it would involve unreasonable expense

LEA appeals to Secretary of State and notifies parents it has done so

SAO made naming school as directed by Secretary of State

self in court for failing to comply with a School Attendance Order. He then has the opportunity to argue his case for educating his child by his own methods and to call witnesses in support. Any parent trying this needs to weigh up the chances of the courts being more sympathetic to his approach to education than the professionals from the LEA who have already rejected it.

2. PARENTS WHO WANT A PARTICULAR SCHOOL

This parent will ignore the first notice altogether. The claim that the child has turned up at school every morning only to be refused admittance is not a proof that the parent is securing his education. Within the fifteen days allowed, the parent must ask for the school he wants to be the one named in the Order. This is the only situation in which the law of education guarantees parents the opportunity to name a choice of school. The LEA presumably have some objection or the child would have been there all along. But their objection is valid only if it is based on one of two specific grounds:

(1) That the school is unsuitable for the child's 'age, ability and aptitude'. An LEA could not use this as grounds for refusing a place at a comprehensive school which, by definition, takes children of all abilities and aptitudes.

(2) The LEA may claim that meeting the parents' wishes would involve 'unreasonable expense'. This argument applies if, for example, the LEA has vacancies in its own schools and the parent is asking them to pay another LEA to give the child a place in a similar type of school.

As Chart 2 shows, the parents will be told if the LEA is objecting to the school the parent wants named in the Attendance Order. This dispute will be referred to the Secretary of State. Parents should make sure that their case is fully presented to the Secretary of State and send in full details themselves if necessary. If the Secretary of State rules that the school named by the parent should be the one named in the Order, the case is won without ever reaching the courts.

If the Secretary of State names the 'wrong' school in the School Attendance Order, parents may decide not to take any notice of it. They will then be prosecuted for failing to comply with a School

Attendance Order, and can argue their case in court. Even if they are acquitted, it means only that they are 'not guilty' of failing to see that their child attends school: the court has no power to give them a place at the school they want. At this point the LEA either has to concede or begin all over again by issuing another School Attendance Order which names yet another school.

3. 'OVER MY DEAD BODY'

The parent whose objection is to one specific school has a better chance of sorting it out before the case gets to court. The first notice does not help him, but the second notice may give him the chance of finding a school to replace the one he objects to. This is the time to compromise. Parents should look carefully at any choice offered to them by the notice. They should write back within fifteen days naming the school which seems to be the most acceptable. If their problem really was to avoid one school they should succeed at this stage.

If the School Attendance Order still names the one school they are determined to avoid they are in the same position as case 2 above, and will have to ignore the order and take the opportunity of a court appearance to state their case again.

4. 'EDUCATION IS A WASTE OF TIME'

School Attendance Orders were designed to get children out of the factories and workshops and in to school. If necessary they can still be used to do this as a protection for children.

All these routes lead to court in the end if parents persist in keeping their child away from school. Parents who lose their case in court will be fined and if they persist in their refusal to send their child to the school named in the Attendance Order, they will become liable to increased penalties and in due course to imprisonment. A maximum fine of £10 on the third offence, followed by a month in prison is unlikely to influence a parent who has set out to establish a fundamental principle. It may stir the feckless parent into sending his child to school.

Once a School Attendance Order has been issued, whether or not the case gets to court, the order remains in force until the child

reaches school leaving age unless the LEA revokes it. So if a
parent who has had an Order served on him starts keeping the
child away from school again, he can be prosecuted without any
of the preliminary notices. The Order can be amended to take account of changes such as a child transferring to secondary school,
and parents may apply to have the name of another school sub-
stituted in the Order or to educate the child at home.

Boarding Education

A child who lives in the Outer Hebrides has the same right to a free
state education as one who lives in the middle of Sheffield, and it is
the duty of his LEA to provide it. The LEA must pay either for
lodgings near a school or for a place at a boarding school for any
pupil who cannot get to a suitable school every day. Where the
LEA does not make satisfactory arrangements for this, the parents
cannot be held legally responsible for the child's failure to attend
school. The question of whether or not the parents could afford to
pay does not enter into it. The LEA has no discretion to refuse to
pay for him any more than they have the right to refuse to pay for a
millionaire's daughter to go to the infant school in the next street.

The duty of an LEA to provide suitable schools for all its
children is stated in Section 8 of the 1944 Act which lists the kinds
of schools an LEA will need to maintain in order to carry out its
duty properly. The list includes 'Boarding accommodation, either
in boarding schools or otherwise, for pupils for whom education
as boarders is considered by their parents and by the authority to
be desirable'. In 1972 141,000 children were at boarding schools,
other than special schools. Very few of these were children for
whom an LEA could not otherwise provide a suitable school
place. Nevertheless, about a fifth of the total were having their fees
subsidized because their parents wanted them to go to boarding
school and had been able to convince the LEA that they had good
grounds for being helped. This help is given under Sections 61 and
81 of the 1944 Act.

When will the LEA Pay for Boarding School?

The DES set up a working party in 1960 to find the answer to this question. Its report suggested that there were four categories of cases in which it would be reasonable to expect help from the LEA to send a child to boarding school.

1. WHERE BOTH PARENTS WERE ABROAD

At the time of the report the group of families most affected were servicemen, but the increase of international companies and the EEC now mean that more families than ever before spend part of their working life abroad. Parents who want to apply for help with boarding school fees on these grounds will need to assure the LEA that they have not emigrated permanently and that the child will be likely to live and work in the UK after leaving school. The LEA will also want to know what kind of schools there are where the parents are posted. A child would be expected to go to a local school near his family if the teaching was conducted in English and pupils entered for English exams.

2. FREQUENT MOVES

The working party did not feel able to specify what occupations or precise frequency of moves should entitle a parent to help with boarding. However, they felt that children over the age of thirteen should have some guarantee of stability in their schooling. A move every three or four years was probably not sufficient justification in itself for a boarding subsidy, but would be an additional supporting argument.

3. HOME CIRCUMSTANCES SERIOUSLY PREJUDICIAL TO THE NORMAL DEVELOPMENT OF THE CHILD

This is the most difficult to define. Some authorities put single-parent families into this category, others will not do so unless the conditions are particularly distressing. Although the working party suggested that bad housing should qualify a child for a boarding school place, some authorities would have to send every child to boarding school if this were the criterion.

4. SPECIAL APTITUDE

A virtuoso violinist needs the right training from a very young age. If a child is offered a place at one of the few reputable specialist schools – usually for music or dancing – it would be reasonable to apply for help with the fees on the grounds that the child has a special aptitude for which proper training can be provided only at boarding school.

Although religious grounds have been accepted by LEAs as a reason for helping with fees, the working party endorsed the view that this alone could not justify a grant.

What Kind of School?

What kind of boarding school can parents choose if they want help from the LEA with paying the fees?

A survey published by ACE (Advisory Centre for Education) in September 1973 showed that state boarding provision – state schools which took all or some boarders – was on the decline. Thirty fewer schools provided boarding places than the previous survey seven years earlier and a number of schools thought the future prospects of their boarding side were uncertain. LEAs are frequently asked to buy places for children at independent schools, while they take up only half the places available in state boarding schools where the fees are much lower. This may be because parents choose the boarding schools themselves and find it harder to get information about LEA schools than about independent schools. A list was published by ACE in *Where*, 84 (September 1973) and 89 (February 1974).

Who Stands the Best Chance of Financial Help?

Royston Lambert, in his book, *The State and Boarding Education**, showed that most grants went to families in the south of England who lived in middle class or light industrial areas. Not where you would expect to find the worst cases of physical hardship. For

* Methuen, 1964.

every nine boys at boarding school there is one who is given help from the LEA, but only one girl in every nineteen at boarding school gets any help with the fees. Although the government working party commented tartly, 'The need of a pupil of secondary school age to have a boarding education will in most cases be entirely independent of the pupil's academic ability . . .', selection for a boarding school place seems to have been another form of selection for a grammar school place. So most of the money spent by LEAs on boarding school places went to clever boys from comfortable, middle class homes.

What Does the Financial Help Amount to?

LEAs tend to consider only the basic cost of tuition and boarding, whereas the real costs include clothing and fares, for instance, as well as all the items which can turn out to be 'extras' at independent schools – anything from swimming to needlework. To avoid hardship to parents other costs need to be taken into account. Although there is no official uniformity of practice on boarding grants between LEAs, a working party of representatives recommended in 1974 that parents whose net assessed income was below £1,400 should not make any contribution to boarding school fees and above that contributions should be increased by £3 for every £15 additional income.

Procedure

The DES working party has some sound advice for parents who want help with boarding school fees. They emphasize that parents are well advised to consult the LEA at an early stage before they make any arrangements with the school; LEAs dislike being faced with a *fait accompli* when they are going to be asked to foot the bill.

Other Sources of Help

A number of employers, government and otherwise, help with grants for sending employees' children to boarding school. Other sources of help may be found through the Educational Grants Advisory Service.*

Break

Break or playtime is officially known as 'the necessary time for recreation'. Schools Regulations do not specify whether that means necessary for pupils or teachers or both.

Any break during the morning or afternoon school session counts as part of the teaching time. Dinner time which divides one session from the other is not counted into the total hours of teaching which have to be provided during the school day. Although an LEA could make a general regulation about when breaks should be taken or how long they should last, they rarely, if ever, do so. Consequently, it is entirely up to the headteacher to arrange break times.

Most primary schools allow a break during the morning and again in the afternoon. Secondary schools expect their pupils to work for longer at a stretch and although the lucky ones get a morning break, it is rare for a secondary school to have a break during the afternoon.

It is common practice to settle for a break of around fifteen minutes. The governors ought to know how the school timetable is arranged and should query any eccentricities, such as half-hour playtimes.

It is the head's responsibility to arrange adequate supervision throughout all breaks including the dinner hour: he must have a good system and be sure that it is always carried out. It is not good enough to have someone on call in the staffroom. Whoever is on duty must patrol the area. The whole point of playtime is to let off steam and no sensible parent is alarmed at occasional bumps and grazes even if there was a certain amount of pushing and shoving going on. But there must be vigilant enough supervision by who-ever is in charge (teachers or helpers) so that they can intervene to stop vicious horse-play or potentially dangerous behaviour before

* At the National Council of Social Service, 26 Bedford Square, London WC1.

anyone gets hurt. A fifteen-year-old boy, who lost the sight of one eye when a group of boys were fooling around with a length of trampoline elastic, brought a case for negligence against the school. The judge said that the school had regrettably fallen short of the standards which the law demands of them in not stopping a potentially dangerous game 'within two or three minutes of its inception'. (Beaumont v. Surrey County Council).

Buildings

Some people leave a warm dry home equipped with all kinds of labour-saving machines and go off to spend their holidays in a cold wet tent without even the most basic necessities. That is their choice. Many children leave a warm dry home each morning and go off to spend the day in a cold, draughty building with toilets on the far side of the playground that freeze over in winter. They have no choice.

It is not the intention of the DES or of LEAs that children should have inadequate schools. It is a measure of the priority given to spending on education, both locally and nationally, that so many school buildings are obsolete, decaying and unsanitary.

A new school building can cost from £130,000 for a small village primary school to £1·3 million for a large comprehensive school in Yorkshire. In fact, the total allocated for school buildings in 1974–5 was £192 million. Whatever the priority given to education, public spending on this scale must affect the state of the economy, which is why the DES controls capital expenditure on education.

Building a New School

Only an LEA can take the initiative in proposing a new school building project whether it is for a voluntary or a county school. So the first stage in getting a new school is to convince the local authority that a new school or a new building for an existing school is necessary. Although the Secretary of State must first approve proposals in principle and sanction the raising of any loan needed, the LEA still has to find the money and pay the interest. The LEA provides the site, all the buildings and other facilities such as playing fields for a new county school. The governors must provide the site and the buildings for a new voluntary aided school. The DES makes a grant of 85 per cent towards the costs, but as the 15 per cent to be raised by the governors will be thousands of pounds, raising funds may be an additional complication in getting a new voluntary school. The LEA has to provide ancillary buildings such as medical rooms, caretaker's accommodation and so on for new voluntary aided schools and these become the property of the trustees of the voluntary foundation. The LEA also has to provide playing fields and all related buildings which remain the property of the LEA. There is no procedure for establishing entirely new controlled or special agreement schools.

Occasionally an LEA does not need to borrow money to build a school because it has raised it by selling off surplus sites, disused buildings or other assets. This cash is known as 'off programme' money and they have considerable freedom to choose what to spend it on.

The Assistant Education Officer for Buckinghamshire had some bitter experience of the problems of building schools when he wrote 'As one who has been in the firing line for some time I have discovered that parents, managers and teachers often agree on one thing – new schools are built too late, too small and in the wrong place.'

ROOFS OVER HEADS

The situation may be that there are not enough school places for all the children in the neighbourhood. Although the need to put 'roofs over heads' gives a project priority it can be surprisingly difficult to prove. It is not, for instance, sufficient to point to 150 new homes; 150 new homes can house 300 children ready for primary school in one area and thirty in another. And even if there are 300 children needing infant places now, those children would be taking their CSEs before a new primary school could be built.

LEAs cannot afford to invest in new schools to cope with a temporary bulge. But an analysis of several census returns for the immediate neighbourhood plus some homework on the housing committee's plans for any new housing estates in the area may show a definite trend over a period of years with considerably more children under five who will be needing places in local infant schools than the schools have room for.

New Schools for Old

A new school building may be needed to replace an appalling old one. The case will be more convincing if the existing building is legally sub-standard according to the Building Regulations (see Appendix Section 10). The Standards for School Premises Regulations 1972 cover the size of school sites and the provision of playing fields. Detailed specifications for accommodation itemize everything from teaching areas, toilets and dining rooms down to storage space. There are standards laid down for acoustics, heating, lighting and ventilation. Any school will need to fall a long way short of the minimum on every count to stand much chance over the competing claims of other schools.

A completely new building may not always be the answer. In an inflationary economy you get less for the same money each year. In one authority it was calculated that they would be able to build four fewer classrooms for a primary school for the same money than in the previous year. So a vast, solid Victorian building may be replaced by a small square open-plan box with a flat roof. (Walls are expensive and sloping roofs prohibitive.) Converting old properties is a popular activity with conservationists and editors of glossy magazines. Converting old schools can be just as successful. There certainly will not be less space and a clever conversion can transform a Victorian rabbit warren into light airy classrooms with scope for inventive activity, even if the outside does still look like a workhouse.

ENLARGING A SCHOOL IN SUCH A WAY THAT IT EFFECTIVELY BECOMES A NEW SCHOOL

The LEA must pay the whole cost of any changes made to a county school. Where the LEA and the trustees of a controlled school agree on a proposal to be submitted to the Secretary of

State, the L E A may be empowered to provide the school with site, school and ancillary buildings. It does not necessarily have to convey its interest in these to the trustees although the terms of the Trust Deed may make it more convenient for it to do so. Governors must provide the site and school buildings for aided and special agreement schools which are to be enlarged, but the D E S makes a grant of 85 per cent of the cost. A change of this kind would require a Section 13 notice (see Appendix, p. 295).

TRANSFERRING A SCHOOL TO A NEW SITE

The L E A provides everything which is necessary for a county school. The L E A must provide the site, school buildings and ancillary buildings for a controlled school and assign them all over to the trustees. However, the L E A is entitled to some or all of the proceeds of the sale of the old site and building. With aided and special agreement schools the governors must provide the new school building. They may get a grant of up to 85 per cent of the cost, taking into account the proceeds from the sale of the old site and buildings. The L E A has to provide the school with a new site to move to and all ancillary buildings and assign its interest in these to the trustees. Similar arrangements apply where minor alterations are made to a school which do not amount to the kind of change which requires a Section 13 notice.

Foundations

Unless a school is at the top of the L E A building programme, it is unlikely to get built. It is no good assuming that projects which start at the bottom of the list will gradually work their way to the top. There are years when no building is started at all; priorities change with the political climate and the state of the economy, and those who are waiting patiently will be pushed aside in favour of those who are pressing harder.

It takes so long to get work started once a scheme is accepted in principle that a new school building is vulnerable to economy cuts until the builders move in. A parents' group in Grimsby succeeded against all the odds in getting approval for a new primary school to replace wartime huts. The letter from the D E S telling them that the school was to be included on the approved list arrived in May 1973. This meant that – having passed through all the necessary stages – 'work on site should be possible after 1st April 1975'. The parents were jubilant. Six months later the government made drastic cuts in capital spending on education and the whole project was shelved.

When the DES has stated its criteria for approving building projects, LEAs can plan more effectively. In December 1970 the government announced that absolute priority would be given to proposals to rebuild nineteenth century primary schools. There was no point in LEAs putting up proposals for rebuilding nineteenth century *secondary* schools because they knew in advance that they would be turned down. In April 1974 a new Secretary of State issued a circular in which he stated:

In considering future proposals for individual major projects at secondary schools he will take account of the contribution they will make to reorganization. He does not propose to include in future building programmes projects at non-comprehensive schools, whether grammar, technical or modern, except where such projects are necessary to enable the schools to become comprehensive.

What Kind of School Building will it be?

The design of a new school will depend on the philosophy of education of the LEA as well as on how much money they have to spend. Increasingly, LEAs discuss the kind of schools they are planning with teachers and headteachers who will work in them. Imaginative schemes in Leicestershire, Nottinghamshire and Manchester, among others, have brought the school and the community together to share the use of sports facilities, swimming pools, art and craft rooms, and much more. Circular 2/70, 'The Chance to Share', gave official encouragement and guidance to this kind of 'dual provision'. If the adult education sector, the Youth Service, the library service are all going to benefit from the facilities, they will be asked to contribute towards the cost from their own budget – a useful additional sum to add on to the amount sanctioned by the DES. Shared facilities are cheaper anyway. The Abraham Moss Centre in Manchester, in which a comprehensive school for 1,200 pupils shares facilities with everyone from babies to disabled adults to old age pensioners, cost 7 per cent less to build than it would have cost to build everything separately. The authority saved £136,000.

The same philosophy may imbue a village primary school. New Nottinghamshire primary schools are helping to break down the barriers between village and school life. They have playing fields which can be used by the villagers, and the school hall is the general village hall and local meeting place.

If local people are going to make good use of the library, pottery and swimming pool, it is just as important to discuss with them what is needed most and how best to provide it as it is to discuss the plans with the teachers.

Repairs and Alterations

The LEA is wholly responsible for any repairs or alterations to the exterior of a controlled or county school building. The governors are responsible for these in the case of aided or special agreement schools although the DES makes a grant of 85 per cent of the cost. Repairs and alterations to the interior of the school, ancillary buildings and playing fields are entirely the responsibility of the LEA in every case.

There is a vital distinction between minor works or alterations which come out of capital and are therefore subject to DES sanction, and maintenance of school buildings which is paid for out of the LEA's current income. For example, suppose a school has such badly designed window frames that the glass drops out. The LEA may be paying around £200 a quarter for new panes of glass from 'maintenance' and decide that it makes better sense to buy new frames than to keep on replacing the glass. Laying out £200 once for all on better designed frames would be an 'improvement' and be a capital payment which comes under the heading of minor works. If they have used up their capital allocation for the year, they are not allowed to pay £200 for new frames out of their current account, even though, by the end of the year, they could have spent £800 on glass.

What can parents do when their child tells them that he is too cold to write, that the toilets are disgusting, that there is nowhere to get a drink? This kind of housekeeping is the caretaker's job, but the condition of the school building is the responsibility of the governors. If they take an active concern they will already be trying to improve it. If they fail to get anything done other agencies can be invoked. Where the toilets or the dining facilities are bad enough to be a health hazard, the Public Health Inspector (Environmental Health Inspector) may be able to insist on immediate improvements so that a school jumps the queue of those waiting for minor works. If it is in really bad condition he may close the school until the improvements are made. Inspectors are employed by the Local Authority, not the Area Health Authority.

The Fire Brigade will inspect any school on request. LEAs frequently reserve funds for dealing with urgent work such as providing a school with fire escapes. The Fire Brigade has emergency powers to close a school until this work is completed. Schools are fourth on the list of five classes of premises designated by the Fire Precautions Act 1971. Eventually, when the Home Office gets as far as that class, they will be required to apply for a fire certificate and will all be inspected. Until this comes into force, which may well be several years, the LEA will not necessarily take the initiative in asking for an inspection of existing school buildings. Parents who are anxious about their school building should approach the governors formally and ask them to call in the fire officer to inspect the building. If they take no action, the matter can be taken up with local councillors.

Use of School Buildings

Whether or not the headteacher has any official authority over the use of school premises out of school hours, as a courtesy, anyone who wants to use a school normally starts by approaching the head. If the head refuses to support a request, application can be made direct to the Education Office. The Education Office probably has a system for dealing with 'lettings' of county schools, but voluntary schools may handle requests individually.

The local authority has control over the use of county schools at all times and of controlled schools on week days. The governors control the use of all voluntary schools on Sundays. With controlled schools the governors can decide on the use of the building on Saturdays unless the LEA or the school needs the premises for some educational purpose or young people's activities. With aided and special agreement schools the governors are responsible for the use of the building except that the LEA has the right to insist on the use of the premises free of charge (other than the cost of light, heat, etc.) for up to three weekdays for an educational purpose or young people's activity for which no other premises are available. So the LEA may be able to support a request for using the buildings or playing fields of a voluntary school if a direct application is turned down.

School buildings are an obvious choice for holding classes in the evenings as a way of making full use of facilities paid for out of public funds. Headteachers have no control over the evening institute and its use of buildings and facilities unless it is the LEA's policy to have one person in charge of all activities which take place in the school, day or evening. Having different groups using the same facilities can cause a great deal of irritation. Headteachers who want to involve parents and extend the school's activities after hours may find they have nowhere to meet. In one comprehensive school the head may have the use of the gym only (not the cosiest place to meet) every other Wednesday. Schools sometimes find they cannot rehearse plays or concerts in the hall in the evenings.

If there seems to be widespread difficulty in getting the use of school buildings out of school hours generally and they are locked up in the evenings and holidays, the LEA may need to re-think its policy, and allow for better rates of overtime pay for school caretakers as well.

Bullying

All children quarrel occasionally and most of them will from time to time bully someone else or be bullied themselves. It is a serious problem when bullying or being bullied becomes a way of life.

Bullying may be widespread throughout a school. Children

exaggerate and so does local gossip, but if parents have convincing evidence that this is happening, they have a duty to bring it to the notice of those who are legally responsible for the well-being of children in school. Bullying in school has been held responsible for tragedies, such as the suicide of a schoolgirl, Tina Wilson, and no one should dismiss the problem as trivial.

If bullying is not widespread in the school but a child seems constantly to be involved in it, whether it is as a bully or as victim, the problem is the parent's rather than the school's, although they should be able to get help and support from the school in dealing with it (see **Child guidance**).

Careers Guidance

'I cannot imagine a ship being built and then such inadequate arrangements being made for its launching that it foundered at that stage.' Sir William Alexander, the venerable chairman of the Association of Education Committees, used this metaphor as a comment on the reorganization of the Careers Service in April 1974. He was stressing the absurdity of the state investing thousands of pounds on a child's education and then grudging the money needed for an effective careers service to launch him successfully into the world. The whole careers service is understaffed, underpaid, under-equipped, under-trained and overworked. The journal *Education* commented on the new Careers Service that 'it would be a stupid or a dishonest Principal Careers Officer who would say that arrangements are likely to become wholly adequate within the next five years'. Six months after reorganization, the Institute of Careers Officers was warning that the service was so seriously short of trained careers officers that it could break down altogether in a period of high unemployment. Seen in this depressing context, it is hardly surprising that the careers service offered to schoolchildren so often appears totally inadequate.

Since reorganization there have theoretically been three sources of help in choosing a career.

1. The School

STAFF AND FACILITIES

The majority of secondary schools – 94 per cent in a recent DES survey – have at least one staff member with responsibility for careers advice and education. But this includes teachers who are given the title of 'careers teacher' and still have a normal time-table for teaching their own subject. In fact, half the large schools in the survey did not allocate so much as one room for careers work. Of those who claimed to have one room or more, most were shared as teaching areas or offices. The most these teachers can hope to do is to keep the pile of publicity and information leaflets tidy. At the other end of the scale, 14 per cent of the schools gave the careers teacher the status of a head of department solely on account of his careers work. And one Staffordshire comprehensive has a special open plan area covering 5,000 square feet for careers work, with a resource centre and facilities for large groups, small discussion groups and individual study.

CAREERS EDUCATION

Careers education is now accepted as part of the whole edu-cational process of 'discovering and using your own potential'. Guidance and help in choosing a career or training should there-fore be seen as part of an overall concern for the welfare, emotional development and education of each individual pupil, not as some-thing which can be done by a total stranger who sees them only to fix them up with a job. In this setting, the function of the specialist careers teacher will be to back up the work of the other staff with a wide variety of schemes for work experience, visits and other re-sources such as films, tapes and books. He will also be able to con-tribute his knowledge of local employment needs to the subject courses in the upper school.

The curriculum must be designed to 'keep doors open'. Schools which allow, encourage or force pupils to drop unpopular or difficult subjects may be seriously limiting the range of careers which will eventually be open to them. Most schools recognize that decisions made at the end of the third year about which courses will be followed in the fourth and fifth years may steer pupils towards or away from particular careers.

There should be sufficient time for teachers and pupils to make sense of discussions on these choices. For example, the Staffordshire school ran an experimental course in which the third and fourth years each had two periods a week designated for careers education as part of an integrated studies course. However, 30 per cent of schools in the DES survey made no provision in the timetable for careers education.

Parents, pupils, teachers and careers officers should have opportunities for discussion with one another and 86 per cent of all the schools surveyed claimed that both pupils and parents are fully involved in discussions about the career implications of courses at the third-year stage. However, the DES working party commented that 'in nearly half the schools visited there appeared not to be secure lines of communication between all concerned, including parents'.

Pupils at both ends of the spectrum of attainment are easily overlooked and those going on from the sixth form to university can be as easily neglected as those going on to unskilled work from the remedial stream. The DES survey showed that the majority of schools made no special arrangements for careers programmes for children with special needs.

The careers teacher in school needs to establish an effective working relationship with the Careers Officer, higher and further education and local employers.

2. Careers Service

LEAs have a duty to provide and maintain their own careers service. Before 1974 LEAs which ran a local youth employment service were acting as agents of the Department of Employment which paid them a grant of 75 per cent of the cost. Since the Careers Service has become wholly the responsibility of the LEA it has had to compete for money with all the other claims on the authority.

The Department of Employment is still responsible for the Central Careers Service Board which employs its own inspectors who can advise the careers officers working for the LEAs. Before April 1974 this was the Central Youth Employment Executive.

The Employment and Training Act 1973 which established the new Careers Service gave the LEA a duty to help anyone receiving education to decide what training they need and to help them find a suitable job. This means they may be asked to help school students; older students doing sandwich courses; anyone attending part-time or evening classes; mature students who have resumed studying after a break, such as housewives working for Open University degrees. The Careers Service is not limited to those in education and anyone may choose to go to them for help in finding a suitable career. It is customary for every school pupil to be offered an interview with the careers officer, which their parents can attend, at some stage during their school career. Careers officers would like to spend at least forty minutes on each interview, but with 400 or so pupils to be seen it is more likely to be a quarter of an hour.

Careers officers are expected to work in close collaboration with the schools. When schools have their own careers teacher the careers officer acts as consultant in planning or developing a careers programme. But if there is no careers teacher in the school the careers officer will have to undertake the careers education himself and this will inevitably be superficial in the limited time available to him.

3. Job Centres

Job Centres are the new version of the Employment Exchange and are run by the Employment Services Agency. They are to be modelled on the more attractive style of the best commercial employment agencies, and, like them, sited in main shopping centres. Anyone over compulsory school age may go to a Job Centre. One part of the service is simply a job supermarket where clients make their own selection from the lists of jobs on display. Staff should be able to advise on training and qualifications. Anyone needing more detailed advice and guidance can make an appointment with a trained vocational guidance counsellor.

Young people who have dropped out of further and higher

education courses are often reluctant to apply to a service run by the education authority. The guidance service hopes to be able to help them pick up the pieces and make a fresh start.

Helping Yourself

Information – even on a simple factual level such as the qualifications needed for a particular course, or the nearest college where the course is held – may be easier to find from the current edition of basic reference books in the reference library. A mass of careers literature is available, the CRAC* and HMSO publications being particularly reliable and objective.

Too many people have dropped subjects on the school's assurance that it is quite all right, only to find they do not qualify for the course or job they want, so it is vital to check the entry qualifications with the Association or Institute or college concerned.

A number of independent agencies, including the Advisory Centre for Education, offer vocational guidance. There is usually a fee which may be quite large.

Charges

Alice in Wonderland told the Mock Turtle that she had been to a day school where French and music were extras. '"Ah! then yours wasn't a really good school," said the Mock Turtle in a tone of great relief. "Now at *ours* they had at the end of the bill, French, music, *and washing* – extra." But he added with a sigh "I couldn't afford to learn it – I only took the regular course."'

Times have not changed much. The 'regular course' has been free in maintained primary and secondary schools since Section 61 of the 1944 Education Act laid down 'that no fees shall be charged in respect of the education provided in any school . . .' This includes the use of the necessary books, stationery and equipment. (See Materials.) But the list of extras is longer than ever: French has been replaced by school journeys to France; there is still a charge for learning a musical instrument in many areas; cooking

*Careers Research and Advisory Centre Ltd, Bateman St, Cambridge.

has taken the place of washing in the home economics course, and pupils are known to miss classes because they cannot afford the materials.

Schools may make a charge for extra subjects but there is no legal definition of the distinction between curricular and extra-curricular activities. In the words of the DES, 'to our knowledge there has been no court ruling on the subject and the commentary on the Education Acts is singularly silent on this point'.

The only compulsory subject on every school curriculum is religious education, so it would be illegal to charge for that. But an authority which started to charge for maths or English lessons in school time could be shown to be acting unreasonably.

In 1944 the Ministry of Education gave authorities some advice on how they should interpret Section 61. It was suggested that it would *not* be contrary to the Act for fees to be charged for special individual tuition, ordinarily given outside school hours, in sub-jects which do not form part of the normal curriculum – such as learning to play a musical instrument, dancing or elocution. But there are wide variations in local practice. Musicians feel that music is as vital a part of a child's education as English or maths but it often continues to be treated as an extra for those who can afford to pay; a number of authorities still charge for teaching individual children to play a musical instrument and expect them to buy their own instruments. Other LEAs take the view that all music is an integral part of the present day school curriculum and provide free individual teaching in school time and lend and maintain instruments free of charge.

Outings which are part of the curriculum should be free. But if outings during school hours are classified as 'extra-curricular' parents can be asked to pay. (See Outings.)

Where the authority is not technically being unreasonable it may be pushing its interpretation of Section 61 to the limit, par-ticularly in times of financial pressure. In 1974, Somerset Educa-tion Authority decided that the following year they would charge pupils for their own examination fees if they took more than seven CSE or GCE O level subjects. The fees are about £1·30 to £1·50 a subject, and the authority estimated that they would save about £2,000 a year. An NUT spokesman pointed out that 'This is quite

clearly another case of the continuing erosion of educational provision and runs contrary to the concept of free education.'

This is the kind of issue where publicity can arouse a sufficient
sense of local grievance to get the policy changed. The principle of
free education for all will be truly established only when pupils are
not excluded from any school activity because they cannot afford
it. Grants to schoolchildren from the LEA are one way to make
opportunities more equal. (See **Grants for schoolchildren.**)

Child Guidance

Child guidance services should be available to all children, including children under five, whose behaviour is causing serious
problems or who have emotional or learning difficulties. The
service may be provided by the LEA, or the Area Health Authority
through the School Health Service and the local hospital service.
Hospital clinics are particularly common in London and are often
called child psychiatric clinics. When the Health Service was reorganized, the DES, the DHSS and the Welsh Office issued a
joint circular (DES 3/74) on Child Guidance. This suggested that
in future 'rather than a self-contained, highly specialized child
guidance service which has operated in some areas, the concept of
child guidance that now appears appropriate is of a network of
services, each providing help for children with difficulties and their
families'. This network would be provided by collaboration of the
school psychological services, the child psychiatric services, the
social work services and the child health services.

Parents who want their child referred to a child guidance clinic
can do this through the school, their GP or the Social Services
Department.

The standard child guidance team consists of a consultant child
psychiatrist, two educational psychologists and three psychiatric
social workers. Official policy (Circular 347, 1959) is for the child
psychiatrist to be the medical director of the child guidance clinics.

Child guidance services are by no means equally well developed
throughout the country. In 1960 the Royal Medico-Psychological
Association issued a memorandum on the recruitment and training

of child psychiatrists recommending that there should be a full child guidance team for every 35,000 schoolchildren and that the national target should be 243 child psychiatrists. By 1972 two thirds of the target had been reached throughout the country on average: London had more than the estimated need and the rest of the south-east and south-west had reached a reasonable number. But this left the rest of England with less than half the number of child psychiatrists thought to be needed.

The average waiting time for a first appointment for a child who has been referred to a child guidance clinic for diagnosis is six months, but the range is from two weeks to eighteen months. The DES has commented that

it would seem that the clinics can make little inroad into the number of children waiting to be seen or the time they have to wait for an appointment so long as every child referred is given a routine 5 to 10 (though it may be 20 to 25) hours diagnostic work-up and only one new case is seen per child psychiatric session.

Once this protracted diagnosis is finally complete, what kind of treatment can parents expect? It is generally recognized that treatment of a child cannot be carried out in isolation from the family. So 'family psychiatry' rather than 'child psychiatry' is carried out in many clinics. The DES explains this by saying that practice and teaching in child guidance clinics focuses 'on the unravelling of psychic processes within the child and on inter-personal relationships within the family'. These inter-personal relationships include the relationship between the parents, who are often expected to attend the clinic themselves.

Their orientation means that child guidance clinics often do not take account of the social, cultural and educational factors which may have been crucial in germinating disturbed behaviour. The DES reports that their assessment frequently ignores physical and physiological factors. It is, for instance, rare for physical tests of the working of the child's central nervous system to be carried out.

The DES has said that there is a very real need for operational research into how resources may best be deployed in providing child guidance facilities for the many children who need it; and that this must be associated with clinical trials into the effectiveness of various forms of treatment. Professor Jack Tizard, Research Professor of Child Development, University of London Institute of Education, has suggested:

> My own prejudices would lead me to look carefully at schools as social institutions possibly influencing the incidence and duration of maladjusted behaviour patterns, at the routines of particular schools which may provide a more or less benign environment for the pupils, at the classroom as a place where children spend long periods of time in a more or less congenial, more or less stressful environment, and at individual, vulnerable or problem children in a naturalistic rather than in a clinic setting . . . (*London Educational Review*).

Choice of School

For the past thirty years parents have believed that, according to the law, they have and ought to go on having a choice of school for their children. Politicians – nationally and locally – have never had the courage to tell them that they have not. Parents were misled in the first place by the best known, most often quoted and most mis-understood section of the 1944 Education Act. Section 76 is headed 'Pupils to be educated in accordance with the wishes of their parents.' But headlines are designed to catch the eye, however dull the news. The full text reveals that parents' wishes are simply to be borne in mind when decisions are made, and even then only 'so far as is compatible with the provision of efficient instruction and training and the avoidance of unreasonable public expenditure'.

So do parents have a choice of school or not? The crunch comes when there are more children applying than places available. Then someone has to decide which children will get the places and who will be turned away. The person who makes this decision is the one who really makes the choice (see **Admissions**).

When Parents *Cannot* Get the School They Want

No one wants a parent to be unhappy about his child's school, and LEAs, or governors in the case of a voluntary school, cannot legally refuse parents a place they want without a good cause, one which the Secretary of State would concede to be reasonable. (See Appendix, Section 68, p. 302.) Schools Regulations say that 'A pupil shall not be refused admission to or excluded from a school on other than reasonable grounds.' So what are reasonable grounds for refusing a pupil a place?

OVERCROWDING

No matter how strongly they support parents' right of choice no authority can give a child a place at a school which is full if there are other suitable schools in the area which have vacancies. When is a school really full? The 'Standards for School Premises Regulations 1972' lay down the minimum teaching space for each school child. Authorities with space to spare in some schools may try to improve on this minimum by reducing the size of classes in all schools and allowing more space for each child.

As a result parents may be turned away from a popular school even though the Regulations technically allow a few extra children to be squeezed in. If the parents appeal to the Secretary of State, the DES has to weigh up on the one hand the parents' wishes and on the other hand the LEA's reasonable aim of making the most efficient use of all its schools and improving standards. Parents cannot win either way on the question of overcrowding: if there is a general shortage of places the LEA has to squash an extra child in somewhere; if it does not suit them they will use the Regulations as a way of keeping a child out. A case was taken to the Queen's Bench in 1962 by two mothers in Hertfordshire who wanted their children to go to a school on the doorstep and had been directed to one a mile away on the wrong side of a major trunk road. The LEA had refused a place on the grounds that the nearby school was overcrowded and the Secretary of State had backed up the LEA. The parents went one step further and appealed to the court on the basis of Section 76. They lost the case. This was the legal principle spelt out by the court: 'A decision by an LEA and the Secretary of State that a school is overcrowded cannot be challenged in the courts by a parent who wishes his child to attend that school and who claims to base his right on the Education Act 1944 Section 76.' (Darling and Jones v. Ministry of Education.)

ZONING

Although Section 76 has not been much help to parents when they get into conflict with their LEA over the choice of school, it has, in practice, restricted the freedom of LEAs to impose catchment areas – to rule that children living in certain streets only will be admitted to a particular school. Section 76 means that they may not zone their schools unless pressure on places is preventing 'efficient instruction'; they may not do so for administrative tidiness or for any social reason. *Where*, 104 (May 1975), discussed an LEA's responsibility to keep the public informed about their current policy on zoning. Although there is no statutory requirement to issue formal notices, Circular 268 (1953) acknowledged that 'the establishment of zone boundaries is a matter of deep public concern'. Parents could therefore appeal to the Secretary of State that it was unreasonable of an LEA to introduce or change zoning arrangements without suitable notice. The local ombudsman might also regard it as maladministration. School governors ought to be consulted *before* any change in the authority's arrangements for their school.

What can parents do if their child is refused a place at a school because it is zoned and they live outside the catchment area? They should start by going to see the headteacher to find out if he has any vacancies. He may be a valuable ally if they particularly want their child to go to his school and he is prepared to back them up by insisting that he does have room. Even if he has room, he cannot agree to admit the child on the spot: he has no authority to overrule his LEA's policy on catchment areas.

If there are no vacancies, the LEA's case for their catchment area is proven and there is nothing to be done about it. But places may become available later as families move out of the district, so parents who are still keen on that particular school should keep in touch with the headteacher.

The LEA is not necessarily acting unreasonably in continuing to zone a school which has one or two vacancies. They may have good reason to expect an influx of pupils from a new housing development or see from their records that there is an increase in the number of rising fives in the district who will soon be needing places. But parents may be able to arrange a concession for one child.

People who move house may still be within reach of the school their child is already attending but may now be outside the catchment area if the school is zoned. It would be unreasonable for an LEA to ask parents to move the child.

NOT SUITED TO THE CHILD'S AGE, ABILITY OR APTITUDE

Parents will not get a place for their child at the school they want if it is not suitable for their child's age, ability and aptitude. In most cases this means that he has 'failed' his eleven-plus and cannot get a place at a grammar school. It would also apply to a child who had been ascertained as in need of special education whose parents wanted a place at an ordinary school. (See **Handicapped children.**)

DISTANCE

It is not unreasonable for an LEA to refuse a parent's choice of school on the grounds that it would involve the child in such a tiring journey that it would 'prevent him profiting fully from the instruction and training given at the school'. On the other hand, ironically, the local authority's own policies may result in children having long and difficult journeys.

When Parents *Can* Get the School They Want

So parents *can* get a place for their child at the school they want – so long as it is a maintained school with vacancies, is not so far away that the journey is impracticable and is either non-selective or suitable. If all these conditions are fulfilled, the authority or the governors have no legal grounds for objecting to a child going there.

Out County

'Out county' or 'extra district' places are places in one LEA given to children whose home is in a different one. An LEA is responsible for securing the provision of enough of the right kind of school places for all the children living within their boundaries. If they cannot provide the places in their own schools they must pay for the children to go to a school maintained by another LEA or to an independent school.

Parents themselves may prefer a school in another LEA to one in their own. They may live so near the boundary that the most convenient school happens to be on the wrong side. Or the area where they live may still have the eleven-plus and they would prefer to send their children to the comprehensive school in a neighbouring authority. The LEA may make difficulties about paying for a place elsewhere if there are vacancies which they consider suitable in their own schools, and if their objections appear to be unreasonable, parents can appeal to the Secretary of State under Section 68 of the Education Act.

The situation is somewhat different in London because the London Government Act 1963 Section 31(8) says that children who live anywhere in Greater London (or in a contiguous borough) cannot be refused a school place solely on the grounds that it is in a different LEA from their own.

A situation could arise in which all parties agree that the most suitable school for a child is in another LEA, but that LEA may have a policy of not giving places to children from other authorities. Parents can appeal to the Secretary of State against an authority other than their own, citing Schools Regulations 1959 7(1) that 'a pupil shall not be refused admission to . . . a school on other than reasonable grounds'.

Denominational schools are likely to accept pupils from several LEAs.

Appeals

It is not always a clear-cut case in which, on the one hand, children have no right to a place and, on the other hand, every right. An authority may make quite reasonable general rules about who may go to which school. This does not mean that exceptions cannot be made where a family has good reason for wanting something different. If the Articles of Government have given the governors of a voluntary school control over admissions, the LEA has no power to give you a place there.

When parents appeal about being refused any school place, it is as well to know that some reasons for choosing a particular school are likely to be more acceptable to the authority than others. After 1944 LEAs were so perplexed about how they should interpret Section 76 that the DES published a *Manual of Guidance* on choice of schools which set out the views of the DES as to what should be taken into account in deciding 'how far effect should be given to the parents' wishes'. A draft circular on choice of schools issued for consultation in April 1976 proposed withdrawing the *Manual* but did not basically alter the principles laid down in it.

Parents have the best hope of getting a place at a school on religious grounds, though not if they go to church just for weddings and funerals. Wanting or not wanting to be taught in the Welsh language is considered a good reason. It will be useful if the doctor supports a request on medical grounds: a child who has to take medicine at midday needs to be within easy reach of home and there are many genuine medical reasons why a child could not cope with a long or difficult journey. Often the nearest school as the crow flies may be more difficult to reach than one sited on a good bus or train route and the *Manual of Guidance* said that the LEA can take account of a tiring journey, although parents have seldom succeeded in claiming on this ground. The preference for mixed or single-sex school is the most important issue of all for some parents but it comes surprisingly low on the list of factors which are likely to get the place they want. It is always worth arguing from the fact that another child from the family is already at a particular school. A notable victory was won by London parents on that point in 1973 when the LEA agreed to change the criteria to make this the first consideration in allocating places at county secondary schools. Since the Education Act lays stress on the provision of 'suitable education' according to age, ability and aptitude of a child, parents can cite special facilities as grounds for asking for a particular school, such as workshops for a girl who wants to be an engineer or cooking for a boy who wants to be a chef.

There is unlikely to be any formal machinery for dealing with appeals from parents whose children do not get places at the primary school they want. It is much more common where secondary transfer is concerned even in a fully comprehensive system. The authority may not give parents unsolicited information about their appeals procedure in case they put ideas into people's heads. The first step is to find out if there is a proper procedure and to use it. Every LEA which has a selective system is bound to have a procedure for hearing appeals. Parents who want to appeal because their child is refused a place at a selective school will have to prove that the school allocated does not meet the child's needs. An educational psychologist's assessment which the LEA will accept, showing that a child's IQ warrants a grammar school place, gives an appeal a better chance of succeeding. A comprehensive school, by definition, caters for all children whatever their aptitude and ability so there are no grounds for appeal if a child is given a place there rather than at the local grammar school, unless it can be shown that the comprehensive does not offer a full range of suitable courses.

Appeals against a refusal of a place at a comprehensive school can be more difficult than appeals against eleven-plus selection. But an LEA must hear a reasonable complaint and will usually be prepared to accommodate individual parents' wishes if there is room in the school. Parents should base their initial appeal on the *Manual of Guidance* principles set out above. If they are trying to get a place at a popular school the problem is likely to be that all the places will have been allocated. However good the basis of their appeal, no one can be given a place which does not exist. Parents will have to weigh up the disadvantages to the child of continuing uncertainty while it is sorted out – possibly many months – against the advantages of making a positive commitment to a less favoured school.

In both county and voluntary schools there is always a right of appeal direct to the Secretary of State or the local ombudsman. In November 1974 when the Secretary of State for Education and Science was asked in the House of Commons how many appeals he had received from parents about the allocation of school places for September 1974, 750 appeals had been received. 'A considerable number' had been settled to the satisfaction of parents. The local ombudsman (Commissioner for Local Administration) has also concluded that there was a wrongful allocation of a child to secondary school in at least one case of this kind.

Anyone who feels that the DES has not given proper consideration to their appeal can ask his MP to complain to the ombudsman – the Parliamentary Commissioner for Administration.

Parents who are prepared to make a real embarrassment of themselves to both the education officers and the Education Committee by keeping their child at home until they get a place at the school they want have sometimes been successful in the end. But if a number of parents do this, the LEA may be forced to take a hard line and start prosecuting parents for their children's non-attendance. (See **Attendance**.) At least this does give parents a chance to name in court the school they want. Whether or not it gets to court parents need to be sure that the school is really worth it. One exceptional mother who did this wrote about her experiences on the education pages of the *Guardian*. In spite of the fact that she was enterprising enough to organize some teaching for her son and a friend who was in the same situation, she found that 'What the children desperately missed was the social world of school . . . the relationship between my son and me grew more tense as he found himself thrown back on a single base, the home.'

If the shortage of places at a local school is so serious that a number of families who live close to it cannot get places for their children it may be worth some urgent publicity. A new school will not be built in time for this year's children, but a mobile classroom can often be installed at very short notice.

Class Size

Confronted with the statement that class size does not mean anything any more and that what counts is pupil/teacher ratio, most people would sympathize with the teacher who told the 1974 NUT conference 'I don't teach a ratio, I teach a class.'

Since 1969 the only DES stipulation is that every school should have 'enough assistant teachers to provide appropriate full-time education . . .' But the Regulations give no guidance as to how many is 'enough' teachers for a particular number of pupils (the teacher/pupil ratio).

Some LEAs have as few as eighteen pupils for each teacher in primary schools, others have as many as thirty-one. In secondary schools the variation is from about fifteen to as many as twenty pupils for each teacher. The details of teacher/pupil ratios for every LEA are given in the education statistics published by the Chartered Institute of Public Finance and Accountancy.*

In their own way teacher/pupil ratios can be just as misleading as counting the heads of seventy children watching a TV programme and assuming that the school has classes of seventy children. One secondary school teacher did a calculation for his own school. His LEA claimed that their secondary schools had on average one teacher for every twenty-one children and that was what his school had. But, to find out what this means in the classroom, allowance must be made for teachers' free periods, non-teaching time taken for other duties, time out of school on in-service training courses. The headteacher is likely to do no teaching at all. Translated into teaching time, there was, on average, one teacher for every twenty-nine children in the classroom. And as that was the average, some classes must have had well over thirty children.

The DES has taken account of all these factors and has calculated that to eliminate teaching groups of over thirty, primary schools would need one teacher for every nineteen children and to eliminate teaching groups of over thirty throughout the school, secondary schools would need one teacher for every sixteen pupils up to the fifth year and one teacher for every 9·5 pupils in the sixth form.

There are some decisions made by the headteacher which affect class sizes in his school; there are some things he cannot do much about. The overall recruiting policy of his LEA will determine how many teachers he has as his establishment. Whether he actually gets them will also depend on the DES salary and training policies. The size and layout of his school may present physical ob-

* The Chartered Institute of Public Finance and Accountancy, 1 Buckingham Place, London SW1E 6HS.

stacles to the way in which he can deploy his teachers. An infant school which has only four classrooms cannot have six classes even if it has six teachers on the staff. So the children will have to be in large groups and will benefit from the extra staff in other ways without the classes getting any smaller.

The headteacher can, however, decide how the curriculum and timetable of the school are arranged. A head may improve the staffing position by making it particularly convenient for part-time teachers to be fitted in. One head may choose to offer Chinese and Russian in the sixth form and allocate a teacher to take two pupils for each of these subjects, while another head might make arrangements for these pupils to take their course at a near-by further education college rather than tie up two of his staff with such a small number of pupils. As the NAS have pointed out in their pamphlet *The Staffing of Schools*, what determines the size of a class *ought* to be the type of activity involved and the kind of pupils doing it. For any subject which needs individual tuition, a forty-minute period with a class of thirty children allows a point-less one and a half minutes help for each pupil. An activity like copying notes, or watching a TV programme, on the other hand, could quite well occupy forty or sixty pupils at a time with one teacher.

Co-education

In 1926 half the nine-year-olds in the country were in single sex schools; today the proportion is 2 per cent. In fact, in the early 1970s less than a third of all maintained secondary schools were single sex and only 10 per cent of comprehensives. The extent of the change in attitudes was described by Mrs Nellie Lunnon, who was born in Islington in 1883. She recalled with great bitterness how when she was eight years old she was caned so hard for being in the boys' playground that she could not use her hand for a week afterwards. Future generations may be just as astonished when they hear that single sex schools were being built in England in 1974, one of the few places in the world where this was still being done.

The definitive work on co-education is a massive research study

which took Mr R. R. Dale of Swansea twenty-seven years of pains-
taking work. His final conclusions were:

It has been demonstrated that the average co-educational grammar
school is a happier community for both staff and pupils than the
average single-sex school; it has equally been demonstrated that this
happiness is not at the expense of academic progress. The greater happiness is reflected in numerous ways in the interaction between pupils
and teachers, boys and girls, masters and mistresses, and these in turn
interact among each other, all contributing to the pleasantness of the
school. There seems to be little reason why this should not be true for
comprehensive and secondary modern as well as for grammar schools.
This finding does not mean that all co-educational schools are good
and all single-sex schools bad; other powerful influences shape a
school's character, such as the personality of the head and of the individual teacher, the social class of the pupils and the nature of the
neighbourhood ... Yet these researches point unmistakably to co-
education as the preferable system.

This is not much comfort for parents who do not live within
reach of a mixed school or cannot get a place for their child at one.
To have any hope of changing the situation, parents need to be
aware of it long before their child is due to go to secondary school.
The actual mechanics of changing a school from single sex to
mixed are not insurmountable: the building will need some modifi-
cation – mainly to supply a different species of lavatories and a
wider range of technical rooms. A Section 13 notice will be required. In the summer of 1974, a group of parents from Westminster CASE realized that there would be no local comprehensive school for their daughters who were then in the second year of
junior school. It had been agreed in principle by the ILEA that at
some unspecified future date the local comprehensive – boys only –
would become mixed. They enlisted the support of the new and
enthusiastic head of the boys school and started campaigning in
earnest. Their scheme involved taking in girls one year at a time,
starting with the first year. This meant that the cost of building
conversion could be spread over several years and the sensibilities
of parents who had chosen a single sex school for their sons were
not affronted. The daughters of the original campaigners will be
among the first group of girls who join the school in September
1976.

One problem is that some parents, Muslims in particular, choose single sex secondary schools for their daughters out of religious conviction and the customs of their community. Where the LEA has decided to make all its schools co-educational, the objections of Muslim parents have been overruled by the Secretary of State. Plans to establish their own schools for their daughters are under discussion.

The journal *Education* summed up the current consensus of opinion:

> The arguments over the pros and cons of co-education which used to be the stock-in-trade of every sixth form debating society have now largely faded away. Faded because history and the changing social scene have made them seem more and more irrelevant.

Combined Cadet Force

Anyone can be a conscientious objector – even in wartime – so official policy is that it should not be compulsory for schoolboys to join the cadet corps. However, this could not prevent a head from making it compulsory for his school because of his control over what happens in the school.

School cadet contingents – over 260 in the country – are under the control of the Ministry of Defence. The Ministry pay more than £2 million a year for officers' pay, cadets' uniforms (they must supply their own boots), equipment, buildings and grants. There is an Inter-Service Cadet Committee (a rear-admiral, a major general and an air vice-marshal) who make policy decisions and a Joint Cadet Executive (a navy commander, a colonel and a retired air-commodore) who carry them out. All contingents belong to the CCF Association which deals with non-military aspects of their work such as insurance policies and competition shooting. The Ministry can turn down an application from a school which wants to set up a CCF if it thinks it is unsuitable – too small, for example. They also carry out formal inspections and can decide to withdraw their support. They can veto or withdraw commissions.

A report 'Corps on the Curriculum', published by the *TES* in January 1976, said: 'The Ministry are careful to point out that they do not meddle in education. It is up to each school to decide whether they will have a CCF and, if they do, how to fit it into their timetable.' This is clearly the kind of decision which governors ought to be involved in: whether, as its supporters claim, this is an appropriate way of teaching boys leadership qualities, responsibility, good discipline and self dependence must be subject to 'general oversight' of the conduct of the school however loosely interpreted. On a more practical level, many governors will want to influence the siting of service huts belonging to the Ministry of Defence on school premises.

LEAs would have power (under Section 23 of the 1944 Education Act) to issue regulations about CCF contingents in county schools. Nearly two thirds of the contingents are in independent schools.

The headteacher appoints teacher-officers who receive a uniform allowance (£110 in 1976) and daily pay for up to twenty-eight days at the rate paid to reservists.

A grammar school head was quoted in the *TES* as saying 'It allows boys to experience service life and develop careers interests.' In view of the evident truth of this (well over 50 per cent of young men entering the Royal Military Academy, Sandhurst, have been a member of the CCF at school) it is curious that the Ministry of Defence is the only official body to recruit in schools in this way; the DHSS, for instance, has not taken up the suggestion from the St John Ambulance Association that first aid should be taught in schools and paid for the necessary facilities and staff.

Compulsory School Age

The law lays down age limits within which children must go to school. Within those limits their parents are breaking the law if they fail to send them to school and the LEA is breaking the law if it does not make sure there is a suitable school for them to go to.

Starting School

Children must go to school when they are five years old. But the

T-C

law explicitly states that 'compulsory school age' is reached only at the beginning of the term *after* a child has had his fifth birthday (Education (Miscellaneous Provisions) Act, 1948, Section 4). So even if his birthday comes in the second week of a term, the LEA is not under any legal obligation to give him a school place until the beginning of the next term. A child who is five at the end of April, just after the beginning of the summer term, may have to wait for the autumn term for a place. However irritating this is, and however damaging, parents have no legal basis for a complaint. (See **Summer-born children.**)

Leaving School

A pupil may leave school when he is sixteen years old. However, he is not necessarily allowed to leave as soon as he has had his sixteenth birthday. If his birthday falls between 1 September and 31 January he may not leave before Easter. If his birthday comes between 1 February and 31 August he may leave at the summer term half-term holiday.

Birth Certificates

Parents are asked to show their child's birth certificate to the school when the child is registered there as a pupil to give the LEA legal proof of his age. If a child was born in Great Britain and his birth certificate has been lost, copies can be supplied on payment of a fee, either by the Superintendent Registrar of the district where the birth was originally registered or from the Registrar General, General Registry Office.*

If parents refuse to cooperate in producing a birth certificate the LEA themselves can apply to the Registrar to get a copy.

Parents whose children were not born in Great Britain may find it quite impossible to produce a birth certificate. In these circumstances the LEA has no alternative than to accept a sworn affidavit from a member of the family, however unsatisfactory they feel this may be.

* For England and Wales, applications should be sent to: St Catherine's House, 10 Kingsway, London WC2.

Choosing to Stay on at School

Although the LEA has to provide places in secondary schools for pupils up to the age of nineteen, pupils have no automatic right to occupy one. They can no longer be made to attend school by law when they are over compulsory school leaving age, but, on the other hand, the school does not necessarily have to follow any legal procedure if it does not want them there any more. Unless the LEA makes regulations to the contrary, the head can probably suspend or expel a pupil without having to prove that he had 'reasonable cause' as he would have to do for a younger pupil. Some schools go so far as to say that pupils can stay at school for a sixth year only if they have passed enough public exams – say four CSEs. Although LEAs are obliged only to provide secondary education for senior pupils who have not yet reached the age of nineteen, many pupils who stay on for a third year in the sixth form have their nineteenth birthday during that year. It would be very unusual for a school or an LEA to raise any objection to their completing their course on the grounds that they were too old.

Confiscation

Whether or not the school rules include a list of items forbidden in school, a teacher has a right to remove from a pupil anything to which he objects. Once the teacher has taken possession of a pupil's property he must take reasonable care to keep it safe from being damaged or lost. Keeping someone else's property is, in effect, stealing, so even if he decides to hold on to it for the rest of the school term, the teacher must return it eventually in the same condition as it was when he confiscated it.

A teacher who is reluctant to return a dangerous object to a child should make arrangements to hand it over to the parents. If there is a particular reason for wanting a confiscated item back immediately (perhaps because it belongs to the parents and not to the child at all) a teacher would be unlikely to refuse a personal request from the owner for its return and would have no legal grounds for doing so.

Corporal Punishment

Anyone who really is a glutton for punishment should read the law reports relating to corporal punishment. A brave attempt was made in 1973 to change the whole system which makes corporal punishment legal in schools. Baroness Wootton introduced a Bill for the Protection of Minors into the House of Lords. The Bill was defeated – but only just. It would have broken new ground: Parliament has passed no laws concerned with corporal punishment in schools and has taken great care to leave teachers out of it when they have passed Bills concerned with young people and their welfare, such as the Acts which stopped the navy from beating young ratings and prison warders from birching offenders. The only binding legal requirement imposed on schools by the DES is the instruction that corporal punishments should be recorded in a punishment book kept by the headteacher who is responsible for its completeness and accuracy (Administrative Memorandum 531/1956).

Most parents, even those who hate the whole idea, have at some time been provoked into smacking their child. The teacher's right to beat a school pupil is founded on the legal assumption that physical violence is a reasonable way for a parent to control a child and is therefore reasonable for anyone who is acting *in loco parentis*. So a teacher has a clear right in common law, in the words of the NUT, 'to inflict reasonable and moderate corporal punishment without more ado'.

What is Reasonable and Moderate Corporal Punishment?

A study of the cases which have reached a court of law enables some generalizations to be made about how a court is likely to decide whether or not the punishment was 'reasonable'.

In the first place they will take account of where the child was hit on the body, what with and how hard. Although the judge commented that being deaf in one ear should not appreciably interfere with a child's hearing, it was ruled that it had not been reasonable to strike a child on the ear (Ryan v. Fildes, 1938). In 1962, when a teacher broke a boy's jaw the stipendiary magistrate said he could not bring himself to say it was right for a schoolmaster to punch a boy on the jaw (R. v. Reid). But ten years later a 'light to moderate blow' which happened to break a boy's jaw in two places was judged to be a reasonable punishment. Mr Justice Ackner, who heard that case, felt he had a special duty to protect society from 'an excess of sentimentality or sloppy thinking'. So although the court will be concerned about where the blow fell on the body, it is not altogether clear what they are likely to find reasonable.

Unfortunately a cane of the approved pattern (or a tawse if you live in Scotland) is not always immediately to hand. So teachers may grab the nearest weapon. Where a cane is not used, any sort of ruler or cane-like object appears to be reasonable to the courts. The teacher who in 1967 whipped a child's legs raw with a wire clothes brush because she couldn't find her ruler had the grace to plead guilty to assault (Asquith v. Proctor).

Bearing in mind that the right of a teacher to hit a child at all derives from the fact that he is acting in the role of a parent, the courts have taken a bizarre view of how reasonable parents punish their children. Although beating a child with a skipping rope until he dies is too hard, caning a child on the hands so hard that she had marks on her hands four weeks later was not too hard for Judge Laski. He was reported as saying that parents must expect discipline in school to be maintained and caning her on the hands about sixteen times was not excessive punishment for the kind of dumb insolence which would have ruined school discipline (R. v. Gilchrist, 1961). What sort of naughty behaviour makes it reasonable in the eyes of the courts for a teacher to beat a child? Using another boy's cap as a football for one thing. In fact when the father who did not think this 'crime' justified beating his eight-year-old son sued the headteacher for assault he not only lost his case but had costs awarded against him to safeguard the headteacher and other heads against such proceedings (Walsh v. Bolwell). In the eyes of the court it is even reasonable to cane a child who may well have done nothing naughty at all. One teacher

whose class got out of hand beat every single child with a black-
board pointer regardless of whether or not they had been doing
anything. The court was most critical of the 'over-excited' parents
who took legal action against the teacher (R. v. Jeffs).

A parent who objects to the punishment meted out to his child
needs to look closely at these depressing precedents before he goes
to court to argue that the punishment was neither moderate nor
reasonable.

LEAS

Under Section 23 of the Education Act, LEAs have the power, if
they choose, to issue regulations controlling corporal punishment
in county schools. Before the reorganization of local authorities
about 25 per cent of local education authorities had not bothered
to make any regulations whatsoever. The majority had rules such
as laying down which categories of teachers were permitted to
exercise corporal punishment. If the LEA has neglected the question of corporal punishment, the headteacher may have made
rules about it for his own school. But if neither the LEA nor the
headteacher has drawn up any code of conduct, then each and
every member of the teaching staff and any prefects who have been
authorized by the school can inflict reasonable and moderate
corporal punishment. Voluntary schools are not necessarily subject to LEA regulations.

Some LEAs have made more ambitious local regulations and
have gone for abolition for some age groups at least. This achievement may disguise a bitter battle behind the scenes with an Education Committee which wants to get rid of corporal punishment
having to fight its own officers in the Education Department as
well as the teachers. When the Chief Education Officer is an ex-
headmaster, such as George Taylor, who was the Chief Education
Officer of Leeds for fifteen years, he may feel that

... it is not for the committee to interfere ... Some members of the
committee wanted to abolish corporal punishment in schools ... I
took the view that it would be very unwise for the Education Committee
to pass any resolutions forbidding teachers to use corporal punish-

ment. It would have caused great conflict between the teachers and the Education Committee . . .*

What Can Parents Do?

It is worth quoting the exact words of the solicitor who discusses the legal basis of corporal punishment in *A Last Resort?*† He writes that

unless there is agreement to the contrary, the teacher has the usual authority . . . the mere fact of sending their children to school implies that parents have delegated their powers of discipline to the school authorities. Where, however, the parents make known to the school authorities that they do not consent to certain rules of discipline the position is not clear . . . A case does not appear to have been specifically decided on whether, if a parent clearly states to a school authority that she does not consent to her child being physically punished, the teacher so punishing the child would be acting without authority.

STOPP (The Society of Teachers Opposed to Physical Punishment) therefore has a form for parents to fill in and send to their child's school which explicitly withholds the right to inflict corporal punishment. G. R. Barrell in *Teachers and the Law* is firmly of the opinion that this form cannot affect the teacher's powers. Nevertheless, in its *Handbook of School Administration*, the NUT plays safe by recommending to headteachers that 'it will be found an advantage to obtain the signature of the parents to a form signifying that, whilst the child is still at school, it is agreed that the latter will be subject to the reasonable rules of the school and to school discipline'. It would be very unwise for a parent to sign any such declaration unless he understood precisely what was in the rules and stated that he agreed only to what he saw at the time of signature. One of the few strengths of the parents' case is that, since education is now compulsory, the concept of a contract freely entered into by parent and teacher is notional rather than real.

In spite of the weight of evidence which shows that corporal punishment is at best useless and at worst damaging to the child and inevitably destroys any good relationship between the child

---

*Kogan, M., and others, *County Hall*, Penguin Books, 1973.
†Newell, Peter, ed., *A Last Resort?*, Penguin Books, 1972.

and the school, it is not opposed by all parents. Parents who do not argue with an occasional caning ought to realize that once the principle that the teachers have the right to inflict corporal punishment is conceded, the parent has no say in how or why it is administered. And if it is reasonable, moderate, not administered for the gratification of passion or rage and is in accordance with the rules of the school, then the child has no redress in law whatever accidental consequences arise from the punishment. What is accidental damage? Aggravating a cartilaginous tumour from which she was known to be suffering by hitting a twelve-year-old girl on her bad arm with a ruler or beating another twelve-year-old girl so that part of her hand was permanently paralysed (Mansell v. Griffin). This sort of accident will continue to happen as long as children can legally be assaulted in schools. That is what parents should remember. That, rather than the occasional slap on the backside to teach a naughty boy a lesson, is the reality of corporal punishment. If you allow one you allow for the other.

Correspondence Courses

Where pupils cannot get the education they need either at school or with a home tutor, a correspondence course can provide individual tuition through the post. LEAs have discretionary power under Section 56 to pay for this. They will need convincing that a correspondence course is necessary and will be carried out if they are to pay the fees. They have been known to pay for children living in remote areas who did not want to live away from home, children who were physically unfit to go to school, children who had school phobia.

There are many correspondence colleges which offer GCE exam courses and a range of further and higher educational qualifications, but the Council for the Accreditation of Correspondence Colleges* has one accredited college which offers full-time courses for pupils of school age.† Their course is intended to provide a basic education; there is a core of compulsory subjects with option-

* 27 Marylebone Road, London NW1 5JS.
† Mercers College, Ware, Herts. (tel: Ware 5926).

al extras. Children are allocated personal tutors who mark all their work when it is sent off at the end of each week. The lessons are intended to be self-explanatory so that the child may do them with or without the help of their parents.

The PNEU – Parents' National Educational Union – has a Home Tuition Scheme.* This is intended to provide guidance for parents who accept the responsibility for teaching their own children. The programme of work includes a timetable and a full syllabus for the whole year, but the parent must undertake the actual teaching. The scheme includes other services such as a library which provides a parcel of books each month for the cost of the postage. They have an examination and report system intended to help maintain standards comparable to that achieved in schools.

Correspondence colleges are very expensive. In 1974 Mercers charged £71 a term for the basic course for a fourteen-year-old child. The PNEU fees for the same age group would be in the region of £100 for the whole year (plus whatever parents think their time is worth). Both colleges have some pupils whose fees are being paid by their LEAs.

Curriculum

The curriculum is the fundamental reason for a school's existence. Grammar schools were schools in which the whole curriculum was Latin grammar. Comprehensive schools not only take a comprehensive range of pupils, they have a comprehensive curriculum: academic, technical and creative subjects are all included. Parents who want to understand the curriculum of their child's school need to know at least three things:

(1) what subjects are on the timetable;
(2) what the syllabus for each subject consists of;
(3) the teaching techniques employed in the school.

Section 23 of the 1944 Education Act says that 'the secular instruction to be given to the pupils shall, save insofar as may be

* Run from Murray House, Vandon Street, London SW1 (tel: 01-222-7181).

otherwise provided by the Articles of Government for the school, be under the control of the LEA'. In aided schools the governors have this control. In practice, LEAs have never attempted to tell heads what to teach or how to teach it and the head has been left with virtually complete freedom over the curriculum in his school.

However, the LEA's control over resources and staffing gives them a practical influence over what happens in schools. One Chief Education Officer has described how her LEA sought to transform maths teaching in their area. After a long process of discussion at professional level the LEA set up a centre for the new maths, ran a series of courses for teachers and sent advisers to visit schools and to encourage teachers who had doubts to go and see it working in other schools. They did not dictate to headteachers what they should do but they encouraged and persuaded them into finding out about it and gave them the most attractive facilities for doing so. The Chief Education Officer said that this had 'electrifying results' on the teaching of maths throughout the authority.*

Although a head has control over what is taught in his school he may find that he has to give a good account of his reasons for choosing certain subjects if the LEA is to provide him with the facilities he needs. A new subject may well call for new teachers and additional equipment. If he wants to get a really ambitious project going such as a computer terminal he may find that he has to convince the committee of elected councillors who decide whether or not to vote him the money. The LEA's policy on supply of equipment will limit the head's independent initiative. The buying may be done centrally so that he can requisition only from their approved list. He can hardly introduce cookery if he cannot get hold of cookers. (See also **Organization and Structure**.)

Subjects on the Timetable

The head has responsibility for deciding which subjects will be studied by which pupils, and the structure of the timetable. One head may build up a strong tradition of studying languages with a choice of as many as six modern languages, another head may concentrate on science; one school may be designing toys for

*Kogan, M., and others, *County Hall*, Penguin Books, 1973.

handicapped children, another may be building a canoe. There is only one subject which the law requires every maintained school to teach: religious education (see **Religion in school**). However, the minimum that a school provides should be adequate qualification for a school-leaver to be able to take up a satisfying job or be accepted for training or further education. Since English and maths are required for almost any training or course of study, irrespective of the subject, schools normally make these subjects compulsory for all pupils during the basic five years in secondary school. But from the end of the third year there will be considerable individual choice of subjects to specialize in, as well as a 'common core'. Parents should be involved when these choices are made and should be able to get advice about the implications of choices made at this stage when it comes to choosing a career (see **Careers guidance**).

Sex Discrimination

The Sex Discrimination Act which became law on 29 December 1975 makes it illegal to discriminate on sex grounds in the admission of pupils to mixed schools (single sex schools were exempted) and in the way they are treated in school. A report published shortly before the Act became law found that boys and girls were separated for some lessons in 98 per cent of the schools studied. It is possible not only that this kind of timetable planning is now illegal but that early specialization could also be seen as a form of discrimination if boys and girls seem to be directed on to different types of courses. It has been suggested that schools may be breaking the law if they use textbooks showing stereotyped sex roles.

Circular 2/76 discusses the effect of the Act on schools. A spokesman from the Department told a *TES* reporter 'In the end it is not for the DES but for local authorities and teachers to interpret the Act in the way it affects the curriculum. Whether the materials used are contravening the Act is up to teachers, parents and others to decide.'

Anyone who wants to make a complaint against a school or LEA on grounds of sex discrimination should first of all send it to the DES. The Department will then decide whether they have powers to act or whether the complaint should be referred to the Equal Opportunities Commission.

Syllabus

Looking at a timetable divided between periods of integrated studies, social studies, integrated science and integrated arts may not tell parents very much about what their child is learning all day. Any school should be prepared to explain which subjects have been combined into a common course. 'Integrated studies', for example, may combine English, history, geography and biology into a general course on the theme of ourselves, our background and our environment. All these subjects will contribute to the course but their contributions will not be separately identified.

It is very difficult to avoid the whole syllabus of every subject in the secondary school being geared to the examination system. By the end of the fifth year, pupils need to have covered the ground marked out by the Board of whatever examination they are entering for. Whatever the constraints of the examination system there is still a choice of periods in history, of set books in English and topics in science, etc.

In theory, pupils who are not working for exams should have a far greater freedom to cover a wider syllabus, but even so, while there are exams for some and not for others, the others will tend to be regarded as second-class citizens.

The syllabus is regarded as a professional matter and seldom discussed with parents. This may be an advantage of homework – interested parents can see their children's books and find out exactly what topics they are covering.

Technique

This is what professional training of teachers is about. In order to gain a knowledge of a subject students study for a degree; to learn how to become professional teachers they have to learn the technique of teaching. Professional questions are the concern of the local inspector or HMI. The teacher is not answerable to the inspector but may depend on his recommendation for promotion, and this could give his advice some weight (see **Inspectors**).

The Governors

The Public Schools Commission of 1861 established many of the principles of school governing bodies. They concluded that

> The introduction of a new branch of study or the suppression of one already established, and the relative degrees of weight to be assigned to different branches, are matters respecting which a better judgement is likely to be formed by . . . men conversant with the requirements of public and professional life and acquainted with the general progress of science and literature, than by a single person, however able and accomplished, whose views may be more circumscribed and whose mind is liable to be unduly pressed by difficulties of detail. What should be taught, and what importance should be given to each subject, are therefore questions for the Governing Body; how to teach is a question for the Head Master.

So according to the Model Articles, governors were given 'general oversight of the curriculum'. But somehow the demarcation between 'what should be taught' and 'how to teach it', which seemed so clear in 1861, has become blurred. A governing body which attempts to ask the head about what is taught, too often faces the prospect of an angry head who assumes that his professional competence is in question. The National Association of Governors and Managers suggests that the relationship between the staff and the governors as regards the curriculum comes under the heading of accountability. Their arguments for it are:

(1) the general need for public bodies to be publicly accountable;
(2) the importance, for teachers, of gaining consent for innovation;
(3) the need to put the governors in a position where they can help to defend the professional integrity of teachers against outside pressure;
(4) the importance of a lay body to whom professional matters have to be explained – if the staff can make it clear to the governors they can make it clear to parents;

(5) the value for innovators in submitting their proposals to comment and criticism (every proposal can be improved by the criticism of those less expert than its authors).

Schools Council

The curriculum is 'a secret garden' which only teachers can enter, said Sir David Eccles in an explanation of his ambitious attempt in 1962 to create a powerful influence from outside the schools by the establishment of a curriculum study group. In due course, the Schools Council was set up with a brief to sponsor research, promote and encourage curriculum development and coordinate secondary schools examinations. It has an income of about £1,700,000 a year, most of which is paid by the LEAs and the DES between them. It is hardly surprising that there is no money left for LEAs to give to any other organization to investigate the curriculum.

The Schools Council has policy committees and panels for individual subjects. On each and every one of these the constitution lays down that teacher members must be in a clear majority. Among the seventy-nine members of the Governing Council of the Schools Council the only ones not directly employed in education are the three representatives from the CBI, the TUC and the National Confederation of Parent–Teacher Associations. Two of the NUT's seventeen representatives were able to sum up the teachers' achievement on the Schools Council 'as having established themselves in an unassailable position against the staff and those clever academics'. So much for the attempt to allow the community to influence the curriculum.

Detention

Detention may be one of the least objectionable ways in which schools can punish pupils: it is not as totally pointless as writing lines, it does not deprive them of education like making them miss art or games, it is not damaging like corporal punishment. 'For', as Mr Justice Field said as long ago as 1888, 'there ought to be some discretion of restraint given to masters in the interest of school order and discipline' (Hutt v. Governors of Haileybury College).

In 1908, Mr Justice Phillimore said (Mansell v. Griffin) 'It is, I suppose, false imprisonment to keep a child locked up in a classroom, or even to order it to stop, under penalties, in a room for a longer period than the ordinary school time without lawful authority.' If detention is imposed without good cause and when there was no precedent in that school, the teacher could be found guilty on a charge of 'trespass against the person', because technically the detention would amount to false imprisonment.

So teachers cannot detain pupils after school hours unless their behaviour is bad enough to deserve it and parents have been warned that the school uses this form of punishment. Detention has to be for a reasonable length of time – thirty minutes seems to be generally acceptable. The NUT says that a 'peccadillo' would not merit detention. But sometimes a peccadillo may be the last straw. Parents would not be justified in objecting to a detention on the grounds that the offence was too trivial, unless they were sure it was an isolated incident. If a parent either informs the school that he does not agree to his child being kept in after school, or goes up to school and asks for the child to be released from detention, the school must comply. However, the NUT *Handbook* suggests to its members that, in that case, 'both parent and child should be told that it will be necessary for some other form of school punishment, e.g. corporal punishment, to be administered as an alternative'.

Detention, by definition, overlaps the moment when responsibility for a child's safety and welfare is handed back from the school to the parent. If the arrangements for detention are not made perfectly clear the child's safety could be in jeopardy: a vital train or bus could be missed; a busy road have to be crossed after the crossing patrol has gone off duty; a journey which should take place in daylight might be completed in the dark; a child who normally walks home with a group may have to walk home alone; parents who meet the child somewhere may have a long cold wait; younger children waiting for an escort from school or for an older brother or sister to come home may be distressed. Parents make arrangements for their child's journey home from school and know when to expect him. They have the right to know if these arrangements have been disrupted. An acceptable code of practice for detentions should include:

(1) parents should be informed that the school imposes detention as a form of punishment;

(2) parents should be given at least twenty-four hours notice of any detention and told that they can state a preference for a different day if, for example, they have fixed a dentist's appointment or a music lesson for straight after school;

(3) parents should be told what time their child will be leaving school;

(4) any child being kept in school should have suitable adult supervision for the whole time he is there;

(5) he should be given some work to do.

Educational Psychologists

Most LEAs employ educational psychologists as part of their child guidance service or school psychological service and also to help carry out their functions under the 1944 Act to ascertain which children need special educational treatment.

An educational psychologist must have a degree in psychology, training as a teacher and some further special training. There are not enough of them available to satisfy the demand from parents and schools for assessment and help with children's learning and behavioural difficulties. In 1968 the Summerfield Report* recommended a ratio of one educational psychologist to 10,000 children. By 1972 75 per cent of this target had been achieved, but even in areas like the ILEA where the target has been exceeded, the increase in demand is such that there are still long delays in getting appointments.

Circular 2/75 especially recommends that schools should normally consult parents before referring a child to an educational psychologist although they have no legal obligation to do so. It

*Psychologists in the Education Service, HMSO, 1968.

also suggests that parents should be given the opportunity of being present at examinations by an educational psychologist. Parents who want a consultation for their child can write direct to their LEA educational psychologist, whose name will be published in the *Education Committees Year Book*.

Where there are long delays some parents may be tempted to speed up the process by making a private appointment. The North London Dyslexia Association, which has considerable experience in this field, had this to say in their annual report for 1973:

Regarding assessments, it is uncertain how much influence the report of an educational psychologist, working in a private capacity, will have with a local education authority. Furthermore, if the child has already been referred to the schools' psychological service, a medical assessment by a neurologist or a paediatrician may be more helpful.

Educational psychologists may be based on the child guidance clinics although much of their work will be carried out in schools. (See **Child guidance**.)

Employment of Schoolchildren

It used to be feared that industrial society would collapse if it could no longer depend on a ready supply of child labour. Even now, daily newspaper deliveries would not survive and service in many retail shops would grind to a halt in the Saturday rush if it were not for working schoolchildren. In some urban secondary schools it is the rule rather than the exception for older pupils to have a Saturday job.

According to Sections 58–60 of the 1944 Education Act, no one is supposed to take a part-time job until they are thirteen years old. On schooldays they may work only after 7.00 a.m. and before 7.00 p.m., but not during the hours that schools are open and not for more than two hours a day. They may work for two hours on a Sunday but for up to eight hours on a Saturday. Certain kinds of jobs are restricted for schoolchildren such as work which involves lifting heavy weights, street trading or taking part in entertainments. (See **Attendance**.) There are some special provisions for children who are working for their family's own business.

Local authorities can make their own more stringent regulations controlling the hours of work permitted and the age at which children may be employed. The local authority can step in to stop any school pupil doing a job which in its opinion is interfering with their welfare or education. They may insist that employers should have a certificate signed by the LEA or the school before they employ a child of school age. These regulations are not so much broken intentionally by parents, employers and schoolchildren as overlooked because no one knows exactly what they are and it is in everyone's financial interests to let the children work if they want to. If this were useful 'work experience' it might be educationally valuable but too often children are exploited as cheap labour. (See **Work experience**.)

Evening Classes

LEAs are responsible for making sure that there is 'adequate provision' for full-time and part-time education for everyone who is over compulsory school age. This does not mean that they have to provide the adult education themselves. Voluntary bodies like the Workers' Education Association and the Women's Institutes have traditionally taken on a good deal of the work and many universities run extra-mural classes for which anyone may enrol.

Older children who cannot fit all the courses they want into their timetable can enrol for evening classes. It may be the most convenient way of re-taking an exam which they have failed or taking a subject which the school does not offer at all – either academic or recreational.

The school's permission will be needed for school pupils to enrol for exam courses at evening classes. Where pupils of school age are asked to pay fees for evening classes, Section 81 of the Education Act gives the LEA discretionary powers to remit these.

Examinations

Everyone accepts that there is more to education than passing exams, but as long as employers, colleges and professional institutions of all kinds insist on exam-passes as an entry qualification, no one can afford to ignore them.

Examinations which may be Taken in Secondary School

GCE

The General Certificate of Education replaced the old School Certificate exams in 1951. It provides the basic qualification for higher education and professional work. There are two levels.

1. Ordinary – O level – is usually taken after five years in secondary school. Although pupils are expected to take O level when they are sixteen years old, the school can get permission for candidates to take it earlier. Subjects in which papers are set at O level range from the conventional English, maths and so on set by all Boards to esoteric subjects like Urdu which may be set by only one. The O level exam results are classified into five grades and ungraded. Although the grades achieved (A to E) are printed on the certificate, D and E are below the original O level pass mark.
2. Advanced – A level – is taken after two years in the sixth form. There are five grades of pass at A level and universities usually specify which grades will be acceptable for entry. It is unusual for anyone to take more than three subjects at A level. Candidates can take one, or exceptionally two, special papers (S) in some subjects on the same syllabus as the normal A level course. A candidate who has not managed to scrape through at A level may be awarded an O level pass on their A level paper. Some Boards set AO papers in the summer designed for A level students doing extra subjects at O level.

The main examinations for both O and A level are held in May and June but a more limited range of subjects can be taken in the winter. Candidates may take as few or as many subjects as they like and there are no compulsory subjects. The exams are set by eight Examining Boards, the majority of which are associated with universities. The names and addresses are given in the *Education Committees Year Book*. Regulations, including a full list of all subjects and syllabuses for every subject, can be bought from the Boards. Most Boards sell copies of old exam papers. All Boards present annual reports giving an account of their year's activities; the Joint Metropolitan Examining Board publishes research papers on its work. Schools may choose which Board to use for each subject as long as their LEA allows this. Candidates have to sit the exams at a recognized centre which is usually the school.

CSE

The Certificate of Secondary Education was set up in 1965 to provide pupils of average and above average ability with a certificate of attainment at the age of sixteen. The CSE course generally takes two years and the certificate takes account of work done throughout the course as well as the results of the final exam.

There are fourteen CSE Boards (listed in the *Education Committees Year Book*) which set up syllabuses and administer the exams. The Boards include representatives from local employers and further education colleges, but are controlled by teachers from the schools where the exam is taken. Schools can take only the CSE courses set by their regional Board.

There are three methods of setting CSE exams, known as Modes:

1. In Mode 1 the papers are set by the examining board and marked by them;
2. In Mode 2 the individual school designs its own course and syllabus but the final exam is set by the board, which marks all the entries;
3. In Mode 3 the school designs its own course and syllabus and examines the pupils itself. The board is responsible for making sure that standards are maintained both in setting the course and in marking the exams.

CSE exams can be taken only in the summer and are available

only to school pupils. They cannot be taken by pupils who are less than sixteen years of age. There are no compulsory subjects. The combined exam results and assessment of class work are graded on a five-point scale, and a certificate is given for Grades 1 to 4. Grade 1 should be accepted as equivalent to a pass at O level by any college or employer. Grade 4 is defined as the standard of performance to be expected from the average sixteen-year-old.

A new higher level CSE exam, the CEE (Certificate of Extended Education) has been introduced in some areas. It is intended to provide a suitable course of study for pupils with CSE who would like to stay on into the sixth form without necessarily wanting to take A level.

COMMON EXAM AT 16+

The present system of having two different exams at 16+ is divisive and wasteful. The overlap is so evident that some schools enter pupils for O level and CSE in the same subject to give them two chances of getting a certificate. Joint experimental exams have been carried out as a means of establishing the feasibility of a common exam at 16+ to replace both GCE O level and CSE. The Schools Council submitted proposals to the Secretary of State in 1975 for a common exam. These could be in operation by 1981 if all those concerned were able to agree on them.

RSA

The Royal Society of Arts was founded in 1754 to 'advance, develop and apply every branch of science in connection with the arts, manufacture and commerce'. Every year more than 500,000 people enter for RSA exams, particularly in secretarial and clerical skills. The elementary exams – Stage One for membership of the RSA – are intended for full-time students either in secondary schools or in colleges of further education. They include subjects like accounts, audio-typing, economics, geography, languages, office practice, shorthand, typing.

Who Decides which Exams can be Taken

The school makes all the decisions about which exam courses will be available. The history teacher may prefer the local Mode 1

CSE syllabus; the head of science may choose to participate in a Schools Council Integrated Science project with an exam set by the Associated Examining Board; the English department may stick to the traditional syllabus set by the Oxford Board; geography may set its own Mode 3 CSE. They have to convince the head and their colleagues that their choice is the right one, and until the Boards finally manage to get together on a common timetable they have to be sure the various combinations will not cause too many complications at exam time.

Do Pupils and Parents Have Any Say in What Exams They May Take?

The choice of subjects in which an exam course is available, the type of exam to be taken and the syllabus to be followed are all professional matters which parents cannot expect to influence very much.

Most secondary schools invite parents to come along towards the end of the third year to discuss the subjects and courses their child will be taking for the next two years. This meeting is an opportunity for parents to find out the school's policy on entering pupils for exams. Some schools enter only those candidates who are certain to pass so that they can boast of a pass rate approaching 100 per cent in spite of the injustice of failing some children before they enter the exam hall. It may be essential for a pupil to persevere with a subject he is not especially good at. The school may decide that he should drop physics and chemistry because he is better at history and French. But parents should give some thought to the future before they agree to let him give up any subject. For instance, if he wants to be a dentist he needs physics and chemistry. Any pupil who already has some idea of what he wants to do should check carefully at this stage, and those who have not given a thought to a career or a further education course could do with some reliable advice about combinations of subjects which are likely to be useful or useless.

What happens if parents and pupils disagree with the school? It is hard to believe that any school would stop a pupil from taking a course wanted for his career. But it is entirely up to them who takes what options, so if all the arguments fail, parents can only try somewhere else – another school or, for GCE, a further education college, if the child is old enough.

It is common practice for schools to set formal exams as a trial run in the spring term before the real thing, often based on the previous year's papers. A pupil may make such a mess of these 'mock' papers that the school decides he will not make the grade after all. The decision not to enter a child at this late stage is very serious. Some schools offer a CSE entry as an alternative but if a folder or project is thrown together at the last minute, it makes nonsense of the aim of CSE to give due weight to the cumulative efforts of two years' work. Parents should insist on discussing any decision like this. They may be able to help or to arrange help with particular problems, although the school ought to be willing to provide this. If the child really does want to sit the exam or really needs it, it is worth putting up a fight for the right to take it. Parents could offer to pay the entry fees themselves. These are usually met by the LEA which may query the policy of a school which seems to be entering children who do not stand a chance of passing.

The school, as the approved examination centre, has the last word as to which candidates are entered. The Boards will not interfere with this decision. If a school will not enter one of its own pupils, no other school is likely to let him sit the exam there. All Boards, except Oxbridge and Oxford, accept private candidates who apply individually and are allocated by them to a convenient centre to sit the exam. However, these arrangements are intended for people who have studied on their own through correspondence courses and so on and regulations often exist specifically to exclude pupils who are still at school. For instance, several Boards will not admit any private candidate who is a pupil at a school which is approved as a centre. The Associated Examining Board gives school pupils the best chance of entering privately: there are no restrictive regulations to exclude them and there are approved centres throughout most of the country.

An additional complication for anyone trying to get round a school's veto is that individual candidates often have to send in their entries before the closing date for schools to submit their lists of candidates. So if the school gives its verdict at the last minute before they send in their own lists it may already be too late to enter privately. There are provisions for late entries which vary from Board to Board. It may cost as much as £12·50 to apply late as well as the normal fee of around £1·50 for each candidate and an additional fee for each subject.

When Something Goes Wrong

Most Boards ask schools to give estimates of the likely perform-ances of their candidates in every subject for which they enter, although many schools do not bother to do this. These estimates are compared with the actual marks given by the examiners and if there seems to be an extraordinary discrepancy – a candidate who was expected by the school to do particularly well who fails or, presumably, vice versa – a senior examiner re-marks the papers.

The headteacher can request the Board to check the addition of a candidate's marks, or for a fee, have the paper re-marked. One Board reported that only four out of 3,500 checks resulted in a grading being changed. Schools can arrange in advance for reports from the Examining Boards on their entries. This may be a general report on the overall work from the school or a report on each candidate. Schools could check on their own performance as well as that of their candidates by making use of this service.

Allowances can be made for anything which might genuinely detract from a candidate's performance. Papers are marked as normal and are then eligible to have the marks increased in the light of special circumstances. This might include an attack of hay fever during the paper or distressing family circumstances, such as a recent bereavement.

It could be that a candidate has a slight permanent disability. For instance, a hearing loss could affect their performance in an aural exam, such as a dictation. It is vital to tell the invigilator as soon as possible, either before the exam or directly after the paper has been written, because they are obliged to include this in their report. There are arrangements for candidates who cannot sit a paper on the day it is set, and for handicapped pupils.

Exclusion

Exclusion is a blanket term used in Schools Regulations to cover a variety of situations in which children might be barred from school. Common educational usage distinguishes between three different types of exclusion:

1. Temporary exclusion because of the child's unacceptable behaviour. The Model Articles of Government call any temporary exclusion on these grounds 'suspension'. (See **Suspension**.) If the school informs parents that a child is to be 'excluded' from school for some time they need to confirm whether this is, in fact, a suspension so that they can claim their full rights according to any LEA suspension procedure. Heads have sometimes bypassed these by claiming that the child is excluded and not suspended because the pupil can come back to school as soon as he cuts his hair/changes his socks/apologizes. The head is given no right in law to make this distinction unless the Articles of Government or LEA regulations specify it.

2. Permanent exclusion is what is generally known as being expelled, although for maintained schools a more accurate description is 'compulsory transfer to another school'. (See **Expulsion**.)

3. This leaves the use of the term exclusion for when a child is debarred from school because his physical condition rather than his behaviour is unacceptable to the school. There are special provisions in the 1944 Education Act which make it legally permissible to exclude children who are infested with vermin or medically unfit to be in school. (See **Health**.) Schoolgirls are sometimes excluded from school in the later stages of pregnancy. (See **Pregnancy**.)

Parents have a right of appeal – which would normally be first to the governors, then to the LEA and ultimately to the Secretary of State – against any exclusion which they feel to be unreasonable.

Expulsion

Headteachers have no authority to expel children from maintained schools. The Articles of Government of the school will determine whether the power to expel a pupil rests with the governors, the LEA, or a combination of the two.

When a child is expelled his name is removed altogether from the school register. Schools Regulations 1959 state that no child is to be excluded from a school on other than reasonable grounds. So parents have a right of appeal to the Secretary of State under Section 68 of the Education Act 1944 if they think that the LEA or the governors have acted unreasonably in expelling their child and they want him to stay on at the same school. The Pupils Registration Regulations 1956 state that if 'the Secretary of State determines that the pupil has been excluded on other than reasonable grounds, the name of the pupil shall forthwith be reinstated in the Admission Register'.

The LEA cannot escape the responsibility of providing a school place for any child of compulsory school age and as soon as the child ceases to be registered at a school as a pupil it is up to the LEA to find another school place for him.

Although a fresh start with new people may be what is needed to solve the problem in some cases, expulsion from a maintained school is seen by all concerned to be generally futile – a game of pass-the-parcel between local heads with problem children as the parcel no one wants to be left holding.

Independent schools have no compunction about getting rid of their mistakes since they have no obligation to make any further provision for the child's education.

Finance

The Education Service is a local service not only because the school buildings are put up by the local authority and the teachers employed and paid by the local authority, but also because it is financed through the local rates.

The pattern of state education was created by William Edward Forster's Elementary Education Act in 1870. One of its most significant provisions was to make education a charge on the rates. The result was two-fold: state education could rely on a guaranteed source of income on the one hand. But on the other hand, rateable values vary considerably from one area to another and consequently so does the quality and quantity of the education services. The proceeds from the rates are no longer sufficient to pay for all local authority services and the rate support grant from central government supplements them. Even though authorities whose yield from the rates is below the national average are brought up to the average level, above average authorities retain their initial advantage. It is worth remembering that the money handed out to the local authorities as rate support grant is collected from the public in the first instance as some other form of taxation. The rate support grant is negotiated between local authorities and the Department of the Environment with the DES taking part. The negotiations are based on the local authority's estimates for expenditure on each of their services as well as their rateable values. The actual expenditure of the previous year is taken into account when the budgets are drawn up provided it was within reasonable limits. For example, authorities have spent as much as 9·08p (Birkenhead) or as little as 5·97p (Liverpool) on the food content of each school dinner in the same year and this will be taken into account. However, an authority would not get away with an extra allowance for school meals because it was spending £1 a head on food.

Once the grant has been authorized it is not earmarked to be spent on the specific items which were the basis of the negotiations. The local authority receives a lump sum from the Department of the Environment and can use considerable discretion as to which of their services will be treated most generously, although DES sanction is needed for major building projects. So a wealthy authority dominated by an elderly population whose children went to independent schools may choose to spend less per pupil of its ample funds on education than an authority with meagre resources but a policy of giving priority to educational needs. There are no legal sanctions against an authority which spends some of the money negotiated on the basis of education spending on some other services, such as housing or social services. One piece of research analysed LEA spending and constructed an index of resources so that they could make valid comparisons between authorities with different rateable values and different numbers of schoolchildren in their population. This showed that Barrow-in-Furness with the lowest resources actually spent more per head on its secondary school pupils than Eastbourne with three times as much money per head available.*

These decisions are political – they will be made by the majority party on the local authority. George Taylor, the ex-Chief Education Officer of Leeds, tells an illuminating anecdote in *County Hall*. He negotiated with the DES and emerged triumphant with approval for spending half a million pounds as a first instalment for a new technical college planned more than thirty years earlier to replace one which was operating from nineteen buildings. The chairman of the Education Committee was delighted. But when he reported to his party they said that building a technical college would interfere with housing. Housing was their first priority. Mr Taylor had to go back and tell the DES that Leeds would not be taking up the offer of loan sanction for half a million pounds. At that time resources were forfeited if buildings were not started by the end of the financial year for which they were allocated, so the DES lost a tenth of their further education building programme for that year.

Education has therefore to compete with all the other services provided by the local authority for their ration of resources. Well over half of all local authority money is spent on the education

*Pratt, J., and others, *Your Local Education*, Penguin Books, 1973.

service. No wonder it has been called the cuckoo in the local authority nest. It is difficult to get support for requests for a larger share of the money when you are already getting more than everybody else put together and difficult to avoid becoming the major victim of any economy drive. The Education Committee may have real difficulty in convincing their colleagues – especially those in social services and housing – that more and better education services are needed.

Local authorities may pay out the money but the government often sets the price. LEAs have to pay teachers on a salary scale which is agreed nationally and they cannot opt out when teachers are given a rise. A substantial backdated rise can play havoc with a carefully planned budget. There are a number of services – careers for example – which the government gives them a duty to provide and pay for. So a large proportion of the budget is accounted for and the authority can express its own educational priorities only with the balance. It is at this point that the authority can choose to put a computer terminal in a grammar school where ten boys will use it for A level work or provide more library books for junior schools.

A study conducted by the Senior Assistant Education Officer for Lincoln, Dr Eileen Byrne, showed that between 1949 and 1963 Lincoln spent two and a half times as much per head on maintenance and repairs of grammar schools as on secondary modern schools. Dr Byrne argues that for the last thirty years

Funds available have tended to be sharply divisive, providing more classrooms, more laboratories, more facilities for older pupils. Pupils of 11 were entitled to more than pupils of seven, pupils of 14 to more than pupils of 11, pupils of 16 and over to more of everything.

Schools are usually provided with money for day to day supplies on the basis of the number of pupils on the school register – their capitation allowance. LEAs vary in the generosity of their capitation allowance and in what it has to cover. Library and textbooks may be supplied as a separate item or have to come from capitation. So the head's ability to transfer resources from equipment for the academic sixth in favour of spending more on the first year remedial group is limited by how rigidly the different items are kept in different budgets. In the ILEA a scheme known as the Alternative Use of Resources gives schools a basic allocation of supplies each year and complete freedom to choose how to allocate all the rest of the available money. The head, in consultation with his staff, can choose to pay for an extra librarian rather than extra library books or decide whether an extra teacher or a video-tape recorder would be better value.

If a child has no textbooks, no exercise books and no pencils, parents need to know if the headteacher is keeping the department short or the LEA is keeping the headteacher short before they start objecting to the wrong person about the shortage. Dr Byrne has concluded 'those who suffer most are the poorer, older, smaller and rural schools, or those governed by non-spending authorities'.

So no one ought to worry about LEAs overspending on education. Parents are more likely to want to persuade them to improve educational provision. Regulations set national standards in various areas – such as buildings – but central government does not put pressure on authorities which fall below the standard to spend more on education. In spite of the fact that the Secretary of State for Education in 1974 was an MP for Newham, the plight of Newham schools would not have become a public national scandal had it not been for the concern of parents who saw their own and other children condemned to a school life-sentence in slum buildings inadequately staffed and under-equipped. Parents' pressure groups throughout the country have been particularly successful in mobilizing support within the local community for improving facilities.

Free Schools

Free schools are founded on the philosophy that since children truly learn only what really interests them, learning depends on them being free to follow their own interests in their own way and in their own time.

Free schools do not automatically fit into any of the legal categories which define the ways in which children may be educated in this country. Children in free schools are not being educated at home, nor are they necessarily being educated in a conventional institution with permanent premises. If a child is attending a free school, parents need to be able to convince the LEA that they are fulfilling their legal obligations in seeing that he gets an efficient full-time education within the meaning of the law either in a school or otherwise. (See **Attendance**.) To do this they need to know what status the free school has opted for.

Independent School

If the free school has five or more pupils they may have decided to register themselves as an independent school. A school is automatically awarded provisional registration as soon as it fills in the appropriate form from the DES. In order to be permanently registered the school will be inspected by HMIs who will look at the building and equipment as well as the timetable and curriculum. Free schools do not charge fees to their pupils even if they are registered as independent schools. They are often registered as charities in order to raise money.

Under Section 78 of the 1944 Education Act, LEAs have the power to pay for meals, milk, clothes and medical treatment for children in independent schools. Unlike the earlier progressive schools such as Summerhill which had to charge fees and could take only those who could pay, the free school movement has a particular concern for the most deprived children in the most derelict urban areas. LEAs often give them help with meals, etc., under their discretionary powers in recognition of this and they may also qualify for help from the Social Services Departments.

Otherwise by Parents

Parents are given the right under Section 36 of the Education Act to educate their children otherwise than in a school. If their children are at a free school which is not registered as an independent school, they would need to claim that they had opted to educate their child 'otherwise'. As long as they could convince the authority that the children were receiving a regular education – by showing them samples of the children's work, timetables, reading lists, etc. – they would be within the law.

Otherwise by the LEA

Section 56 of the 1944 Education Act allows LEAs to make arrangements to educate children 'otherwise than at school' in 'extraordinary circumstances'. It is possible that Local Education Authorities could legally finance free schools under this section of the Act if they felt that the free school was fulfilling a valuable social function or (under Section 82) was an interesting research experiment. Any project which has been classified as an LEA's 'otherwise' scheme must presumably be acceptable by them as a way of providing a child's education so parents whose children are attending any free school which has been classified in this way must be fulfilling their legal responsibility as far as securing their child's education is concerned.

How to Set Up a Free School – a Handbook of Alternative Education* explains exactly what is involved legally and practically. The Children's Rights Workshop has a list of free schools.†

Governors

The 1944 Education Act says that every primary school must have a body of managers and that primary schools 'shall be conducted in accordance with the rules of management'; every secondary school must have a body of governors and the school 'shall be conducted in accordance with the articles of government'. So anyone who tries to find out how the English educational system works by reading the 1944 Act may come away with the totally false impression that managers and governors are the 'board of directors' who run the school.

The legal differences in the powers of managers and governors are so insignificant that the tendency now is for writers to call them all governors, which is what we have done throughout this book.

---

* Available from White Lion Street Free School, London N1.
† Available from 73 Balfour Street, London SE17.

Grouped Boards

Every school has to have governors, but not necessarily its own separate governing body. Section 20 of the 1944 Act allowed schools to be grouped together under one board of governors. The only restriction on this arrangement was that the authority should not act unreasonably in the view of the Secretary of State. It was not thought to be unreasonable for LEAs to designate a sub-committee of their Education Committee as the collective governing body for all their schools and, as recently as 1968, a survey showed that twenty out of seventy-eight County Boroughs did this. Even the very smallest of these had at least eight secondary schools and many more primary schools. Where an LEA groups its schools in this way, it is quite out of the question for the governors to know the schools well enough to do a good job or even to fulfil the function which has become a standard joke – turning up to sit on the platform on Speech Day.

Some groupings may make sense, for instance, grouping a first school with the middle school or secondary school to which the pupils will transfer in due course. But on the whole, every school deserves the standard of individual concern from its governors which was visualized in the Education Act. The intention was to give the community a voice in the functioning of its schools and large groupings of schools completely invalidate this purpose.

The Education Authority does not need to go through any legal or statutory processes in order to introduce separate governing bodies.

The government published a White Paper in conjunction with the Education Act which sets out the principles for governing schools, and which was accompanied by Models for the Instrument and Articles of Government for county and voluntary schools.

The Instrument

The instrument sets out how many governors there should be and how they should be appointed. The rest of the instrument is the standing orders of the governing body which, like the standing orders of any committee, settle the details of when and how they can meet and so on.

The LEA draws up the instruments of government for county schools and makes all the appointments (although it has to allow some places on primary school boards to a 'minor' local authority – a district within an authority). So it is entirely up to the LEA which special interests are guaranteed some representation.

The Secretary of State lays down the formula for voluntary schools to ensure that the interests of the charity which founded the school are properly protected. The LEA appoints the majority – two thirds – of the governors in controlled schools, leaving one third for the foundation. The LEA appoint one third of the governors in aided and special agreement schools, leaving the foundation a majority of two thirds.

The headteacher does not necessarily have a right to be a member of the governing body of his school. Some LEAs do not even expect him to come to the meetings but base their comments and suggestions about the conduct of the school on the written report he sends in to them.

Local authorities are political bodies and the party currently in power jealously guards its control over every committee. As local authorities are responsible for nominations to governing bodies it is normal practice in almost every LEA for the places to be shared between the major parties in proportion to their strength on the council. In 1971 the Wolverhampton Liberal Association produced a list of appointments to local governing bodies. The situation there was typical:

Some councillors and non-councillors held as many as 6 or 7 appointments; endearingly, the husbands of women councillors and the wives of men councillors sat on several boards of schools in the same wards; a considerable number of failed council candidates and former councillors held posts ...

Some authorities make provision for nominations from industry and commerce and religious bodies. Primary schools and secondary schools which are linked may have representatives on the other governing body. Where there is a local university or institute of education it is very common for them to be offered a place for a representative. In most cases care is taken to preserve the political majority of the party controlling the local authority itself.

In 1944 a strong body of parliamentary opinion was in favour of parents being formally represented on governing bodies, but this too was left to the discretion of the LEAs. This is where the most recent changes have taken place, especially since local government reorganization in 1974. The National Association of Governors and Managers (NAGM) undertook a survey in May 1975 and discovered that seventy of the eighty-two LEAs giving information (85·4 per cent) had parent governors. Parent governors are nominated in a variety of ways: nomination by the headteacher, the PTA, election by all the parents in the school and other variations. NAGM's recommendation is that parent governors should be elected by parents and that every parent in the school should have a proper opportunity to cast a vote.

Teachers, ancillary staff and pupils have been claiming a place on governing bodies. Although the model instrument specifically prohibits the appointment as a governor of a 'master or other person employed for the purposes of the school', a number of LEAs have revised the instruments to allow LEA employees to participate and in the NAGM survey sixty-one LEAs (74·4 per cent) had teaching staff as governors. Nine LEAs had non-teaching staff on the governing boards. Twenty-six LEAs had made some kind of arrangements for pupils to attend governors' meetings.

Governors cannot be any sort of link between the school and the community if the parents – and often the teachers too – have no idea who they are. Even if the LEA does not encourage or direct them to make their names known, the governors would have to discuss a formal request to do this. Such a request would be taken far more seriously if it came from a PTA. It is up to the governors themselves how they choose to make their names and addresses public. This may mean that the school or the education office will be prepared to divulge this information on request, or it may mean that their names and addresses are on the notice board in the entrance hall or are sent to parents by the school. The local political party whip is often in charge of party patronage which includes the appointment of school governors and ought to be prepared to tell members of the public whom they have nominated to any school.

The clerk or correspondent is the secretary to the governing body and acts on their behalf in the Education Offices. In county schools he is often an LEA officer and the delegate of the Chief Education Officer.

The Articles

The articles determine the respective functions of the LEA, the governors and the headteacher. Although the Act said that every school has to have its own articles, these were expected to follow the guidelines of the Model. The Articles of Government for all primary schools are made by the LEA. Articles for county secondary schools are made by the LEA but have to be approved by the Secretary of State. The articles for voluntary secondary schools are made by the Secretary of State alone. Some local variations are allowed, but the Secretary of State can veto any extraordinary departures from the standard form. Once they have been agreed by the Secretary of State – known as 'sealing' them – school articles have just as much force of law as the Education Act itself.

The Model Articles give the governors responsibility for 'oversight of the conduct and curriculum of the school'. A more precise idea of what this means in practice is the clause which states that 'All proposals affecting the conduct and curriculum of the school shall be submitted formally to the governors' and in fact, their powers may be more formal than real. More specifically, the articles are likely to involve the governors when decisions are to be made on finance; care and use of the school premises; appointment and dismissal of the head, assistant teachers and non-teaching staff; school hours and holidays; suspension of pupils. The Model Articles for voluntary schools give the governors control over the admission of pupils. Copies of the articles for county schools ought to be available from the Education Office.

The effectiveness of a governing body depends on many factors of which their legal power is only one. The National Association of Governors and Managers has said, 'even the most limiting articles can be used for the benefit of the school if governors are prepared to think about them and use them'. At least as important as legal power is mutual confidence and goodwill between the headteacher and the governors. Without this they can be kept completely in the dark about what is happening in the school and may feel as diffident as parents in a confrontation with the head.

Committee of Inquiry

In February 1975 the Secretary of State announced that he was setting up a committee of inquiry into the management and government of schools (the Taylor Committee). The terms of reference were

To review the arrangements for the management and government of maintained primary and secondary schools in England and Wales, including the composition and functions of bodies of managers and governors, and their relationships with local education authorities, with head teachers and staffs of schools, with parents of pupils and with the local community at large; and to make recommendations.

The committee is expected to complete its work within two years. The committee is unusual in having three members who have been invited to serve in a personal capacity as parents (one of these is a co-author of this book).

Grants for Schoolchildren

There are two categories of grant which may be paid by LEAs:

1. Grants which LEAs are required to make by law. These are controlled by central regulations and allocated according to a national income scale.
2. Discretionary grants which LEAs may or may not choose to provide.

Discretionary grants are mainly sanctioned by Section 81 of the 1944 Education Act which states that (subject to regulations made by the Secretary of State) LEAs may defray expenses, pay the whole or any part of fees and make a variety of grants so that pupils can take advantage without hardship to themselves or their parents of any educational facilities available to them.

The justification for giving LEAs discretion in these awards is that it allows them to respond to local needs and interests. It is also a form of economy because the LEAs could not possibly afford to pay them all. There are two basic flaws in this system. Firstly, discretionary grants embrace too wide a range of objects from luxuries to basic necessities. It may be legitimate for one authority to be more generous to children wanting to travel abroad while another gives special help to sports enthusiasts. But if a school is permitted by the LEA to insist on a uniform, a family's right to a grant to pay for it should not be affected by where they live any more than their right to draw family allowances varies from one area to another.

Secondly, because these grants are discretionary they are the first to be cut in times of financial stringency. While it may be reasonable to cut back on such extras as travel abroad when times are hard or authorities chronically hard up, it is inexcusable to cause real hardship by withholding grants intended to help children from poor families to benefit from their education.

How to Apply for Grants

Many of the grants listed below have to be applied for on complicated and confusing forms (a different one for each separate grant) backed up by supporting evidence such as recent pay chits, rent books, insurance books and so on. Forms and information should be available through the school. If the school cannot help or parents are unwilling to discuss their financial situation with them, all LEAs have someone responsible for welfare to whom parents can apply direct through the Education Office. The welfare service may be no more than one section of the Education Office or it may be a well-developed Education Welfare Service with education welfare officers (EWOs) linked with every school. (See Welfare.) They will have specialist knowledge of all benefits in cash or in kind which are available to schoolchildren and can help with filling in application forms.

The local Citizens' Advice Bureau or branch of the Child Poverty Action Group should also know what help is available in the area and will be able to give advice on when and how to appeal if a grant is refused.

The best authorities and schools make sure that families know about the benefits to which they may be entitled. They circulate every parent at the beginning of each stage of the child's career with details of what is available and how to claim it. Even so, many of these perks must depend on the vigilance of heads, class teachers or education welfare officers in spotting distress signals. Gill Frayn, a voluntary care worker, has commented

I suppose it's a microcosmic glimpse of the drawbacks of our society in which a well-informed family down on its luck will find out about boarding grants, for instance, while an equally needy child doesn't receive help because of family/school ignorance of what can be done.

NET INCOME

The national scale for allocating free school meals depends on net income. This is calculated by taking the family's gross income and deducting: mortgage or rent; rates; tax and insurance; super-annuation; fares and other expenses to do with work; wife's 'dis-regarded' earnings; all other earnings from other members of the family; allowances for special cases such as handicap. Many authorities now use this scale for calculating whether families are eligible for other grants although the level on the scale at which families qualify for benefit varies.

However detailed and specific the rules, they still tend to operate unfairly. The honest family in reduced circumstances may well be denied help with dinners or uniforms by their sheer honesty in describing their resources, whereas a messy, complicated family, with father defecting one minute and then returning the next, may continue to enjoy benefits because they do not report changed circumstances.

Boarding Education

If boarding or lodging near a school is the only way a child can be provided with a suitable education by the LEA, then they must pay the full cost, and the cost of travel to and from the school at the beginning and end of term. Fares for mid-term visits are dis-cretionary. Under Section 81 of the 1944 Education Act LEAs may pay part of the cost of boarding education for children whose parents particularly want them to go to boarding school. Suitable grounds may include both parents living abroad, frequent moves in this country, prejudicial home circumstances, special aptitudes. But LEAs vary widely in their willingness to pay for independent boarding education. (See **Boarding education.**)

Clothing

UNIFORM

LEAs may make grants towards the cost of a school uniform insisted on by the school, but the amount given varies widely and some authorities give nothing at all. The grant may bear no relation to the actual cost of the uniform that has to be provided.

The system for paying the grant is as variable as the amount. Some authorities make a once-for-all grant when a child starts secondary school; others give further grants as the child grows older and bigger. Parents may have to buy the uniform and produce bills before they can recover the cost. One authority went so far as to insist on a signed statement from the headteacher that the uniform was being worn.

Some heads have used the existence of uniform grants as a reason for not getting rid of compulsory school uniform. The argument is that if no 'distinctive clothing' is specified, then no one is eligible for uniform grants and needy families would lose a benefit. Heads who are prepared to end compulsory school uniform have got round this by producing an optional list of recommended clothing. The grant can then be used for clothing on this list. The following extract from one school's list shows how flexible this can be:

BOYS   Terylene mixture or cord trousers
       Plain shirt
       Anorak or duffle coat or raincoat or reefer jacket
GIRLS Plain trouser suit
       Dark skirt
       Stockings, tights or socks in the following colours: beige, black, royal blue or white.

ESSENTIAL CLOTHING

If a child's lack of suitable clothing prevents him from taking full advantage of the education provided at the school, the LEA may either make a grant for buying essential clothing or provide the actual clothes. Some LEAs think that essential clothing means underwear, others that the most basic need is overcoats and shoes. A generous authority may provide clothes from the skin out at regular intervals, others may never provide anything at all. If the clothes are given to the child outright LEAs are supposed to charge the parents for some of the cost if they think they can afford to pay. If the child is given only 'user rights' there is no charge but the clothes do not officially become the family's property to dispose of as they wish.

In some authorities all those receiving supplementary benefit or free school meals receive an essential clothing grant as well. Others insist that families on supplementary benefit apply to the DHSS for money for essential clothing for schoolchildren. The DHSS itself recognizes this anomaly. Their report *Families Receiving Supplementary Benefit* quotes two mothers living in different areas. One mother received a regular grant once a year from the LEA for several items of clothing. The other reported 'I went to the Education Department but they sent me to the Assistance and they only gave me £1·50.'

The Education Welfare Service may be given the responsibility for deciding whether or not a child is entitled to an essential clothing grant. As one education welfare officer put it 'This can embarrass the child if not handled with tact' and she quoted the case of a child whose clothing was inspected in front of the whole class. Procedures for making the grant may also cause distress. Clothing may have to be ordered sight unseen from a central stock and it is hardly surprising if it does not fit. Sometimes vouchers have to be presented at shops named as official suppliers.

GAMES KIT

Games kit is usually compulsory even in schools where uniform in general has been abandoned. The fact that this can be a source of particular difficulty to poorer families was recognized as long ago as 1948 when the Provision of Clothing Regulations specifically gave LEAs the power to provide for pupils' general use 'such articles of clothing as may be prescribed suitable for the PT provided at the school'. The Regulations show that these include 'plimsolls, running shoes, football, hockey and cricket boots, bathing suits, shorts and singlets'. Nowadays it would also cover judo suits and leotards.

There are two ways in which an LEA can help towards the cost of games kit. It can take it into account when determining the amount of uniform grant or it can provide a common stock for use at each school. It is distressing, therefore, to find that children who cannot afford to buy it are still being punished for not having the right games kit – openly, for instance by caning, or covertly, by exclusion from school sports teams.

Clubs

If schools charge a fee for membership of the music society, the orchestra, the drama society and so on the LEA can pay the fee so that pupils can join without hardship.

Maintenance Grants

LEAs can pay maintenance allowances to pupils staying on after they reach compulsory school leaving age at sixteen. The purpose, according to Mrs Thatcher when she was Secretary of State, is 'to encourage children who wish to stay on at school beyond compulsory leaving age by enabling them to do so without hardship to themselves or their parents'.

The DES leave complete discretion to LEAs as to what level, if any, of allowance they will pay. In 1975 the ILEA, for example – a generous authority in this respect – paid a maximum of £192 a year to a family with one child whose net income was £15·50 a week or less. When you consider that a sixteen-year-old school leaver could earn £18 at the local chainstore, the financial incentive to stay on at school is minimal.

A sub-committee of the House of Commons Expenditure Committee recommended in September 1974 that allowances should be

paid on a nationally agreed scale and should be paid to all those
eligible for free school meals. More controversially, the committee felt that part of the allowance should be paid direct to the
pupils. The DES are carrying out a review of the working of
maintenance allowances before any changes are made.

Meals

Parents whose children are at maintained schools have a legal right
to free dinners for all or some of their children if their income is
within the income scales specified by the DES. For example, in
November 1975 when school meals cost 15p each a family with
three children whose net income was £33·20 a week would get free
meals for all three children wherever they lived. Families drawing
supplementary benefit or family income supplement are automatically entitled to free meals for all their children. Children who
are granted free school meals will normally receive them for twelve
months, irrespective of improvements in the family's income,
before they need to re-apply.

A number of surveys have concluded that around 20 per cent of
children entitled to a free meal do not take it. Every school ought
to know exactly how families should apply for this and an education welfare officer can always help parents to get this benefit
even where he is not directly responsible for organizing grants for
free meals.

Some people are put off applying for free meals because of the
embarrassment caused to the children when dinner money is collected in school. Any school governors ought to be prepared to
look into the system used by a school for collecting the money to
make sure that children having free meals are not identified in
public. (See **School meals service**.)

School Journeys and Field Study Trips

LEAs have discretionary power to make grants to pupils who
might otherwise be prevented from taking part in school trips. If
the trip is a necessary part of the curriculum no charge ought to be
made. Not all authorities are as generous as Haringey whose rule

of thumb is 'No child is ever left behind because of lack of money.'
In fact, at least one grammar school organized a hockey tour for
the team at a cost of £35 a head and dropped the team members
who could not afford to pay in favour of children who could afford
it, whether or not they were good players. PTAs sometimes subsidize this kind of activity and the head may have charge of a
voluntary school fund from which he can make payments to help
in individual cases of hardship.

Special Talents

This is another discretionary area in which there are wide variations between one LEA and another and policy may reflect the
special interest and enthusiasm of an influential local councillor
or officer rather than any rational use of resources. Authorities
may offer tuition in music for promising pupils, grants for those
with special talent in ballet and the arts to attend schools like the
Royal Ballet School, modern language awards to enable pupils to
spend time abroad, training for sport. The difficulty for parents is
that the awards do not always cover the true cost. A sports award
that pays for coaching but not the cost of travelling to and from
the lessons or the equipment could prove expensive. Information
about these grants should be obtainable through the school but if
the head does not seem very interested in music or Spanish it may
be worth asking the Education Office direct about what is
available.

Travel to and from School

The LEA is obliged to provide transport to and from school if the
journey is longer than two miles for a child of under eight or three
miles for a child who is over eight. They must pay for the whole
journey if the distance is above the limits. They cannot, for instance, pay the train fare to a place near the school but not the
remaining bus journey. Authorities may be more lenient than this
but in all cases the criterion is distance, not financial hardship.

Children over fourteen who are not eligible for free transport or
travel passes and would normally have to pay the full fare, may be

allowed (free or for a small sum) to obtain a 'half pass' which entitles them to travel at half fare to and from school. (See **Transport.**)

Trust Funds

Many authorities inherited trust funds when the 1944 Act came into force. As trustees they can use the interest on the capital invested for helping cases that do not fall into the official categories of need. Local organizations such as the Rotary Club will occasionally help special cases. A resourceful education welfare officer will often have a list of unofficial sources of help at his fingertips.

Handicapped Children

One of the bleakest diagnoses for a parent to hear about his child must have been 'Your child is ineducable'. Since 1970 every child, however severely handicapped, has a right to an education in school. A committee, known as the Warnock committee after the name of its chairman, Mary Warnock, was set up in November 1973 to consider the future of special education. When she announced the inquiry to the House of Commons, Mrs Margaret Thatcher, who was then the Secretary of State for Education, said:

Against the background of the reorganization of local government and of the health and youth employment services in 1974, I believe that the time is ripe for a general inquiry which will go somewhat beyond the specifically educational needs of the handicapped. I propose therefore, in conjunction with my rt hon. friend and Secretary of State for Scotland and my rt hon. and learned friend the Secretary of State for Wales (and after consultation with my rt hon. friends the Secretaries of State for Social Services and Employment), to appoint a committee with the following terms of reference: 'To review educational provision in England, Scotland and Wales for children and young people handicapped by disabilities of body or mind, taking account of the medical aspects of their needs, together with arrangements to prepare them for entry into employment; to consider the most effective use of resources for these purposes; and to make recommendations'.

Of twenty-six members only one is there just because she is the parent of handicapped children.

The Law

It is the duty of every LEA to find out which children in their area need special education and to make suitable arrangements for providing this.

The DES lays down the standards for accommodation and organization of special schools. These regulations are set out in *Handicapped Pupils and Special Schools Regulations 1959* (SI 1959 No. 365, amended by SI 1962 No. 2073 and SI 1966 No. 1565). If boarding education is recommended for a handicapped child, the LEA must normally pay the full cost. It may make use of suitable independent schools, whether or not these are special schools. Since 1964 no LEA may send a handicapped child to an independent school which is not recognized as efficient by the DES. A list of all maintained special schools – List 42 – is published by HMSO and is available in reference libraries together with a list of all independent schools which have been recognized as efficient – List 70. The independent schools are arranged by area and details are given if they cater for any handicap.

Handicapped children used to have an extra year of compulsory schooling but since the school leaving age has been sixteen years for all children they now have the same leaving age as everyone else.

Ascertainment

All kinds of organizations may notice that a child needs help and ask the LEA to look into it. So children may be referred to the LEA as possibly in need of special education by their parents, from the register of children 'at risk' kept by many Area Health Authorities, by the Family Health Centre, GP, hospital assessment centre, audiology or other special unit, or, particularly in the case of ESN (educationally subnormal) and maladjusted children, by the schools.

In order to put the problem into perspective, we have looked at the figures given to us by the health authority for one London borough. In 1967 there were 3,520 births in the borough, but by 1972 when it was time for the children to start school only 2,226 were still living there. Of these, eighty-eight had been kept on the observation register throughout the five years, but sixty-two of them went straight into ordinary schools in the normal way. Another eight started their school career in ordinary schools but were kept under special observation. So only eighteen children were finally ascertained as needing special education.

The sooner problems are diagnosed the better, but some handicaps do not become evident until a child is ready for secondary school. Parents may ask for their child to be examined at any time if they feel that he may need special education. Parents who are requested to let their child be examined for this purpose cannot refuse. When a child is assessed to decide whether he needs special schooling, the community physician arranges a medical examination at which all available reports on the child – educational, medical and psychological – are taken into account. Parents are entitled to be present at this medical examination and in Circular 2/75 the DES says that, although it is not required by the Education Act, parents should also be given the opportunity to be present at any examination by an educational psychologist.

After considering all the information, the LEA will decide whether the child needs special education. If so, it must give notice to the parents together with full details of the medical report.

The DES issued a circular on 'The Discovery of Children Requiring Special Education and the Assessment of their Needs' in March 1975 (Circular 2/75). This stressed that

Parents should be brought into consultation even before – and certainly not later than – the time when initial medical and psychological investigations take place; these can be arranged quite informally without reference to the legal basis for the medical examination. Parents should also be encouraged to visit the special school, unit or class suggested for their child. In these ways any questions or problems which they have can be brought into the open and dealt with.

It is deplorable that the National Council for Civil Liberties receives a number of requests for help from parents of handicapped children who have not been allowed to see the report which is the basis of the decision about their child's future. It is quite clear that the Education Act (Section 34) intends them to have this right and parents should take any difficulties to their local councillors or MP. They could also write direct to the Secretary of State objecting to the action of the LEA on the basis that it was unreasonable (Section 68).

The LEA ought to provide special education for any handicapped child over the age of two, although it is not compulsory for parents to take it up until the child is five years old.

If a parent insists on it, or if a parent absolutely refuses to send his child to a special school, or if a child who is registered at a special school has a very poor attendance record, there is a statutory ascertainment procedure to be followed which is set out in the Education Act. A certificate is issued, setting out the nature and extent of the child's disability and his need for special educational treatment. A parent can appeal against the issue of the certificate to the Secretary of State who can arrange for the child to be re-examined. If a certificate is cancelled, either by the Secretary of State, or by the community physician, the LEA must notify the parents and must not provide special educational treatment any longer.

Once a child is registered as a pupil at a special school, whether or not the statutory ascertainment procedure has been carried out, he may not be withdrawn from school without the consent of the LEA. Here again, the parent can appeal to the Secretary of State if the LEA refuses to let the child leave. The Secretary of State cannot direct a child to attend a special school unless a certificate has been issued.

LEA Provision

Lists of all officers and education committee members for each LEA are published in the *Education Committees Year Book* which is available in every reference library. This will show whether an authority has any committees specifically concerned with special schools and whether they employ any inspectors, advisers, organizers or officers with a responsibility for special education.

Some big cities have only a handful of children who were born totally blind. Some handicaps are so rare that there are fewer than twenty children in the whole country suffering from them. Parents may find there is no school in their district or even in the whole authority which can cope with their child's handicap. In that case the LEA must offer the child a boarding place, but if parents do not want their child to go to a boarding school it may be a long hard struggle to get a satisfactory education for the child.

At the other extreme, the demand for places for mentally handicapped and maladjusted children may be so great that the schools have long waiting lists. Parents may jump the queue with a specially hard case but the long-term solution would be to contact other parents – through the local branch of any voluntary society – and try to get more places provided somehow. One solution – regarded as experimental in Britain although it is the usual system in Sweden – is to integrate handicapped children into normal schools. A special unit may be the home base for those who need special equipment, but the children can take part in many school activities and avoid some of the social isolation which compounds the distress of the original handicap for so many children and their families.

Examinations

A variety of arrangements are possible for candidates who are blind or have some physical handicap. Extra time is usually allowed and candidates may be allowed to use typewriters or to dictate their paper to someone who writes it down. Surprisingly, the simpler expedient of dictating into a tape recorder does not yet seem to have been accepted.

Health

School Health Service

The School Health Service has a magnificent record. In 1939, when it had been running for just over thirty years, an official report was able to record that the death rate of children of school age had fallen by more than half. Life improved out of all recognition for the survivors as well. In *Century of Growth in English Education 1870–1970** H. C. Dent recalls

> I lived as a child at school amidst the adenoids, the decayed teeth, the 'earache', the rickets, the 'rheumatism', the ringworm, the erysipelas and the ubiquitous fleas and lice that were such common afflictions among elementary school children in the first decade of the twentieth century.

The School Health Service used to be the responsibility of the LEAs – part of the education service – because it was clear from the start that you cannot hope to educate ailing children. As the concept of a community health service developed the health of schoolchildren was seen to be an integral part of it. So the School Health Service was taken away from the LEAs and became part of the National Health Service on 1 April 1974. It is now run by the Area Health Authorities (AHA) which were then set up. Outside London the boundaries of the Area Health Authorities coincide with the local authorities. In London they operate within the boundaries of one borough or a combination of them. In his final report on the old School Health Service, the last Chief Medical Officer of the DES, Sir George Godber, pointed out with obvious misgivings that whatever facilities are available for children under the National Health Service 'they are not enough without a staff associated with the schools and devoted to securing that the best that can be done in schools to promote the health of all children is done'.

HOW IT WORKS

The National Health Service Reorganization Act 1973 (Section 3) took over from Section 48 of the 1944 Education Act with a detailed specification of the functions of the School Health Service. Each Area Health Authority has had to appoint a senior doctor to have special responsibility for the School Health Service, in agreement with its matching LEA. A senior dentist and nursing officer are appointed by the same procedure. The doctor (community

*Longmans, 1970.

physician) is to be a specialist in community medicine and is to be in charge of the whole range of health services for children. But, in addition, he is directly accountable to the LEA for a number of functions.

The Department of Health and Social Security (DHSS) issued a circular to help Area Health Authorities and LEAs to sort out exactly who was to do what after reorganization. Broadly speaking, the AHA appoints all the staff needed for the School Health Service and is responsible for all medical and dental inspections and treatment. However, the LEA must continue to provide medical rooms in schools for the use of the School Health Service. The AHA must supply the LEA with the staff and services it needs to carry out specific duties where medical personnel are called for, such as assessment of handicapped children. There are to be joint committees of the AHA and the LEA for planning and consultation.

Medical Inspections

The lynch-pin of the School Health Service has always been regular routine medical inspections for every child in school to discover and treat preventable diseases in their early stages.

All children are likely to have at least three routine medical examinations during their school career. These are spaced out from when they start school (or just before, through the Infant Welfare Clinic) to when they reach compulsory school leaving age, with another probably around the age of twelve. These inspections are compulsory and any parent who refuses to allow a child to be examined may be fined £10 unless there are exceptional circumstances. The school can refuse to admit the child until they have the medical. In the case of Fox v. Burgess (1922) a father was convicted for failing to secure his child's education because she refused to have a medical and was therefore not allowed in when she arrived at school.

School Health Service Regulations 1959 state: 'An authority shall, so far as is reasonable and practicable, give the parent of a day pupil the opportunity of being present at every medical inspection, and at the first dental inspection, of the pupil.' It is quite clear that parents have the right to be at their child's medical and the responsibility has passed from the LEA to the AHA to make sure that they are given proper notice in time to make arrangements to be there. If parents miss a medical because their child forgot to give them the note or lost it on the way home, they should point out to the Area Community Physician that unless notices of medicals are sent by post parents may lose the chance of attending.

A problem could arise if it was not 'reasonable and practical' to arrange a child's medical for a time when parents could get there. School doctors are in school only for certain sessions, so although the Authority ought to cooperate if parents ask to come at a slightly different time or on another day, there would be a limited choice of days and times when the doctor would be available. If a child is given a full medical examination without parents being notified or given an opportunity to be present, they really ought to write a formal letter of complaint. They should start with their local community physician, if there is one, and if they are not satisfied take it up with the community physician for the whole Area Health Authority. They should not give up if they are not taken seriously: the Community Health Council should support this kind of case. Although they are not intended to be a channel for complaints, they would take up an issue like this if the normal channel for complaints did not get anywhere, and they would also help parents to sort out to whom they should be writing in the first instance. It may be too late for their child but it should at least ensure that other parents are not denied this basic right through an 'oversight' or misunderstanding.

The School Health Service Regulations say that medical and dental records must be kept for each child. So parents who have filled in the date of the triple booster and attack of chicken pox once, do not need to rack their brains all over again the next time they receive the same questionnaire. They can add any new information and mark the rest 'Same as before'.

Parents or teachers can ask for a child to have a special examination if they are worried about him in any way. If any examination shows that treatment is needed, it can be arranged either through the School Health Service or through the GP. The School

Health Service should check up to make sure the child is being treated even if parents decide to do it their own way.

Eyesight Tests

Almost every LEA tests pupils when they start school for variations in eyesight, but not all of them have a programme for retesting them at regular intervals. These routine vision tests are mostly carried out by nursing staff and any children who appear to have a defect are referred to an ophthalmologist for a full test.

Eye tests almost certainly include a test for colour blindness.

The vision test carried out in schools is a primitive one, but it ought to detect really serious defects in vision. Parents should not rely on it if they suspect a child has difficulty in seeing properly. They should arrange to have an examination by a qualified practitioner even if the child has just 'passed' the school test. The GP will supply a form which entitles patients to a full test.

Hearing Tests

Severe deafness ought to have been diagnosed long before a child gets to school but a slight hearing loss can easily be overlooked. All AHAs have a responsibility to carry out a hearing test on a child at some time in his school career; how it is done is left to each AHA. In 1971, 60 per cent of schoolchildren in their first year of school had a routine hearing test, carried out by some recognized technique using proper equipment. A further 26 per cent were screened in school in this way during their second year. Parents should not wait for a routine test if they suspect that a child has a hearing problem – the sooner they get advice the better.

Inspections for Cleanliness

Inspections of hair and feet are carried out regularly by school nurses. Parents are not expected to come to these and are not normally told when they are to be held. They will be told if treatment is needed and, once again, offered an appointment through the School Health Service if they want one.

Cleansing

Every local authority has a duty to make facilities available for cleansing children who are 'infested with vermin or in a foul condition'. Children who are suspected of having nits or some other infestation, or else so dirty that they have become objectionable and unhygienic, may be legally compelled to have a special examination and can then be excluded from school until they are cleaned up. The parents of a child excluded from school because of nits, who has applied for treatment at the cleansing clinic, cannot be held responsible for the child's absence from school. But parents who do nothing about getting the child cleansed and either keep him at home or try to send him back to school in the same condition can be taken to court for failing to secure the child's education and the medical officer can make an order for someone to collect him and take him to be cleansed compulsorily. Once a child has been cleansed he is expected to stay that way. If he gets into a foul condition again, his parents may be fined.

Clinics for Schoolchildren

Certain problems, such as bedwetting, obesity, dietary problems and behaviour problems not severe enough to need child guidance, are so common amongst schoolchildren that the local School Health Service may have set up special clinics to treat them. Staff at these clinics should have special know-how in dealing with children. The scope and name of these clinics varies from one area to another.

School Dental Service

The School Dental Service has not been able to achieve any dramatic successes in saving teeth and preventing dental disease. Recent reports show that while nearly every schoolchild needs some treatment, less than 20 per cent of them go to the School Dental Service for it. But wherever they go for their treatment, ideally every child will be seen by the school dentist once a year for a check-up.

As well as chronic staff problems, the School Dental Service seems to have difficulty in coming to grips with the administrative problems. In answer to an inquiry about the School Dental Service, the Inner London Groups for the Advancement of State Education were told that in 1972 in Inner London 55·15 per cent of children for whom a first appointment was made failed to turn up for it. Assuming that ten minutes were allowed for each appointment, this means that dentists were hanging around with no patients for 17,770 working hours in that year. Or, in other words, nine years of the working life of one dentist. The dental service have tried various ways of solving the problem, including taking the dentists to the children (mobile surgeries) if the children will not go to the dentists. The official report for 1971–2 on the School Dental Service concluded that 'Although the increase in the number of children treated in the past 20 years has been small the pattern of treatment has greatly improved. The brief visit for an extraction to relieve pain is much less common than hitherto.' So at least the people who do turn up are benefiting and parents who have difficulty getting an appointment with a National Health dentist, or are not satisfied with the treatment, should give the School Dental Service a chance.

Orthodontics

Orthodontics is a branch of dentistry specializing in correcting misplaced teeth. Children are normally treated when they are about eleven years old to coincide with losing their first molars and a child who is self-conscious about having wires on his teeth will soon find he is not the only one with them.

Although the number of dentists with orthodontic training is increasing, there may be areas where it is hard to find one. As well as specialist practices, some hospitals have orthodontists on their staff and in some areas a dentist in general practice will give advice on orthodontic treatment.

The school dentist or family dentist may recommend orthodontic treatment for a child under the National Health Service. If parents are convinced that their child is growing up to look like Dracula and the dentists are too busy doing fillings to notice, the GP may be able to get them a referral to a hospital.

Orthodontic treatment frequently takes two years or more and parents need to be strong-minded to see it through. A child's speech should be quite normal when he has had a week or two to get used to a brace, but he may not be able to play the trumpet.

Methods of treatment vary, so parents who are not happy about the course of treatment suggested should try and get a second opinion.

Vaccinations

In accordance with the DHSS schedule current in 1974, certain vaccinations are offered through the School Health Service. Parents can have them done by their own doctor if they prefer, but the School Health Service will want to keep a record of when they were done.

AGE	VACCINE	COMMENT
At 5 years of age or school entry	Diphtheria/tetanus and polio	Can be given at 3 years
Between 10 and 13 years of age	BCG vaccine	For tuberculin-negative children
All girls aged 11 to 13 years	Rubella vaccine	To be offered irrespective of history of an attack of rubella
At 15 to 19 years or on leaving school	Polio and tetanus	

Hygiene

Many infections, such as dysentery, and parasitic infestations, such as lice and worms, are spread amongst schoolchildren through lack of elementary hygiene. Both teachers and children need to understand the life cycle of parasites and how infection and infestation are spread. Education about these matters can never be effective unless every school cloakroom is adequately provided with toilet paper, hot water, soap, nail brushes and disposable towels.

When is a Child Fit for School?

When a child has a temperature of 102° parents do not need anyone to tell them he should not go to school. But a child who looks perfectly fit may still not be welcome there. Parents are not always clear as to when a child may go back to school after an infectious illness, whether he should stay at home throughout the incubation period if he has been in contact with an infectious illness, what the school's attitude will be to a whole range of other complaints which commonly afflict schoolchildren.

INFECTIOUS DISEASES

The community physician (previously the principal school medical officer) is responsible for setting up procedures in his area for monitoring epidemics of common infectious diseases among schoolchildren. He is likely to ask headteachers to report to him when children are absent with one of these, whether or not they are on the list of notifiable diseases. (In the case of an officially notifiable disease it is the doctor's responsibility to make a report to the Area Health Authority.) So if a child is off school with something like mumps, measles or chicken pox, it is helpful to let the school know straight away rather than waiting to send a note when the child goes back to school. Schools are not conscientious enough about asking parents to give them information about illnesses or about recognizing the significance of absences, which could be a warning of a serious epidemic such as dysentery.

It is much worse to catch almost any childhood disease as an adult and some illnesses, such as mumps, may have serious effects in an adult which do not occur in children. Many fellow parents would be pleased to get it all over with and may not mind at all if other children go back to school with swollen or spotty faces as soon as they feel well enough. However, old habits die hard and most authorities expect children to stay away from school until they are no longer infectious. How long must they stay off school?

A useful guide for parents is the minimum time recommended in 1971 by the DHSS that a child should be regarded as infectious with each disease. The community physician for any area can make his own regulations which may vary slightly and any individual child may take longer to recover.

Disease	Minimum period for staying away from school
chicken pox	six days from onset of rash
diphtheria	until nose and throat swabs are bacteriologically clear
dysentery	until complete recovery. The Area Health Officer may insist on complete bacteriological clearance, i.e. three consecutive stool specimens collected at intervals of not less than two days all proving negative
food poisoning	until complete recovery and bacteriological examination is clear
German measles	four days from onset of rash
infective jaundice	seven days from onset of jaundice
measles	seven days from onset of rash
acute meningitis	until clinical recovery and until nose and throat swabs are bacteriologically clear
mumps	until swelling has subsided
poliomyelitis	until clinical recovery
smallpox	until declared free of infection by Area Health Officer
streptococcal infection (this may take several forms, e.g. respiratory infection, scarlet fever or tonsillitis)	until treatment given. If a child has had rheumatic fever or is susceptible to streptococcal infection parents must make a point of asking the school to let them know of any epidemics of this illness so that they can consult their doctor
TB	until declared non-infectious

Disease	Minimum period for staying away from school
typhoid/ paratyphoid	until bacteriological examination is clear
whooping cough	twenty-one days from onset of cough

Whether or not the GP says a child is free from infection and fit to go back to school, the school is entitled to exclude him if the medical officer recommends it and issues a notice stating that the child is to be excluded from school on health grounds. In that case, the child will not be allowed back to school until the medical officer himself certifies that he is in the clear.

Does a child have to stay away from school when he has been in contact with someone who has an infectious disease? With most children's 'normal' illnesses nowadays it is quite all right to send them to school until they develop the first symptoms themselves. The only exceptions are where they have been in contact with diphtheria, polio, smallpox, TB and typhoid.

German measles (rubella) is a special case because if a pregnant woman catches it her baby may be affected. Children with German measles may be infectious before the rash actually appears. Parents ought to warn the school if their child has been in contact with it so that any staff members who could be at risk can consult their GPs. The DES recommends schools to tell all mothers of pupils if German measles occurs in the school and to advise them to consult their GPs if they are pregnant. Regrettably, schools do not appear to make any attempt to carry out this advice.

Other Medical Problems Common in Schoolchildren

Children can suffer from a whole range of unpleasant ailments which do not make them really ill but look unsightly or could create social problems. Parents may not know whether children should go to school with them. The doctor should be consulted about persistent spots, skin rashes or bald patches on the head. The advice here is only about how such conditions may affect a child's school life.

If a child has a complaint which is unsightly but not contagious parents should explain to the teacher what the matter is and make sure that the child himself knows all about it so that he can answer questions from parents or other children. Although treatments are available for some conditions without a doctor's prescription, it is better to get the doctor's advice in any case. As prescriptions for children under sixteen are free it will be cheaper too. If a child has any chronic condition which is likely to make him miss a lot of school, it is always helpful for the school to be kept fully in the picture. A letter from the doctor could be useful.

ACNE

Acne affects four out of five teenagers and can make them absolutely miserable. It is not contagious. However, do not hesitate to go to the doctor. Severe acne can leave the skin permanently scarred if it is neglected and even if it is only a few pimples or blackheads it is worth getting all the help possible to clear them up quickly.

ALLERGIES

Allergies may take many different forms. Sufferers may sneeze or wheeze, their eyes may stream, they may come up in all kinds of rashes. It is often difficult to pin down what has triggered off the allergic reaction.

However much a child sneezes no one else can catch his hayfever nor will they come up in spots if they sit next to him while he has nettlerash (urticaria).

The school needs to know about any allergy a child may have and the cause if it has been identified. It is particularly important to tell the teacher in charge of a field trip or school journey about known allergies. If a child is going to be staying away from home remember to warn the person responsible about allergies to antibiotics.

Warn the school if a child is having antihistamine treatment for an allergy as this can make him sleepy.

ATHLETE'S FOOT

Athlete's foot is a form of ringworm in which a fungus develops between the toes. It may spread from the feet to other parts of the body. It has more to do with the changing room than the sports field. Provided it is treated the DES says that pupils do not need to be excluded from swimming or other barefoot activities on account of athlete's foot.

BITES

A child who keeps developing a fresh crop of bites may have been in contact with animals which have fleas, lice, mites or ticks. These not only itch, but can produce an allergic reaction. If there are no pets at home and parents know that the child has been handling animals at school, they should tell the teacher about the bites.

The DES recommends precautions which should be observed when handling animals: washing the hands after every contact with the animal; constant supervision of young children through-out the time they are handling animals; no child to handle any animal while they have any cuts, abrasions or open sores; dis-couraging all hugging and kissing of animals; referring any serious animal bite to a doctor with information about the animal which bit the child. This advice is just as valuable for families who have animals at home.

CONJUNCTIVITIS

The conjunctiva is the delicate membrane which lines the inside of the eyelids and covers the exposed front surface of the eyeball. It can become inflamed as a result of infection with bacteria or viruses. The eyes become completely blood-shot – which is why this condition is commonly known as pink-eye – and the eyelids swell. All of this combined with a discharge of pus often causes the eyelids to stick together during the night and the child cannot open them in the morning until the eyes are bathed. This can be very alarming the first time it happens.

Conjunctivitis is highly contagious and can be transmitted by fingers, towels, flannels and so on. Although there is no official guidance from the DHSS, the local School Health Service may have its own rules about keeping children at home when they have conjunctivitis. It is certainly very antisocial to send a child to school with conjunctivitis unless he is mature enough to understand how to avoid infecting anyone else.

CONSTIPATION

The doctor should always be consulted about chronic constipation in case there is a physical cause. But this may have become a problem because the school lavatories are so disgusting that a child refuses to use them or difficulties are made by staff about letting pupils go to the toilet. This is something parents should discuss with the school. It may be a question of closer supervision of what goes on in the lavatories which are a notorious haven for troublemakers. If it is a more basic question of the condition of the toilets or of whether the facilities are adequate, it becomes a problem in which the school governors ought to be involved.

DEAFNESS

Parents must make sure that every teacher knows about a child who is at all deaf so that they can sit near the front of the class. Learning languages may present particular difficulties but there is no need to give them up solely on account of some hearing loss. Pupils who could hear well enough to learn to speak English quite normally can learn other languages too, although they may need some special help.

ECZEMA

Eczema is not contagious however unpleasant the skin may look. It is often associated with an allergic reaction, although emotional stress is sometimes thought to be a factor. Parents should be sure to tell the school doctor about a history of eczema before the child is given any vaccinations.

ENURESIS

Parents are always asked at school medicals whether their child wets the bed. Treatment is often available through school clinics. The school must, of course, be told that the child wets the bed before applying for a place on a school journey.

It is generally regarded as a symptom of stress if a child who has been dry at night for some time suddenly starts wetting the bed again. It would be nice to think that if the teachers knew about this they would try and find out whether any situation in school was causing the anxiety and at the very least avoid making it worse. So if parents have sufficient confidence in the sensitivity and tact of their child's teachers they should discuss it with them.

FOOD POISONING

If a number of children from the same school develop nausea, vomiting, diarrhoea or acute stomach pains, food poisoning should always be suspected. It is surprising that there is no official request for parents to let the school know immediately if their child has developed these symptoms. Unless the school knows the following morning that all forty children who are absent were ill all night with the same symptoms there may be serious delays in tracing the origin of the outbreak.

IMPETIGO

Impetigo is a highly contagious skin infection. If a child has no more than a couple of sores, completely covered by dressings which he can be trusted not to interfere with, he may go to school according to DES advice. But it can spread all over the face, hands and limbs and in that case the child must stay at home.

LICE (PEDICULOSIS)

Even the cleanest child can become infested with headlice at school and other members of the family are quite likely to catch them from him. Lice are small wingless insects about $\frac{1}{16}$—$\frac{1}{8}$ inch long which can be seen moving in the hair. They feed on the blood of the scalp and in doing so make bites which irritate so much that constant scratching may lead to infection. Children with headlice can be made to stay away from school until they have been treated. (See 'Cleansing' above, p. 118.) The whole household needs to be examined to make sure they do not keep reinfesting one another.

NITS

Nits are the eggs laid by headlice. The eggs are sticky and become firmly cemented to the strands of hair near the scalp. Although they hatch out in nine days, the empty shells of the eggs remain stuck to the hair as it grows, unless they are removed with a fine tooth comb designed for the purpose.

Chemists certainly have the combs and the special shampoo for getting rid of nits and lice but parents may still find it reassuring to get the expert advice of the cleansing clinic on how to eradicate the infestation thoroughly and safeguard the whole household against further infestation.

OBESITY

It is known that 80 per cent of fat children grow into fat adults. A survey in Cornwall in 1972 showed a 'striking increase in obesity during the period that children are attending primary school': only 3 per cent of five- and six-year-olds were seriously overweight as compared with 15 per cent of the eleven- and twelve-year-olds. Part of the cause may be that they are now old enough to get pocket money and go to the sweetshop to spend it. Part of it must be caused by the meals they eat at home. But the Principal School Medical Officer for Cornwall concluded that 'when all reservations are made it still seems clear that school meals are, in general, unsuitable for the overweight child owing to the large carbohydrate content'. What cooperation can parents expect from the school if their child is overweight? There is no reason why a diet suitable for an overweight child could not be accommodated within a normal school meal. There is no need to go to extremes like one school near Leeds: a slimmers' club was formed in which all the members sat at one table which quickly became known as the fatties' table, to the humiliation of the children. The school meals organizer for Nottinghamshire, Joan Whitham, described in *Education* in May 1974 how non-fattening meals could easily be made available in schools:

Even in schools with single menus there is very little problem in providing a meal for obesity diets. In most cases the child can take the main meat dish, omitting any pastry or batter mixtures. School meals now generally provide two vegetables and a good serving of these, excluding, of course, potato, and a piece of fresh fruit, cream crackers and cheese or yoghurt to follow will provide a suitable lunch for even a low calory diet.

This modest aim may sound too ambitious for the kind of school where the head told the school meals organizer 'If we make an exception for one child [a diabetic], they'll all want to do it.' So if the school will not provide any alternative to starchy puddings, offer to send an apple from home instead. Some schools insist on the dinner, the whole dinner and nothing but the dinner. The school meals organizer for your LEA may be able to help. (See **School Meals Service.**)

PLANTAR WARTS

See 'Verrucae'.

RINGWORM

Ringworm is highly contagious and can be caught from towels, combs or other objects as well as from direct contact. It is a skin infection – not infestation by a worm – called ringworm because the middle of the sore frequently heals while the outside is still infected and forms a ring around it. Children are not allowed to go to school until treatment has been started. Then they can go back provided the ringworm patches are completely covered.

SCABIES

Persistent itching is the main symptom of scabies and parents should consult the doctor about intense irritation whether or not they can see a rash. This infection is caused by the itch mite and is so highly contagious that if one member of the family is affected all the others usually are too. Children must not go to school until the whole family has been treated.

SCHOOL PHOBIA

A phobia is defined as an extreme and abnormal fear, particularly one so overpowering that the victim cannot function in a normal way. School phobia, or school refusal, is not the same thing as nervousness or reluctance about going to school for what may be a perfectly rational cause. In those cases the child himself probably knows what is wrong – whether it is a difficult lesson, not having the right clothes, being frightened of the playground, fierce dinner ladies – and he could explain if his parents or his teacher can persuade him to. A child with school phobia may not know himself what makes him so desperately frightened of school. In fact, the origin of the phobia may not be in school at all. It could have more to do with being away from home all day, fear of separation from the family or some other unconscious cause.

If a child is terrified of going to school parents must get psychiatric help. They should go to their GP and if he does not believe in school phobia insist on referral to a consultant. Ask the consultant to write to the school stating that the child is medically unfit to be in school so that there is no question of attendance proceedings being taken because he is not receiving his education. A mother in Haringey has been threatened with court action in these circumstances.

If the treatment does not involve any formal teaching and seems likely to last for several months the LEA may be prepared to provide a teacher at home or pay for a correspondence course.

STOMACH ACHE AND SICKNESS

When is a stomach ache not appendicitis? When it comes on only first thing in the morning every Tuesday. A little research on the timetable may reveal that it is games all the afternoon or double French in the morning. Parents should, of course, get their GP to give a thorough physical examination to a child who suffers from persistent stomach aches or sickness. If he can find nothing organically wrong, it may be deduced that the pains are psychosomatic. Do not write them off unsympathetically for that reason. It is well known that anxiety and stress play havoc with adults' ulcers; it is just as common for them to cause sickness and stomach ache in children and the pain and malaise are as real. If parents succeed in identifying the cause they must discuss it with the school whether it is a general problem or one lesson. The school may be able to help the child to overcome or adjust to his difficulties.

VERMIN

Infestation by scabies, lice, nits and fleas is generally described as verminous. (See under separate headings.) The DES reports with concern that there has been a steady increase in cases of verminous infestation of schoolchildren over the past few years, reaching at least a quarter of a million in 1971. This seems to be due to ignorance on the part of parents and children about the causes of these conditions and how they are spread; one determined publicity campaign by a Midlands LEA brought about a reduction of 80 per cent in cases of headlice.

VERRUCAE

Verrucae, or plantar warts, are a type of wart which occurs on the sole of the foot. They are caused by a virus and are so infectious that schools may find themselves dealing with an epidemic. In 1971 one LEA found that 10 per cent of its school population had verrucae. Children are unlikely to notice a verruca until it is bad enough to make walking painful, but regular foot inspections in schools could prevent epidemics by discovering them at an earlier stage. Although the DES says that pupils need not be excluded from swimming and other barefoot activities once adequate treatment has been instituted, many schools and LEAs will not allow children to join in any barefoot activities until the verruca has been cleared up completely. Children have even been excluded from school journeys because they had a verruca.

WARTS

Ordinary warts, mostly on the hands, are caused by a virus which can spread only in moist conditions. They are not normally considered serious, so unless they get in the way or are unsightly they can be left alone and they may gradually disappear. If they are causing any trouble consult the doctor.

WORMS

Dr Spock has summarized advice to parents about worms in one sentence: 'Worms are no disgrace, but need treatment.' Two million treatments for worms were taken in 1972 and the Medical Officer of Health for Reading estimated on the basis of some pilot studies that about one in three children may have threadworms, which is the most common form of infestation. Female threadworms emerge from the anus to lay eggs on the perianal skin. This causes irritation and when the child scratches himself he infects his hands with the eggs which are transferred to his own mouth or food or to somewhere else where they can infect other children. Children with threadworms often wake up in the night disturbed by the irritation. The worms can then be seen around the anus or inside the vagina. They look like thin white threads about one third of an inch long. Chemists sell an effective medicine without a prescription. The only way to prevent young children from infecting one another is to be very strict about hygiene, supervising them closely. Cutting their nails short may help. The whole family may need treating to get rid of the worms altogether. There is no official advice on children going to school while they are infested with worms.

Health Education

Health education may be on the curriculum of the school but parents may have missed it because they expected it to be somewhere obvious like biology. In fact, it may be masquerading under the guise of a modern religious education syllabus. The DES mentions some of the topics which might form part of a health education syllabus: health hazards of different modes of working life; information about health and social services facilities; problems of mental and physical illness; child development; nutrition and diet; dental care; the importance of hygiene and how infections and parasitic infestations are communicated. That part of a health education programme would be uncontentious. But any honest attempt at health education could not avoid sensitive areas with moral and social overtones: alcohol, drugs, smoking and sex.

What has a parent a right to expect when the school enters the area of morality? Undoubtedly, that they will give pupils the information they need to reach their own conclusions. It should not be the school's function to seek to indoctrinate pupils with any particular attitude, whether or not parents happen to hold the same view as the school. Parents who think the school ought to 'sell' a particular moral line should think what they would feel like if they did *not* hold the same view on it as the school. They also have the right to expect that the school will not misjudge its audience and actually encourage them to experiment with the hazard they are being warned against. Research by such bodies as the National Association of Youth Clubs and the Drug Dependency Discussion Group has shown that schools which offer a programme without considering all its implications are going to do more harm than good.

The extent to which parents can have any say in how schools tackle this kind of subject depends on how it is classified. If it is part of the ordinary curriculum – for instance, part of a biology course – parents would have no legal say at all. However, if it is called religious education, parents have a legal right to withdraw their child from classes altogether. In practice, in such an uncertain area teachers may be more prepared to listen to a sensible approach from parents about a course than they would be for a straightforward academic syllabus. Schools have sometimes covered themselves by telling parents in advance when a sex education programme was planned and some have taken the trouble to invite them to come and watch the films to be used and discuss them. One piece of research showed that more than 80 per cent of parents appreciated the value of sound, factual sex education. Nevertheless, a school would be unlikely to insist that sex education was compulsory if parents strongly objected.

There is some comfort for parents who would rather take responsibility for their children's moral education themselves. A government survey on smoking showed that of children who came from homes where parents took a very strong line against smoking only 11 per cent defied their parents' disapproval and did it just the same. Where parents condoned smoking, 51 per cent of the children were confirmed smokers. Perhaps parents have the last word after all.

Holiday Playschemes

> Two more days of school
> Two more days of sorrow
> Two more days in this old dump
> And we'll be home tomorrow.
> One more day of school . . .

Schoolchildren are expected to count the days till the end of term. When holidays arrive at long last the reality can be disappointing and many children end up bored and frustrated. Holiday playschemes can be fun, useful, give children the chance to use specialist equipment and facilities and can arrange excursions on a more enterprising scale than are within the scope of most families.

LEAs can offer all kinds of support to holiday playschemes if they want to. (Section 53, 1944 Education Act.) Encouraged by growing publicity for the need for holiday provision, LEAs in some areas have set up their own holiday playschemes where they plan all the activities and employ all the staff.

Benevolent authorities with less initiative or resources may give help in the form of a grant or the use of school buildings and playing fields, etc., to voluntary societies or community groups.

The National Playing Fields Association* tries to keep track of all holiday schemes being planned so as to include them in their register, published annually. The local authority – the social services or the education department – ought to know about any plans to hold local holiday playschemes although it may be hard to contact the person who has the information.

All sorts of help and information may be available from the Fair Play for Children Campaign† about existing schemes, many of which are members of the campaign, and about getting one going in your own area, with useful local contacts.

Holidays

Children are convinced that everyone else's school has longer holidays than their own. Parents, on the other hand, may get the impression that their children are nearly always on holiday In fact, Schools Regulations state that maintained schools must be open for at least 400 sessions each year. A session is a morning or afternoon. Schools are allowed to take another ten days holiday which are described as 'occasional closures'. So the total term time is 190 days a year which looks at first sight almost equal to the 175 days holiday. However, the 175 days includes all the week-ends and it works out at about forty weeks at school and twelve weeks holiday.

* 25 Ovington Square, London SW3 (tel: 01-584-6445).
† 237 Pentonville Road, London N1 (tel: 01-278-5314).

Schools Regulations do not fix the actual holiday dates. In county schools standard dates are normally laid down by the LEA for all their schools. They are fixed in advance for the whole school year and parents can always ask for a complete list of holiday dates from the school or the Education Office. Many schools send every parent this list routinely. Governors may have the right to apply for a variation for an individual school and to hand out the occasional holidays. Some give teachers a day off for Christmas shopping, many add the odd days onto the half-term break to make them all a full week. Occasional holidays must be taken during the term and may not be added on to the main school holidays.

Voluntary schools are also subject to Schools Regulations. Governors of aided secondary schools can make their own choice of holidays within the total allowed. Church schools in any area often coordinate their dates. The LEA must not make any arrangements which interfere with reasonable provision for religious instruction in any voluntary school.

In spite of variations of a week or so between different areas, school holidays are very much the same throughout the country. This is partly because no one wants to be in school on Christmas Day and partly because the academic year has traditionally started in the autumn and consisted of three terms. In 1966 a special regulation was issued to make it possible to stagger holiday dates or to divide the school year into a different number of terms. But over the years so many other arrangements have been based on the traditional pattern that so far no radical changes have been made except in a handful of special schools. Public exams, held in May and June, are the greatest stumbling block to making any drastic changes and the GCE and CSE examining boards are unlikely to change their whole timetable for the benefit of one or two LEAs who want to try something different. However, there is a revival of interest in the idea of alterations to the standard pattern, including the four-term year.

Where there is a strong local case for a particular choice of holiday dates the education authority will usually accept it. For instance, Oxford school holidays coincide with the annual 'stop weeks' of the Nuffield motor works.

Families with children in separate schools can find it infuriating if all the children are at home at different times. Unless a significant number of families is affected a request for coordination of the dates is unlikely to carry much weight. But where for instance one voluntary school is out of line with other schools in the same authority the governors ought to listen sympathetically.

Schools Regulations allow children to take two weeks off school in term time once a year to go on holiday with their parents. This concession does not apply to a holiday a child wants to take without his family. However exciting an opportunity the holiday may be, a head has no legal authority to agree to it unless the pupil is already over the compulsory school age. The best he can do is to turn a blind eye. If he actively objects parents would have to weigh up the possible consequences of antagonizing him against the value of the holiday. These consequences may be anything from an unpleasant atmosphere to suspending a child of school age or telling a pupil who was over the compulsory leaving age that he cannot return to school next year. Parents can appeal to the governors, the LEA, and, ultimately, to the Secretary of State if they think the action taken by the head is unreasonable.

There is always the possibility of a diplomatic illness.

Home Teaching

In 'extraordinary circumstances' an LEA has the power to provide a free education for a child at home rather than in school (Section 56, 1944 Education Act). The maximum home tuition time recommended by the Secretary of State is five sessions (half days) a week. Most LEAs have some system for arranging this. The LEA decides whether a child's circumstances are extraordinary enough. The sort of cases which qualify are schoolgirl pregnancy, where a child has a prolonged convalescence from an illness or accident, or where it is taking an exceptionally long time to find a place at a suitable school. Mere distance from a suitable school is not in itself the kind of extraordinary circumstances covered by this section since the authority should provide board and lodging in those cases. However, parents who do not want their child to live away from home could ask for home teaching to be considered under Section 56. If the child is a registered pupil of a school the headteacher ought to help parents to apply for home tuition during a long absence. Parents should ask about this if the information is not volunteered. Applications can always be made direct to the Education Office.

Where LEAs claim that it is impossible to provide home tuition, parents should not accept too readily the standard alibi of staff shortages. Many teachers who would not want a part-time job in school – those who are either retired or housebound with young children – might be able to manage a temporary home teaching job with one pupil. If the LEA accepts that there is a good case but cannot provide a teacher, parents should advertise locally at LEA rates of pay and see if they can find one for themselves who could then be employed by the LEA.

Where the need for home tuition is agreed and all attempts to find a teacher have failed, the LEA may be prepared to pay for a correspondence course. (See **Correspondence courses.**)

Homework

The only legal case on record about homework was in 1884 when the parents of a child who was punished for not doing his homework sued the teacher. The barrister won the parents' case on the basis of his argument that 'The parent's liability to have a child educated ... extends only to sending the child to school during school hours for instruction. The order to the child to do home lessons was unauthorized ... the child could not lawfully be punished for breach of it.' (Hunter v. Johnson).

Although no later court case has changed this ruling G. R. Barrell in *Teachers and the Law* expresses the diffident opinion that

It is probable that the courts would decide, at least in the case of pupils of secondary school age, that a requirement that a child should do a moderate amount of homework is a reasonable requirement and that, where such a rule exists, a parent may not order his child to break it.

There seems to be no legal grounds on which a primary school can insist on formal homework. This does not mean that schools will never ask children to look things up, find material for a project or learn their multiplication tables. It does mean, however, that the school would be quite wrong to punish a child in any way for failing to complete the work set.

As far as secondary school pupils are concerned NUT policy is 'That it is necessary for children in secondary schools wishing to sit for examinations, to do homework, but the work given should not be excessive and should be governed by the headteacher, taking into consideration the local circumstances.' So pupils who demand the freedom not to do homework may find that they are offered the freedom not to stay on an exam course.

Parents often have very strong feelings about homework: there is too much, too little; it is too hard, quite pointless. But what worries them most of all is not the actual task but the implications of homework being set. The reasoning seems to be based on two premisses: children who take exams are clever; children who take exams get homework. So parents feel that getting homework is a visible sign that the school knows and cares how a child is getting on and not getting homework shows that no one is bothering to get their child on and he is out of the running for exam successes.

Parents and pupils ought to have a clear explanation of the school's homework policy: how much should be set and how long should be spent on a serious attempt to complete it.

Hospital Teaching

In theory, it is impossible for a child to have a long stay in hospital without the LEA knowing about it. The school, the education welfare officer, and the hospital are all supposed to notify the LEA that a child in hospital is in need of teaching. In spite of this, parents may find it worth contacting their local office themselves in case everyone else is relying on one of the others to do it.

It is not the responsibility of the hospital to provide education for children, however long they are likely to stay there. But they are expected to cooperate in making arrangements so that the teaching can take place. Section 56 of the Education Act says that LEAs have the power to provide education for children who cannot go to school. The fact that they are given a power rather than a duty means that they are not in default of their duty legally if they do not do anything about it. 'Provide' means either finding and employing a teacher and sending them along or paying for a teacher if a child is in hospital outside his own area.

The teaching set-up in any particular hospital will depend on how many long-stay children they have. A children's hospital will almost certainly have enough long-stay patients to justify a permanent hospital school with a headteacher in charge and its own board of governors. Where there is a school the Department of Education has recommended that every child in the hospital should have the opportunity of joining in classes, even if it is only for a week or so (Circular 312 1956).

One research worker from Chester College whose field was 'the therapeutic role of teachers in hospital' conducted a small survey and found

wide differences in facilities provided by LEAs and hospital authorities from one area to another – differences in acceptance of teaching staff on wards and differences in teachers' attitudes to what they felt they could or could not do on a hospital ward not only from hospital to hospital but also from ward to ward within a hospital.

If there are problems, not with the LEA in getting a teacher, but with the hospital itself, the LEA should approach the hospital to sort it out. Parents can also ask their Community Health Council for help and advice, particularly in clearing up any misunderstandings about what the hospital can be expected to do.

Parents should not lose touch with the child's school and the class teacher can be very helpful in suggesting work and encouraging contact with friends.

Arrangements can be made for candidates to take exams in hospital.

Hours

The 1944 Education Act gives the LEA the right to decide the times for beginning and ending school sessions. But they would not be able to opt for the continental system of schools opening from 8.30 a.m. to 1.30 p.m. and then closing down for the day, because the 1959 Schools Regulations stated that all British schools should have two sessions – one in the morning and one in the afternoon except in extraordinary circumstances. The only legal exception to this is in nursery schools or classes for children below compulsory school age where children may go to school for one session only.

The DES lays down that children of under eight years must have at least three hours of 'secular instruction' and children over eight years must have four hours. The dinner hour and the time taken up marking the register do not count towards the total number of hours but time taken up by breaks and medical inspections can be included. LEAs may make their own regulations which lay down a longer school day than this national minimum.

The times of school sessions must be shown on a timetable in every school. This timetable could be cited as evidence in a law case which turned on whether a child was in the care of the school or the family at a particular moment of time. In one such case (Barnes v. Hampshire County Council, 1969) a five-year-old girl was dismissed from school five minutes early before her mother arrived to meet her. She set off on her own and was knocked down by a lorry and seriously injured. The Barnes family were awarded damages against the education authority. The judgement made it quite clear that the children's safety was the legal responsibility of the school up to the 'appointed time' and the parents' responsibility only after that time. So even if a school does not follow a rigid timetable for lessons during the school day, for their own legal protection they ought to publish the times of the sessions as the law requires.

Although the LEA may decide on standard sessions for all its schools, the Articles of Government will usually allow for variations to be made by the governors if an individual school argues a special case. For instance, if a number of schools in an area all start and finish at the same time it may lead to rush hour conditions on public transport which could be alleviated by minor changes in hours. The authority must be asked to give approval to any changes. Hours are controlled by the governors of voluntary aided secondary schools, subject to Schools Regulations.

It is unfortunately true that where there are no parent governors, governors have been all too ready to endorse requests for changes from the head without asking the parents how the proposals will affect them.

Inspectors

The 1944 Act laid on the Secretary of State the duty of causing inspections to be made of any educational establishment, from primary schools to further education colleges, from youth centres to borstals. This included independent schools. Local Education Authorities can appoint their own inspectors if they wish to do so.

Her Majesty's Inspectorate (HMI)

The first national inspectorate was established by the Privy Council as long ago as 1839. The independence of inspectors from schools, LEAs and the DES itself is still symbolized by the title, Her Majesty's, and the formal appointment by the Queen. It was made perfectly clear from the start that the independence of schools from central control was not to be threatened. HMIs are organized as an independent group based at the DES led by the Senior Chief Inspector. About thirty HMIs work at the DES; some may be seconded to other organizations, such as the Schools Council, or abroad; the remainder are assigned to territorial divisions covering England and Wales. In addition to general responsibility for a group of schools an HMI will have a special interest in one particular field, perhaps a subject such as English, or remedial teaching. A District Inspector will also have responsibility for liaison with LEAs in his district.

In their role as the eyes and ears of the DES and in their regular visits to schools up and down the country they can spread ideas about curriculum, practice, and organization, and can report back to the DES on standards, both in facilities, buildings and numbers of teachers, and also in what is being taught. When an inspector visits a school his aim is to assess the work being done there, not to report on individuals, although he may give advice and encouragement. Any written reports on the school would be shown to the staff and governors of the school concerned as well as the LEA. An HMI should be able to build up good relations with the school and the LEA that enable them to speak their minds. He can bring pressure to bear on the LEA if he feels that a school is seriously understaffed, under-equipped or badly housed. The LEA will find it helpful to have the HMIs on their side when putting in claims for new buildings and extra money during negotiations on the Rate Support Grant.

Parents have no direct right of appeal to HMIs; they cannot ask for the HMI to visit any particular school or that he does anything about it when he has. But it is certain that any complaint to the inspectorate about a particular school will end up on the desk of the HMI concerned and, if the complaint is reasoned and substantiated, it will not be ignored.

Apart from visiting schools HMIs are responsible for running training courses for teachers, publications on various aspects of subject teaching, and more general educational surveys, such as the one on parent–teacher relations in primary schools. They are closely involved in the work of the Schools Council. They are responsible for approving new teachers on probation.

As the new LEAs develop their own full inspectorates, is there any future for the HMI? No doubt, LEAs would prefer to present their own picture to the DES of what was happening in their areas rather than that of the impartial witness of the HMI, but the HMI's independence and breadth of experience can prevent LEAs from becoming too parochial, and can allow one authority to benefit from the experience of others. The teachers themselves would prefer that inspectors should be under the control of the teachers' professional organizations.

Local Inspectors

More and more LEAs are now taking advantage of their power to appoint their own local inspectorate. Some large urban areas have a very highly developed system of inspection, others may employ a couple of special advisers. The scale of an LEA's inspectorate can be judged by looking up the numbers and posts in the *Education*

Committees Year Book. It may be described as an advisory service in deference to teachers' sensibilities.

Although local inspectors carry out many of the advisory functions of HMIs they have other roles as well. Sir W. Houghton identified seven special functions to a select committee of the House of Commons on Her Majesty's Inspectorate in July 1968:

help with staff requirements and promotion;
encouragement and help to young teachers;
development of in-service and induction training;
transmission of current educational thinking;
advice on new buildings and equipment;
appraisal of individual schools as a whole;
channel of communication between school and administration.

There is a significant difference between HMIs and LEA inspectors: the local inspector has the same employer as the teacher, and is closely concerned with the teacher's career prospects. The local inspector may, therefore, be in a better position to exert influence. The staff and the school may have to rely on him to present their case at County Hall on all kinds of matters: promotions, extra staff, minor works, new equipment. Conversely, it is the inspector's duty to ensure that the LEA's policy is being carried out in schools, whether on corporal punishment or coaching for selection tests. One example of how an inspector can help a school in a difficult situation was given by an ILEA inspector. He was visiting the school once a fortnight, talking to teachers, discussing problems. He was persuading the ILEA to divert extra resources to the school. He arranged for the Chief Education Officer to come on a special morale boosting visit. He could draw the school's attention to all the special help and services available.

As far as parents are concerned they have no general right of access to the local inspectorate, although they may be involved in some individual cases such as appeals about transfer to secondary school. However, there is nothing to stop any parent from writing to their local inspector if they think he could help.

It is worth bearing in mind the definitive description of the power of the inspector given by Mr W. R. Elliot, then Senior Chief Inspector, to the House of Commons Select Committee:

When you meet a teacher or a head and you feel that his methods are misguided, you have a debate with him; you use sweet reason; you cannot use more than sweet reason. If you have persuaded him by the logic of your demonstration or perhaps invited him to attend one of the Inspectorate's courses at which he can spend a week or 10 days discussing this, well and good. If at the end of that time he is still thinking his methods are better, God bless him.

Learning Difficulties

Parents have a right to expect their child's progress to be appropriate to his age, ability and aptitude; the law says this is what his education should ensure. When a child falls behind in school he may react by being disruptive in class. The problem may then become how to decide whether the failure in school is the cause of disturbed behaviour or whether some kind of emotional trouble caused the failure to learn in the first place.

Failure to learn means different things according to the expectations of parents, teachers and pupils, although it can also be measured by comparing a child's performance with what average children are expected to do at that age. This may be done by testing him with standard tests, such as those for testing reading age and so on.

What can parents do if they feel their child is failing to progress as he ought or cannot catch up because he has missed a great deal of schooling? It is crucial to establish whether a child's work is up to the standard of the rest of his class or not. If the school agrees that he is behind they may be able to help. The class teacher, however hard-pressed the timetable in school, ought to be prepared at least to offer advice or to set work for the child to do at home which will be marked in school. This would be a reasonable request for a parent to make. The NUT makes a point of recommending that schools should be staffed and organized so that extra help can be arranged for children with difficulties.

Many junior schools and virtually all comprehensive schools have special arrangements for remedial teaching. Children may spend part of each day being taught on their own or in small groups.

In some schools there is a remedial stream and children are taught all day in a class of children at a similar stage to themselves.

Where a child seems to have serious permanent learning difficulties, the solution will be more complicated than a few extra sessions to learn tens and units which the class 'did' while a child was away with measles. A specialist assessment will be needed. The school should arrange an appointment with an educational psychologist (see **Educational psychologist**) to discover whether the child is achieving less than he is capable of or has the capacity to go only at a slower pace than the rest of his class.

If, as a result of the investigation into a child's learning problems, parents find that he has some specific learning disability, there are several voluntary parents' associations, such as the British Dyslexia Association,* who have experience and practical help to offer.

Schools and LEAs are at last beginning to realize the importance of dealing with learning problems as soon as they arise. The secretary of the North London Dyslexia Association has written

everywhere there is recognition that existing special provision is unsatisfactory for all concerned. The will to improve is strong. Money is being made available to the authorities. For parents who are dissatisfied with help provided for a child in difficulty, or feel that it is ineffective, or even adverse in effect, the climate has never been better. Seek to become thoroughly informed on the specific handicap, press for the best help that is available, and make sure that any shortcomings in procedure or provision are made known to senior officers of your authority.

Lost Property

The LEA is not legally responsible for a child's belongings, even those given to the teacher for safe-keeping, unless they were lost through fraud, gross negligence or a breach of the school rules. For instance, there may be a rule that money and valuables given to a teacher to be looked after should be kept in the office safe. If the teacher leaves them in the classroom and they are lost, the teacher would be liable.

*18 The Circus, Bath BA1 2ET (tel: Bath 28880).

What children mostly lose is clothing. Children do not stop to read the name-tape before they grab the nearest green parka and it may have been accidentally swopped rather than stolen or lost. Every school has a huge box of lost property which no one bothers to claim.

Dr L. F. H. White, writing in *'Where' on Parents and Law** gave the opinion that LEAs may make an *ex gratia* payment (without admitting liability) where an expensive new item of essential clothing, like an outdoor coat, was irretrievably lost in school in spite of being marked with the owner's name.

There is no hope of getting compensation from the education authority for losing something in school which should not have been there in the first place. A child may be expected to wear a watch to school and to take his own pen, but it would be his own responsibility if they were very valuable.

A householder's comprehensive insurance policy often includes a 'temporary removal' clause (look in the small print). This would cover the loss of any belongings from the school building by fire or theft.

Musical instruments should be insured separately with an all-risks policy if a child is going to take them to school, because that will also cover breakages or losing them through carelessly leaving them on the bus.

School Property

Parents could not legally be made to pay for school property lost by their child. However, if he left a school team football strip on the bus or lost an expensive textbook for the second week running, the school might put moral pressure on parents for a contribution at least. Parents who are thinking of holding out for their legal rights should be prepared for their child to be dropped from the school team or for the school to refuse to allow him to take textbooks home to revise for O level. Most parents will think it is quite reasonable to pay what they are asked if they can. Musical instruments may involve large sums of money. Parents should check with the school whether any instrument is covered by the school's

* ACE, n.d. [1973].

insurance while it is on loan and take out an all-risks policy if not.

Materials

'No fees shall be charged in respect of the education provision in any school or college' (Section 61, 1944 Education Act). Education is not free if parents are expected to pay for the textbook 'in respect of' their child's maths lesson, so they should not be charged for materials necessary for their child's school work any more than paying fees for the teaching. Children often like to have their own pens, pencils and geometry sets which they can take home, but the school ought nevertheless to have a supply.

Anything supplied by the school remains their property.

Some schools have interpreted this so crassly that they have destroyed exercise books filled with children's work sooner than make them a gift of school property to take home. One seven-year-old in an Essex infant school watched the destruction of his detailed diary of the school holidays and all his stories. He said 'It's a bit like war – burning books is just like killing them. I wish I could do some magic to bring them all back.' The Advisory Centre for Education heard from at least seven different parts of the country where this was the practice. Any parents who are worried about this happening should make a special point of asking well before the end of the summer term whether they can have their child's books.

The real difficulties arise over practical subjects with an end product which can be worn, eaten or given away for Christmas. Many LEAs have a stated policy of recovering the money laid out on materials for practical subjects, whether or not the pupils are making something they would choose to keep. A survey conducted by the Association of Teachers of Domestic Science found that some authorities insisted on recovering up to 80 per cent of food costs and 100 per cent on needlework. Although almost every authority said that children from needy families should be given the opportunity to take part in home economics courses, in practice, the authorities provide very little food or fabric for these pupils. In this situation, parents need not be surprised if their children's home economics is based on the sales appeal of what they produce rather than teaching them about sound nutrition.

Parents who are annoyed at having to pay for ingredients more expensive than they would normally buy to feed the family should not assume it is the teacher's fault. It could well be the unrealistic demands of the examination boards. One infuriated mother wrote to the *Guardian* that her daughter's O level course had nothing to do with home economics and should be renamed 'How to prepare party food in a hurry'. For an examination in needlework pupils are sometimes asked to produce one part of a garment or something they would not be seen dead in. Yet the teacher will still be obliged to ask them to supply and pay for the fabric themselves. Children working for exams in needlework and cookery may have to pay over a pound a week for materials. The survey found that a lot of pupils skipped classes rather than face the embarrassment of not being able to pay. One teacher who didn't want this to affect her pupils' choice of project for CSE exams told them to choose what they would most like to make and see her privately so that she could arrange to provide the ingredients and recover the money by selling the end product. She commented 'Quite understandably, they all wanted to take their work home, so they paid for the ingredients out of their Saturday job money.' Do the sixth form scientists have to work on Saturdays to pay for the chemicals they need for their A level course? The report concluded that 'Home economics and needlework are becoming subjects children from wealthy families only can afford.'

Parents need to find out if the policy of making home economics and craft subjects self-supporting is the school's or the authority's. The best way is to write to the authority and ask them what is their policy on costs, sales and provision of materials.

It may turn out that it is up to the head whether or not the school finances consumable materials for practical subjects, and he has so many other demands on school resources that he has decided craft and home economics will have to pay their own way. In that case, a primary school teacher who does not want the craft materials to be limited to toilet rolls and cereal cartons for ever may have to ask parents for money, or other materials. Without supplies from parents, pupils in secondary schools would be copying out recipes instead of cooking the food.

There would be an outcry if pupils were regularly charged for their O level history textbooks, yet the ingredients are as essential to the O level cookery class. One of the basic principles of comprehensive education is the recognition that practical and creative subjects are an integral part of a true education. But until they are given equal treatment they will never achieve the status which has always been accorded to academic studies. One solution is put forward by the Association for Teachers of Domestic Science who argue that LEAs should make schools an adequate grant, separate from any capitation allowance, earmarked for food, craft and needlework materials.

Milk

Free milk – a third of a pint each day – is provided to all schoolchildren until the end of the summer term of the school year in which they have their seventh birthday. If a child's seventh birthday falls in the summer holidays or at the beginning of September they should still be getting free milk when they are almost eight years old. If the LEA finds it impossible to provide fresh or longlife milk, they must supply dried milk or milk tablets instead. All children aged up to sixteen attending special schools are entitled to a third of a pint a day of free milk, and children at special schools for the delicate may get an extra third of a pint as well. Children in special units which are part of an ordinary school do not get these concessions. Handicapped children aged five to sixteen who are not at school are entitled to a pint of milk a day free, regardless of their parents' income. Parents have to apply for this on leaflet FW20, which is available from Social Security Offices.

Any child of any age may be supplied with free milk in school if the school doctor examines him and certifies that it is necessary on medical grounds. Some LEAs who regard the provision of free milk to primary schoolchildren as an essential welfare service have made strenuous efforts to find a pretext for supplying it free to as many children as possible. One solution is to pay out of the rates for free milk for all children up to the age of eleven under the clause of the Local Government Act 1972 which allows the product of an old penny rate to be used 'for a purpose which is, in the council's opinion, in the interests of the area and its inhabitants'. Other LEAs give all children under eleven a medical examination, which shows that children who have said they want milk need it. So when the Secretary of State told the House of Commons in December 1974 that 76,000 primary schoolchildren over seven were receiving free milk on health grounds, many of them will have been getting it because their LEA were determined to give it to them. There is no guarantee that the children throughout the country who most need the milk to supplement inadequate diets are in fact the ones who are getting it.

The school must make arrangements to supply the milk in school on the doctor's recommendation even if it means getting milk for one child in a school of 2,000. Parents who would like their child to receive free milk can ask the school to arrange a medical examination for this purpose. A child has a right to have a medical on request.

The Education (Milk) Act 1971 gives LEAs the power to sell milk at an economic price to all pupils in all maintained schools. If the Education Bill, 1975, is enacted LEAs will be able to subsidize the sale of milk in schools.

Moving House

Not all moves involve children changing schools. Many people move because their family is growing or shrinking and they want a home which is a better fit. A parent should not be asked to take a child away from a school at which he is already registered as a pupil just because moving house puts him outside the catchment area. However, the LEA may argue that they cannot pay a child's fares if there would be vacancies at a school nearer to his new home. (See Transport.)

Whatever scope there is in choosing exactly where to live, it is worth looking at a map to get some idea of the pattern of the whole region. A study of the *Education Committees Year Book* in the reference library will show which education authorities are involved. Everyone has their own views on what makes one LEA better than another and this preliminary survey of LEAs in the region may narrow the field. For instance, if within a reasonable distance there is one LEA which retains the eleven-plus while another has a fully comprehensive system, parents may want to eliminate one of them before they start.

The next step is to write to the Chief Education Officers to find out more specific details. Even if only one LEA is involved, it is still worth writing because there may well be differences within the authority, inherited from the old authorities which existed before local government was reorganized in 1974. Ask for precise information about the type of school organization throughout each LEA. It is also important to find out how children are admitted to the various schools. This is equally relevant for children going to a nursery class or a grammar school. But it may be particularly significant for families transferring to an area which still has the eleven-plus from one which is comprehensive. Will a child have to take an exam? What kind of report will be acceptable? Eleven-plus selection procedures are always fraught with anomalies, but in this situation a child is less likely to do justice for himself than if he has been groomed for selection from an early age.

The Chief Education Officer must be asked about the exact catchment area of any school, and whether or not a child within the catchment area is guaranteed a place there. Families should not assume that it is safe to buy a house in a nearby road, however close: it may not be within the catchment area.

If a child's school career is likely to be punctuated by a series of moves, parents may be able to do something to minimize the disadvantages the child faces of always being the new one. The choice of school will be less dependent on long-term considerations, more on whether the set-up enables the child to settle down quickly. This is where the internal organization of the school is crucial. The child will start with a marked disadvantage each time in any school which has rigid streaming or, worse still, class places. Whatever the pros and cons of 'family grouping' in the primary school, families who move frequently have found that it is an ideal system for children who are going to be in a school for only a couple of years. Among all the other changes they have to make, at least they stay with the same teacher and the same group of friends for the short time that they are settled in one place.

Non-teaching Staff

Parents may not realize the importance of the non-teaching staff to the life of the school until the caretaker says 'You're not having any play-centre in *this* school' and that's the end of the play-centre. What happens in the classroom is only part of a child's experience of school. What happens in the dinner hour, in the cloakrooms, in break time are all just as significant. The quality of life in the school depends on the whole experience and the non-teaching staff who are involved in and out of the classroom all contribute to this.

Employment

How many non-teaching staff are employed in a school will depend partly on the staffing policy of the LEA and partly on the practical problems of finding people for the jobs. A survey conducted a few years ago discovered wide variations in the practice of similar authorities. Caretakers, maintenance and secretarial staff are employed by the LEA at county, controlled and special agreement schools. At aided schools they are appointed and employed by the governors but the LEA pays the salaries, and settles the numbers and conditions of service.

Although non-teaching staff are employed by the LEA, recruitment of helpers like dinner ladies is often left to the headteacher to organize.

School Secretary

Anyone who has tried to speak to the headteacher at their children's school and failed to get past the defences of the stalwart school secretary will understand how important this job is. Whether it is one lady in for the morning at an infant school or a large general office in a comprehensive school, for many parents they will be the first point of contact with the school. Take dinner money as an example. At one primary school parents who do not send the exact amount, in separate envelopes for each child, are told off in no uncertain terms. At the school up the road the children can pay daily, weekly or by cheque in advance for the whole term, whichever suits them best. Why is it that what is impossible at one school is no problem at all at the other? The answer is very likely the difference in the personality and attitude of the school secretary. It is as improper for the school secretary to answer problems about a child's education or attendance at school as it would be for the doctor's receptionist to diagnose a child's illness. However difficult the secretary tries to make it, parents must insist on speaking to or being given an appointment with the teacher concerned to sort out difficulties.

Caretakers

Every school has a caretaker who is responsible for the house-keeping. In some areas he lives on the site of the school. In a large school he may have a considerable staff of assistants and cleaners responsible to him for the work they do. Apart from seeing that the school is kept clean, the caretaker is usually in charge of the heating system, responsible for ordering repairs and supplies of consumable materials for cleaning and for equipping cloakrooms, etc., and for protecting the school and its property from thieves and vandals.

A supervisor for school caretakers in Yorkshire described their job as 'creating a caring environment'. He felt that

improved physical conditions can actually change people, make them more aware of their surroundings and determined to improve them even more. The opposite, of course, is true also: untidy and dirty conditions can breed a lack of caring and further spoiling of the environment . . . Take the problem of litter . . . It is the first sign that we have ceased to care and it quickly affects the way we live. In a school it makes it all the easier to deface the walls, first unseen in the toilets then blatantly throughout the school until outright vandalism develops . . .

This may seem rather remote from the harassed man rescuing footballs from the primary school roof, but we should recognize how fundamental their job is to making school life worth living.

The caretaker's conditions of service should make it quite clear if he is expected to be on duty for evening meetings. The governors should be prepared to look into any dispute about his obligations and take it up with the LEA if necessary.

The caretaker has no authority over the children and should not take it upon himself to punish them even when he catches them red-handed. He must contain himself and hand them over to a teacher.

Dinner Ladies

Parents worry about their children being in a class of forty with one qualified teacher in charge. But for nearly two hours out of the school day they may well be with 299 other children in the playground in the charge of one lady who happens to live near the school and wants a part-time job.

Teachers are not under any legal obligation to supervise the children while they eat their dinner. Where they have decided to 'opt out' of voluntary dinner duty, the whole responsibility rests with the head. So any head will welcome the chance to employ 'dinner ladies' to come and help out. It does not always work. For instance, a primary school may have a philosophy of allowing the children considerable freedom but the dinner ladies may be ferociously conformist so that mealtimes are completely out of tune with the rest of the school day. Good dinner ladies are not just born, they could be made. The PE inspector of the ILEA drew up a programme showing the kind of training which would be suitable. She would like to see the dinner ladies

(1) tutored in simple first aid with access to their own equipment;
(2) taught the proper supervision of children handling playground equipment, e.g. climbing frames;
(3) instructed in ideas for informal games and imaginative play when children seem bored, but also instructed in the desirability of children making their own games for themselves whenever

possible, and especially the preservation of old traditional play-ground games;

(4) attend a yearly refresher conference and, as a long-term aim, the establishment of a short training scheme which would carry enhanced status and more pay.

Help for Teachers

A working party of eleven professional bodies produced a memorandum on the employment of ancillary helpers for non-teaching duties in schools. In their view the main aim was 'to conserve the time and energy of the professional teaching staff for those duties which can properly be undertaken only by qualified teachers'. How much time could be conserved? One research team followed a group of teachers around with a stop-watch. On an average school day they found that 53 minutes (11 per cent) was spent on mechanical tasks; 47 minutes (10 per cent) was spent on supervision; 13 minutes (3 per cent) on clerical tasks; 10 minutes (2 per cent) on school administration and messages. This adds up to the impressive total of 123 minutes or 26 per cent on average of the teacher's day which was being spent on duties which could quite properly have been undertaken by non-teaching staff, had they been available.

Modern methods of teaching make tremendous demands on teachers to produce their own materials. Making up the work programme is the job of a professional teacher. Duplicating sheets, copying out cards and covering them with plastic is a mechanical skill which any reasonably deft person can do once they have been shown how.

If an education authority wants its schools to get away from 'chalk and talk' they must budget for sufficient ancillary staff in schools to relieve teachers of mechanical tasks. Most schools could rely on there being some mothers who would be prepared to come and help out if they were made to feel welcome. Most teachers have not wanted them. Perhaps that is why *The Times Educational Supplement* called it a 'novel solution' when the National Association of Schoolmasters told the Secretary of State in 1974 that schools should 'recruit an army of mothers'. Teachers, they said, need 100,000 helpers to deal with the routine work, including 'supervising outside visits, helping children to read and write, and marking work'. It is difficult to sympathize with schools which complain about being overworked and short-staffed, if at the same time they are barring the school gates against parents offering help.

Specialists

In primary schools, non-teaching staff are most useful if they can offer general help with all kinds of odd jobs. In secondary schools, specialist help may be needed. A large school may need a full-time professional librarian. The science block will need technicians and laboratory assistants. These categories of staff are not counted as part of a school's allocation of teachers.

Open Days

Schools do not have to have an open day but when they do and it is what it claims to be it can be a pleasant occasion: a day or evening (preferably both) when families can come into school and see a whole range of work and activities. This is a chance for parents to see what can be done by other children of their child's age and what they can expect him to be doing in two or three years' time. They can see the topics the children are studying and may get a better understanding of the school's methods and techniques when they see them in action and the results they produce.

It is when this kind of open day is the only chance for parents to talk to the teachers about their child and is used as a justification for keeping them out of the school for the rest of the year that it all turns sour. When parents commiserate with one another over the horrors of school open evenings, they mean the kind of evening when they tried to have a serious conversation about a whole year's school work, about problems and progress, with forty other families jostling for position, trying to pretend they were not eavesdropping. Exhausting for the teacher, frustrating for the parents.

If a school never holds open days and parents are hoping to per-

suade the head that it would be a good thing, they must be sure to
get these two functions distinct: an open day to which all comers
should be welcome is not the right occasion for serious talk.

Organization and Structure

The basic unit in any school is the class: however large the school
and however the pupils are grouped for lessons or leisure throughout the day, a group of anything from twenty-five to forty pupils
will meet as a class at the beginning of each session when the
register is taken. Putting a child in the right class is certainly regarded by most teachers as a wholly professional matter for which
the headteacher has absolute responsibility (see p. 256). In primary
schools he is likely to draw up all the class lists himself, in secondary
schools a number of other staff will be involved.

Primary School

In a primary school children spend most of the day with the same
teacher. Sometimes two or three classes are combined with several
teachers. This is often called team-teaching. For play and dinner
the whole school gathers together in the playground or the hall.

Classes may be streamed by attainment; divided by age; or have
some mixture of children of different ages and abilities, known as
family grouping. Some of these arrangements are more in-
trinsically flexible than others. For example, one small primary
school may have only one class for all the eight-year-olds, so there
is no parallel class for a child to move to if he cannot get on with the
teacher or the other children. Another school, the same size, may
have arranged the children into 'family groups' in which children
from three different years are mixed together in three classes all
more or less parallel. In that case a change is possible if the head is
willing to agree to it.

Secondary School

There are two kinds of systems most commonly used by secondary
schools for dividing pupils into groups: they may be divided

horizontally or vertically. Horizontal schemes mean that all pupils are divided into groups in which everyone is the same age. There may be an upper, middle and lower school or each year may have its own group. Vertical organization means that each pupil belongs to a 'house' with members from every year in the school on the lines of the houses of the traditional public schools. Some schools with a house system separate off the first year and the sixth form.

The intention of every system is to give each child individual attention from a number of people who know him and can help him to find his place in the school. Its success depends fundamentally on how well the class tutor knows the children in his class. If he sees them for registration only – ten minutes twice a day – he will have to make an enormous effort to achieve anything more than fitting the right name to the right face by the end of the year.

In a typical year system, a pupil will have his class tutor, a head of year, head of lower/upper school and the deputy head and head, all of whom have some sort of responsibility for him ranging from the most personal to the most formal. In a house system the most personal contacts will be with the tutor and then the head of house through to deputy head and head. The head of year, middle, lower or upper school or the head of house will have the responsibility to deal with a whole range of issues without reference to the head or deputy head. His special concern is to know the children in his care as individuals. Where a teaching problem is involved he will contact the department head or subject teacher. However much power has been delegated to the year heads or heads of house, the headteacher retains the ultimate responsibility for what goes on in his school.

The internal structure of a school is entirely the responsibility of the headteacher. Although some variant of these systems is in use in most schools, the head is quite at liberty to change one for another, invent a new one of his own or decide to have no internal structure at all. The LEA may impose its preferences by the way it designs its schools so that one scheme fits into the building better than another. Where a school's buildings are on more than one site, the lower/middle/upper school arrangement is more or less obligatory.

Streaming

Streaming children is a method of grouping them for all their lessons according to their attainment. In secondary schools some streams may be groomed for GCE, others for CSE and the lowest streams may be labelled non-exam. A great deal of research has shown that children live up to their labels. If they are labelled 'top ability' and their teachers believe that they are 'top ability' they do better as time goes on at everything from art to calculus to football, while those who are labelled as failures deteriorate at everything. Experiments have shown that if you pick children at random and classify them as clever, average and stupid, they will be treated by their teachers according to these labels and will begin to fulfil the expectations made of them. In a streamed school a parent who thought his child was in the wrong class would have to convince the head that there had been a mistake in the child's assessment and that he could cope better with more, or less, demanding work.

Banding

Banding is a form of streaming with fewer groups. A school with 180 pupils in each year may stream into six streams with each class carefully graded from one to six. Under a banding system they might be grouped into three bands with two parallel classes in each band. Splitting children into only two bands is more objectionable: those at the bottom of the top band and at the top of the bottom band are virtually identical in attainment and ability yet they are divided by an indelible label affecting their entire school career.

Setting

This is a system in which children are grouped according to their attainment in a particular subject. So a pupil may be in the top set for English and the bottom set for maths. It is quite common for a school to use mixed ability teaching for most subjects but to retain setting in English, French, maths or science.

Mixed Ability

The basic assumption behind comprehensive education is that you
cannot measure a child's attainment at the age of eleven and pre-
dict from that his potential academic achievement. More than ten
years ago when selection at eleven was far more widespread than it
is today, the National Foundation for Educational Research followed up the subsequent academic performance of children who
were selected for a particular type of education at the age of eleven;
one in eight of the children surveyed (12 per cent) were wrongly
allocated at the age of eleven judging by their subsequent performance.

The same applies to streaming. A mixed ability class is a group of
children with a wide range of attainment. No assumption is made
at the age of eleven that some of them will be capable of taking
public exams and others will not. Each child should be given the
scope to progress according to his level of understanding and the
rate of development and maturation. The teaching techniques required for this kind of class group are quite different from class
instruction which assumes that every child will work at the same
speed with the same understanding and will gain the same benefit
from the same set of exercises in the same textbook. In a mixed
ability class the teacher cannot even pretend that this makes any
kind of educational sense. He knows that he will need a wide range
of teaching materials to meet the needs of pupils and will have to
develop methods of working which make it possible to help individual pupils as and when they need it. Without these kinds of
skills and resources mixed ability teaching, instead of meeting the
needs of each individual child, can fail to meet the needs of any of
them.

Outings

John Holt, the author of *How Children Fail*, once envisaged
travelling 500 years into the future and talking about education.
'But where are your schools?' he would have to ask. 'Schools?
What are schools?' 'Schools are places where people go to learn

things,' he will have to explain. They will not understand. 'People learn things everywhere, in all places.'

Outings from school can be as valuable for the children's education as what goes on inside the classroom and we do not have to wait 500 years for a trip to the zoo or a visit to the fire station.

While outings which are an integral part of the curriculum should be free, many schools could not afford to take the children out at all unless they were able to ask for contributions. Parents may not be charged the whole cost and this is one of the ways in which voluntary school funds may be used to help pupils.

LEAs and schools usually claim that children do not get left behind because they cannot afford to pay for an outing. However, the offer of help is frequently left to the discretion of the class teacher and parents are not always automatically told that they need not pay if they are in difficulties, nor are they told how to apply for a free place if they need one. An example of good practice, with notices for outings, was set by one Sunday school. They sent a letter to every parent which could well be adapted by ordinary schools:

Dear Parent,
    As you will appreciate, the arrangements for the outing described in the accompanying letter will involve considerable expense to the Congregation.
    If you are able to make a contribution towards these additional expenses, will you please complete the slip below and return it, together with your contribution in the enclosed envelope.
    If, on the other hand, you feel that you are not able to make any contribution, please do not hesitate to send your child(ren) in any case.
    Yours sincerely,

When an outing is planned schools may ask parents to sign a letter of permission purporting to indemnify the organizers for any claims arising through illness, accident or any other cause. They may even refuse to take any child whose parents do not send the letter back. Parents should go ahead and sign: their signature gives the letter no legal force. It does not absolve the teacher from any part of his legal and professional responsibility to take proper care of the children.

T–F

Most LEAs make regulations about the ratio of teachers to pupils on school outings to comply with their insurance policies. The NUT suggest a maximum of twenty pupils to each teacher. The ILEA, for example, require one teacher and one extra adult at least to accompany any visit for each class of children of secondary and junior age and at least two extra adults for each infant class.

Schools may claim that they cannot organize outings because teachers and helpers cannot be spared from school to supervise. Parents could volunteer to help out. Even heads who will not have parents inside the school are often happy to use them outside.

Parents' Associations in Schools

The fact that there is no official parents' association does not mean that a school has a bad relationship or no relationship at all with the parents of its pupils. You cannot pass a regulation decreeing that there must be goodwill – and goodwill is the one essential condition for making an effective link between parents and teachers. Nevertheless there are definite advantages in having some kind of formal structure. In the first place, its survival does not depend on the enthusiasm and goodwill of individuals alone and so it is more difficult for a head quietly to dispense with parents altogether. A second advantage is that communications from a committee are more formal and less personal. One emotional parent putting up a fight on behalf of his own child may provoke an aggressive reaction from the head. A formal request from a committee who have reached a consensus calls for a rational reply.

Getting Started

The National Confederation of Parent–Teacher Associations* can help any new association to get going and has suggestions for a non-controversial constitution. Plenty of advice has been offered to parents about how to get some kind of parent–teacher co-operation going in their child's school if the head does not want anything to do with parents at all. And this advice, whatever the

* 1 White Avenue, Northfleet, Gravesend, Kent.

source, is always substantially the same. Approach the head with tact, delicacy and sensitivity. One eminent educationalist advises parents to 'concentrate on doing something for the school' while another adds 'underemphasizing at first the good you think it will do the parents'. For parents the prospect seems to be 'all give and no take' until the head sees that parents are not as dangerous as he thought, at which moment, according to the theory, he may agree to a PTA. How long might this take? Optimists suggest a year; realists warn parents that it will 'often take longer than the school life of any one child'. But sometimes tact and delicacy can simply make it easier for someone to avoid committing himself. After all, received educational wisdom – personified in the Plowden Report – insists that parents are a good thing, essential to the progress of any individual child and the general well-being of a school. All that may be needed to make a diffident head take the plunge is a push off the edge of the fence where he has been balancing for years. One primary school headteacher in the Wirral had procrastinated successfully for many years about whether or not to have a PTA in spite of numerous tactful approaches from individuals and small private groups. He finally agreed to call a parents' meeting two days before the election for the first parent governors so that the candidates could introduce themselves. Parents had never had a meeting in school before. First one, then another spontaneously seized the opportunity to ask the candidates whether they would support a PTA. Put on the spot by the unanimous demand of thirty parent-voters and all fifteen parent-candidates, the head had to say *something*. He managed a bold statement that he was 'not actually opposed in principle to a PTA'. Before he had time for second thoughts, the parents set up a special meeting to arrange the details. The moral of that is, if you have spent a long time tactfully laying siege to Jericho, the time comes when you must 'blow with the trumpets and shout with a great shout' if you want the walls to come down. Having committed himself at long last the headteacher and parents are now working together with mutual goodwill to get things done for the school.

Parents should not squander reserves of tact by trying to talk an adamantly hostile head round to their viewpoint or by 'selling' him all the things the parents could do for the school if they were given a chance. It is more productive to coax the head into explaining precisely what his objections are. He may be worried by the fact that a committee, by its very nature, involves only a small group of people and all the rest may begin to feel as if they do not belong to 'the club'. This is a real danger. Any parent, however well-educated and normally articulate, may become tongue-tied and inhibited when they turn up to a meeting and find all the regulars, parents and teachers, on Christian-name terms. How does a parent address his child's 'Miss Smith' when everyone else is calling her 'Mary'? So if the development of 'in-groups' is the head's main objection to a PTA (and, indeed, even if it is not) it is worth giving a lot of thought to a programme of activities which will not exclude anyone, and to the arrangements for welcoming newcomers to meetings. Parents can try approaching the head again when they can present him with positive solutions to the problem.

As far as teachers are concerned PTA activities are unpaid overtime. The NUT has said 'such giving of time must be on a voluntary basis. It is normally very gladly given but it is for the teacher to determine how far he or she can participate' (*Handbook of School Administration*, NUT). Parents should always make it perfectly clear that they understand that teachers should choose freely whether or not to take part. Heads have often underestimated the support their staff would give a PTA because they have never asked them. A teacher governor may be able to help by finding out what the staff really feel.

There may be an answer to procrastinating heads and to rationally wary heads. But what about blind prejudice? The kind of head who dredges up the tired myth about American parents running the schools or the head who told the National Association of Head Teachers at their conference in 1969 'I prefer to return to the old idea of parents feeling a little honoured to be invited into school,' – and was warmly applauded. With a head like that the first step is to take a detached look at the people involved: the head and the parents who have been conducting the negotiations. Perhaps the prejudice has been exacerbated by a clash of personalities which could be resolved. There is nothing to be done about the head but the parents may be able to appoint a new ambassador. Although it is awful to have to say it, a headmistress may be more ready to listen to a successful and authoritative professional or business man; at least he will not get stuck with the label 'fussy mother' as soon as he opens his mouth.

Schools are not homogeneous: primary schools sometimes have separate infant and junior departments, secondary schools have houses or year groups. A sympathetic housemaster may be prepared to get together with his parents; the infant head may be interested in having parents' help. In one infant school a solitary class teacher used to invite her parents in for her own meetings and made them welcome in her class, although the staffroom made it clear that they were harbouring a viper in their bosom. (She is now a headteacher.) One cell may multiply in time.

Organization

'The first thing to determine is not the name of the organization but the purpose for which it is to exist . . . a vehicle for raising funds . . . an educational centre for lectures and discussions.'* Too many parents have ignored this advice: they have been sidetracked into the wrong means to the end they want and have learnt too late that 'money can't buy you love'. Of course, fund-raising is a very practical way for parents to give help to a school. But a parent could have bought a place at Eton by the time some heads are won over to a PTA by this method. They may well start with jumble sales which raise £30; years later they may be running garden fêtes and donkey derbys and raising £3,000 and still never have the kind of contacts with the school and the teachers they really wanted. In some schools the staff do not even come to the bazaar so laboriously organized by the parents.

What's in a Name?

Do not worry about the name; it is not worth making an issue of it. A PTA can be set up only with the cooperation of the headteacher and his staff. But if they do not want to get involved there is nothing to stop parents from forming themselves into some other kind of organization to do the things they want to do on their own. A

* White, Dr L. F., *'Where' on Parents and Law*, ACE, n.d. [1973].

Parents' Association can work very well as long as the teachers do
not make a conspicuous fuss about being absent from all the events
and activities. In any case, the parents' association versus parent–
teacher association question can be ingeniously resolved by calling
it a 'school association'. No parents or teachers can pretend that it
is none of their business and grandparents, ex-pupils, future
parents and local tradesmen can all join in.

What can be Done?

The NUT wants the individual headteacher to decide for himself
how best to 'achieve rapport' between the school and the parents.
But for too long too many headteachers have not even tried. For
parents to have access to the school and to be consulted about their
child's education is a fundamental right. Individual headteachers
should not be allowed to withhold it according to their personal
whims. Parents are entitled to expect real help from school
governors, from the LEA and the DES. LEAs could take more
positive steps than they do to encourage headteachers to form a
good relationship with parents by making a firm policy commitment. Practical steps by the authority could include:

> (1) Allowing any group of parents from a school free use of
> school premises in the evening without requiring the consent of
> the head.
> (2) Making it clear to headteachers when they are appointed that
> spending occasional evenings and week-ends with parents on
> informal as well as official and formal occasions is part of the
> conditions of service.
> (3) It has been suggested ('*Where*' on Parents and Law) that LEAs
> could draw up a model constitution for the guidance of em-
> bryonic PTAs. As teachers would, no doubt, be consulted while
> this was being prepared, their objections could be dealt with in
> advance. Then heads need not worry about a newly formed
> PTA in their school trespassing over professional boundaries.

Any parents' association in a school, however modest a part
fund-raising plays in its activities, must have its own treasurer and
bank account. If the money goes into school funds even the best

and friendliest of heads has been known to go off and spend it without a word to anyone. Some heads never tell parents afterwards what it was spent on. If yours is the hand that signs the cheques, at least the head will have to tell you what he wants to use the money for.

As far as the quality of school life is concerned, nothing can improve it so much as genuine, warm goodwill and the informal, unforced friendships which arise spontaneously when parents, children and teachers work and learn together.

Play-centres

The first voluntary play-centre was founded in London by Mrs Humphrey Ward as long ago as 1898 to care for children after school and in the holidays. And yet we still have 'latch-key kids' with no one to look after them when school is over.

In 1944 the Education Act (Section 53) instructed LEAs that it was their duty to secure the provision of 'adequate facilities for recreation', and that to do this they may establish, maintain and manage, or assist the establishment, maintenance and management of play-centres. LEAs are specifically urged to cooperate with voluntary groups in this field and they may defray the expenses of play-centres or make a contribution towards them.

Spending on play-centres is not subject to the stringent DES controls which apply to capital spending on buildings, so the decision about how much to spend on play-centres depends entirely on the local authority's own priorities.

The Home Office's urban aid programme specifically invites LEAs to apply for grants in order to set up 'schemes for the development of play in deprived areas'. Details of the programme can be obtained from the Home Office on request.

Playing Fields

Section 10 of the 1944 Education Act gives the Secretary of State power to lay down national standards for school premises – in-

cluding any detached playing fields – and to make LEAs conform
to them. The Secretary of State is able not only to insist on new
schools meeting the standards but also on existing schools being
brought up to the standard. However, if the nature of the site or
the shortage of sites makes it 'unreasonable' for the standards to
be enforced, the Secretary of State can direct that premises are
'deemed to conform to the prescribed standards'.

Where schools have facilities for swimming and any other
activities which might replace outdoor games, this is taken into
account and an area less than the minimum would be approved for
actual playing fields. These facilities are not to be at the expense of
gymnasia but are to allow for a wider variety of games. One
example would be squash courts. Schools in urban areas often use
sports grounds some distance from the school and these are all
taken into account.

The Regulations which are currently in force are the 'Standards
for School Premises Regulations 1972' (SI 2051). These set out the
size of the paved or hard porous area which should be available in
every size school (laid on suitable foundations, properly graded
and drained).

It also specifies that every school other than an infant school
should have playing fields, either separately or jointly with another
school or schools. Boys' schools are entitled to larger playing
fields than girls' schools with mixed schools splitting the difference.
Nursery schools are supposed to have a garden playing space, and
less than half of it should be paved. Special day schools for educationally sub-normal pupils are covered by a separate section in
the regulations and their playing fields are normally supposed to
adjoin the site of the school.

Playing fields must be provided by the LEA for every type of
school, county or voluntary. Control over use of school premises
out of school hours includes use of the playing fields and so on.
(See **Buildings**.)

In 1964 the DES issued a circular (11/64) jointly with the Ministry of Housing and Local Government which outlined ways in
which education authorities could cooperate on schemes for sports
facilities with other sections of the community. The circular
pointed out that combined provision meant better value for money

and a wider range of both outdoor and indoor facilities. Authorities were asked to look into ways in which facilities for sport and physical education in schools could be shared with other users.

Police Investigations in Schools

According to Judges' Rules 'A child or young person should not be arrested, nor even interviewed, at school if such action can possibly be avoided.'

Children are bound to be interviewed if the police have been called in to investigate something which happened in school. The headteacher has to use his own discretion about whether an incident is serious enough to justify calling in the police. So playground scraps are dealt with as part of normal school discipline, but if the injuries might amount to 'grievous bodily harm' the police are likely to become involved. On the one hand, no one wants the police in school for every lost raincoat; on the other hand, no head can risk the accusation that he has covered up for crimes in his school.

There is a lot to be said for the police carrying out the investigations of offences such as serious thefts. After all, pupils are not the only possible culprits and as staff are hardly likely to cross-examine colleagues, it is a protection for all concerned if police rather than amateur detectives attempt to solve the case.

When the offence has been committed outside school there is no reason why the school should become involved in identification. In September 1974 the fire brigade committee for Tyne and Wear Metropolitan County decided to ask teachers to identify the voices of children recorded making malicious fire calls. The local NUT opposed the scheme saying 'There is at present a proper process which involves the police and they as far as possible quite rightly involve the parents rather than the schools.' This principle ought also to apply to identification of pupils from films of political activities or demonstrations.

However, the police may approach the school for information about a pupil. Headteachers may supply the police with a pupil's name and address. But the ILEA goes so far as to say – without any qualifications – that 'When police are making investigations, heads should, as far as they are able, furnish them with any information that may be required, either from school records or from personal knowledge about the pupil concerned'. Parents and pupils may well have no knowledge about what is in their school record nor will they have had an opportunity to check its accuracy, so this information may influence the police against the child quite unfairly. (See **Records on pupils**.)

Police sometimes go to school to question pupils in the course of their inquiries. A spokesman for the Schools Action Union told *The Times Educational Supplement* that they turn up hot on the trail of stolen library books. The NUT considers that police officers who go into school to question pupils ought to be in plain clothes. The headteacher would be entitled to know what the inquiry is about so that he could judge whether or not the urgency justified the investigation being carried out in school rather than at home.

Interviews

As far as practicable children (whether suspected of crime or not) should only be interviewed in the presence of a parent or guardian, or, in their absence, some person who is not a police officer and is of the same sex as the child ... Where it is found essential to conduct the interview at school, this should be done only with the consent, and in the presence, of the headteacher, or his nominee. (Judges' Rules)

So parents are always entitled to be informed before their child is questioned. The NUT suggests that headteachers should find out whether the parents of a child have been informed of the investigations and given the opportunity to be present for the questioning before he agrees to let the police proceed with the interview in school. If the parents have not been informed, they consider that the head should object to the investigation continuing until they have been contacted. Mr G. R. Barrell, an authority on teachers and the law, has said that if the parents are not present the head may give the child such counsel as he would give his own child. But the NUT says 'it would not be advisable for the headteacher to intervene in the questioning, suggesting to the child what questions he should or should not answer'.

Going to the Police Station

If the police arrive with a warrant for the arrest of a pupil or are acting under the authority of an Act of Parliament, such as the Children and Young Persons Act, the school must cooperate or risk a charge of obstructing the police. The NUT believe that children should not make written statements in school and that parents should be asked to go with the child to the police station to do this. In any case, parents should be contacted before a child is taken from school to the police station for any purpose.

Complaints

If parents feel that the intention of the Judges' Rules has been thwarted and their child denied their protection, they should approach the local police authority. This is the kind of case in which an MP might take an interest where individual complaints fail.

Pregnancy

When it becomes noticeable that a schoolgirl is pregnant home teaching is often arranged, either because the girl herself prefers it or because the school does not want her there. The LEA has an obligation to see that a child under sixteen continues to get an education suitable to her age, ability and aptitude. Pregnancy is generally taken to be one of the extraordinary circumstances which qualifies for home teaching. (See **Home teaching.**) The problem would be when a girl wanted to continue at school or go back to the same school after her baby was born – possibly to complete an exam course – and the school refused to have her. In those cases the outcome would depend on whether being pregnant or having had a baby was considered reasonable grounds for excluding a pupil. (See **Exclusion.**)

   Two surveys of LEA provision for schoolgirl mothers both found that the majority of pregnant girls of compulsory school age were allowed by their LEA to abandon their education even though this was illegal. Of those in the survey, the only authority with a comprehensive policy for schoolgirl mothers was the ILEA which claimed that

Girls were given home tuition for two months before the birth, and also afterwards if they were breastfeeding. A girl could return to school – either her own, or another – or college if the baby was satisfactorily cared for. If there was no one to care for the baby, the mother would receive home tuition up to A level standard if requested.

Pre-school Provision

Children under the age of five have no automatic legal right to an education unless they are ascertained as handicapped. According to Section 8b of the 1944 Education Act LEAs only have to 'have regard to the need for securing that provision is made for pupils who have not attained the age of 5 years'.

In 1972 the DES published a White Paper called *Education: a Framework for Expansion* which claimed to be 'the first systematic step since 1870, when education was made compulsory at the age of 5, to offer an earlier start in education'. The paper commented on the considerable evidence that, as well as the value of nursery education in promoting the social development of young children,

given sympathetic and skilled supervision, children may also make great education progress before the age of five. They are capable of developing further in the use of language, in thought and in practical skills than was previously supposed. Progress of this kind gives any child a sound basis for his subsequent education.

The government's aim was

that within the next 10 years nursery education should become available without charge . . . to those children of 3 and 4 whose parents wish to benefit from it.

The government did not, of course, make it compulsory either for LEAs to provide nursery places or for parents to take them up where they exist. But they hoped that local plans would reflect local needs and resources and that

in preparing for the expansion of nursery education, local authorities will need to take account of other facilities for under fives, existing or planned, so as to prepare a scheme for their areas in which nursery classes and schools, voluntary playgroups, day nurseries, and other forms of day care all play their part.

It is government policy to encourage part-time rather than full-time education for children below the age of five on the grounds that it is not only cheaper but actually preferable. The result is that in 1973 of the increase of 11,000 pupils receiving education in nursery classes and schools more than 10,000 were part-time.

There have been changes of political control since the White Paper but the priority given to building projects designed to increase places for the under-fives was preserved, although the programme has suffered from the cut-back in spending by local authorities. In many areas, especially rural authorities, there remains a chronic shortage of every kind of place and, as the need seems to have been underestimated in the first place, even the steady increase in places every year since 1960 seems to have done little to close the gap.

Nursery Classes

A nursery class means a class mainly for children who are over three years old but not yet five. Schools Regulations 1959 say that children should not be admitted to a nursery class under this age or allowed to stay after the end of the term in which they have their fifth birthday unless 'exceptional circumstances require it'. Nursery classes are part of a school the majority of whose pupils are over the age of five, which normally means an infant or first school. Educationally, this has the special advantage that children do not have to change schools when they are ready for full-time schooling. Nursery classes attached to LEA primary schools have two sessions which start at the same time as the rest of the school but over half the children in maintained nursery classes and schools attend for one session only.

Nursery Schools

A nursery school is a primary school which is used mainly for the education of children who are over two years old and under five.

Legally, therefore, a child may go to a nursery school a year younger than to a nursery class. Nursery schools are not classified as either county or voluntary as other primary schools are and their staff may not be appointed by the same procedures as ordinary primary schools.

Ever since 1918 the government has had the power to make grants to nursery schools. In 1973 ten nursery schools qualified for the grant and were classified as direct grant schools. At the same date there were 114 independent schools registered with the DES solely as nursery schools. However, nurseries which include the word 'school' in their official name are sometimes classified as playgroups, not schools, and in that case they will be registered with and inspected by the Social Services Department rather than the LEA.

Playgroups

Playgroups not only offer children under five good play materials, space, stimulation and companionship, they may also offer support, companionship and education to the mothers who help in running them. Most playgroups rely on the involvement of parents as well as the leaders who are expected to have as a minimum a playleader's qualification. Some playgroups are independent voluntary groups, some have help from the LEA or Social Services Department. There is a fundamental difference between a playgroup in which parents are the managing body, whether or not they help there on a day-to-day basis, and a nursery school or class in which the day-to-day running is in the hands of the professionals and policy decisions are made by the LEA. Playgroups normally charge – anything from 10p to 35p a session. The Social Services Department may pay for places in a playgroup for children in need.

Day Nurseries

Day nurseries take babies from the age of six months until they start school. They are normally open early enough in the morning and late enough in the evening for parents to fit in a full working day. They do not close for school holidays. Day nurseries are either administered by the Social Services Department or are registered with them, so the ultimate responsibility for regulations controlling them rests with the DHSS, not the DES. Day nurseries give priority to cases of particular need and single parent families are usually in that category. Their aim is social – a service for the family – rather than the education of the children, although the NNEB (National Nursery Examination Board) qualification, which is the most popular one for people doing this kind of work, involves a knowledge of all aspects of the needs and development of young children.

Pupils' Rights

It is easy to forget that when compulsory education was introduced in the nineteenth century it was a move to *increase* the freedom of children who otherwise would have been sent to work at the most menial tasks with no opportunity to acquire any of the skills by which they could improve their lot.

Children are being denied freedom if they are denied an education which involves 'systematic learning of basic skills, a challenging programme for acquiring knowledge and more advanced skills; continuity, assessment of individual needs, the encouragement of persistence and recording of progress'. This, in fact, is the programme of the White Lion Street Free School who comment 'It is hard to see how anyone could want to do less than that.'

So, you cannot give children the right to choose whether or not to be educated without giving them a responsibility for their own future which they do not have the maturity or experience to cope with. But there is a wide gap between allowing children to opt out of education altogether at the age of ten or eleven and denying them the right to decide how long they should wear their own hair; between allowing them to drop maths when they are thirteen because it is too difficult and involving them in discussions about which courses they should take in the sixth form.

The issue of whether schools should be run by democratically elected school councils consisting of representatives of teachers, pupils, parents and workers may remain an unattainable idea until we have a social and political revolution. But there are many basic principles of civil liberty, guaranteed by law to adults in society, which should be guaranteed by law to pupils now in schools. The right not to be subjected to legal physical assault; the right to decide what hair style and what clothes to wear; the right to present petitions or requests for changes in school rules without being subject to sanctions. Recently, a headteacher suspended a hundred senior pupils because they had signed a petition asking that fifth form pupils should be allowed to wear their hair longer. He would not allow them back into school until their parents signed a letter certifying 'I have dealt with my child and I continue to support the school in all its aims and standards.' It was suggested to parents that 'if your child feels – and you do too – that a school offering other standards is more acceptable to your child then a transfer to another school is the only course of action to take'. It would be unthinkable for an employer to sack employees who petitioned peacefully for changes in conditions of work. Such is the power of the headmaster, and the respect it is given by parents, that they all meekly signed.

In June 1973 an English boy missed an important public exam because he was sent home to change his shirt which was the 'wrong' colour. Three years before that a Federal Judge in Wisconsin USA overruled a school decision that a High School junior pupil should be excluded because his hair was too long. The judge said, 'It is time to broaden the constitutional community by including within its protection younger people whose claim to dignity matches that of their elders.' (See **Rules and discipline**.)

Things They Want You to Do

'We have ways of making you . . .' so if pupils refuse to give up evenings to rehearsals for the play, Saturday mornings to playing in the first eleven and two weeks of the summer holidays to playing at soldiers at the Combined Cadet Corps camp, they are bound to be dropped by the selectors altogether. That is fine for those who have no team spirit anyway, but very hard on enthusiasts who need to take a Saturday job to pay for their own clothes or have to baby-sit in the evenings while their parents are out. Headteachers have been known to suggest that lack of cooperation in participating in out of school activities for the glory of the school may affect the reference given to the university.

The courts have ruled that it is part of their education for children to run personal errands for teachers in school. In 1959 a fourteen-year-old girl who was seriously scalded while she was making tea for the staff sued the school for negligence (Cooper v. Manchester Corporation). She had to carry half a gallon of boiling tea along twenty-five yards of narrow corridor and staircase, around three blind corners and past the doors of several classrooms. The barrister who argued that 'If the school desired free labour a greater burden of care was placed on it' lost that case. Pupils can be asked by the teacher 'to perform small acts of courtesy to herself or others' on the same basis as they are asked 'to read or write, to sit down or stand up in school, or the like' (Smith v. Martin and Hull Corporation, 1911).

Confidentiality

Confidentiality should never be promised or implied to pupils if it is impossible to keep to it. No one can be expected to collude in serious law-breaking and one school counsellor wrote to *The Times Educational Supplement* that, from the point of view of helping the child 'an assessment of (and possible support through) the consequences of action is more constructive than unthinking protection'. Nevertheless, there should be ethical safeguards about how information is collected and to whom it is given. For example, information derived from questions answered in school medicals has sometimes quite improperly been used as grounds for suspending pupils. If information is likely to be passed on to anyone the pupil should be told before he answers any questions and the normal standards for medical confidences should apply.

School Councils

Whether or not a school should have a pupils' council, who its members should be, who should elect them, who should be chairman, when they should meet, what they may discuss and whether any notice is taken of it are all matters which are determined by the headteacher. Some systems have built-in advantages, such as dividing a large school into year councils so that the younger pupils are not submerged. But the fundamental need is for proper channels of communication to be established and real responsibility to be given.

Pupil Governors

Although no one can legally hold a public office until they are eighteen years old LEAs are beginning to appoint pupils on to governing bodies or to allow pupil observers to attend governors' meetings. (A survey published in May 1975 showed that twenty-six LEAs had made some arrangements for pupils to attend governors' meetings.) Schools which have pupil governors or observers generally seem to have found that it works to the benefit of the school and the pupils. The difficulty is to ensure that the pupil represents not just himself and not just the sixth form, but the whole school, and that there is some feedback to the rest of the school (this problem, of course, is the same for parent and teacher governors). Because governors meet infrequently and the procedures are unfamiliar, a pupil often leaves school just as he is beginning to understand something about how the system works.

Where an authority insists on pupil governors or observers for every school it makes it much more difficult for headteachers to ignore the aspirations and feelings of pupils in the school.

Records

'The keeping of school records is still in an experimental stage' wrote the Ministry of Education in 1947 (Circular 151) and offered excellent advice on how to go about it. But it seems to be a long-drawn-out experiment – no further pronouncements on the subject have been made since then. Yet almost every LEA requires schools to keep individual records on their pupils from the age of five onwards, and supplies its primary schools at least with a standard card or folder to be used for this purpose.

This record is the basic source of information on any pupil throughout his school life and, indeed, after he leaves. School records are not only about which reading scheme a child has been taught by, whether he has learnt traditional or new maths, what topics he has covered so that he does not do dinosaurs four times and miss the Middle Ages altogether. They are much more pretentious than this. The personality, appearance and attitudes of the child and his family may be assessed. Subjective opinions are often given a spurious scientific status by being presented in the form of entries on a five-point scale.

Records sometimes include a passport-type photograph. Parents will not necessarily be asked to supply this. Photographers who come into school to take photos of each child for sale to parents may provide the school with an identity photo as part of the service – 'invaluable for record purposes in the modern school' according to one photographer's advertisement. Asking parents for a convenient-size photograph, provided they know to what use the record will be put, is one thing. Acquiring an identity photo without the knowledge of either parent or pupil is another kind of thing altogether and one that most people would agree is objectionable.

The most contentious aspect of school records is that they are often secret, anonymous and confidential: secret in the sense that parents are not officially told of their existence; anonymous in that the teachers writing the entries do not always have to sign them and cannot be held to account for anything they say, however unjust, prejudiced or quite simply mistaken; confidential in that neither the pupils nor their parents are allowed to see what has been said about them.

When a suspect is to be questioned by the police he is cautioned that anything he says may be taken down and used in evidence. A parent chatting to his child's teacher is given no such caution. One teacher who regards records based on friendly conversations as a betrayal of trust says 'Parents are often surprisingly frank with teachers. They blurt out intimate facts about themselves.' Parents ought to know if a permanent record is being kept of these spontaneous confidences.

It can be argued that records have to be confidential because they may cover intimate areas of a child's home life so that a teacher can make allowances for this in her treatment of a child. But provided the details are factual, however delicate, there would be no reason to leave them out if the reports were to be read by parents. There is all the difference in the world between writing on an open report that mother has been receiving treatment from such-and-such a psychiatric hospital, and the teacher's unqualified opinion, entered under 'Parental attitudes' in a confidential record that mother is fussy and neurotic. Moreover, parents can correct any factual inaccuracies if they see their child's record. As the Ministry of Education said in their circular: 'The validity of many of the entries in the record will depend to no small extent on the help which parents can give to the teachers.'

What Should the Records be Used for?

The chances are that neither the school nor the teacher for whom the records were intended will get to see them in spite of the fact that Schools Regulations 1959 require that 'such educational information as the authority considers reasonable' should be supplied on request to any new school or place of education or training to which a pupil transfers. One piece of research conducted at Bristol University showed that, while all lower school heads interviewed accepted the necessity for passing knowledge about new entrants to their teachers, in practice, only a quarter of the schools in the survey did anything about it. Fifty-three per cent of the teachers in the survey wanted data about new pupils due to start in September before the end of the summer term: only 10 per cent of the schools produced it in time. This ignorance can have tragic repercussions. The official report published in September 1974 on the death of seven-year-old Maria Colwell concluded that

Vital information about Maria was not entered on her record cards and that these were not regularly consulted in the schools she attended . . . If record cards are made out they must be used properly or abolished otherwise their existence creates a false sense of security.

What are the Records Used for?

Local education authorities claim that the confidentiality of the records is strictly preserved, that they are kept under lock and key and seen by no one. But one teacher reports that in her authority records had to be completed in black ink 'so as to be suitable for reproduction'. Parents and pupils may be the only people who do *not* see what has been said about them.

The Children and Young Persons Act (1969) lays on local education authorities the duty of providing information about children brought before the courts and this is usually done by producing their school records.

Schools have to supply the Careers Service with a standardized form of information about the health, ability, educational attainments and aptitudes of all pupils when they are nearly at school leaving age. This information is intended to help careers officers to give sound advice and is supposed to be treated as absolutely confidential and not passed on to employers or anyone else. Parents may ask to be shown the information which has been given to the Careers Service. The standard form used by the Careers Service has no space for any comments on character, personality or attitudes but one mother wrote recently to the *Guardian* claiming that the Department of Employment had quoted remarks to her nineteen-year-old son which he was supposed to have made at school six years earlier.

In the United States in 1974 The Family Educational Right and Privacy Act was passed by Congress. The Buckley amendment, named after its sponsor, gives parents 'the right to inspect and review any and all official records, files and data directly related to them, including all material that is incorporated into each student's cumulative folder and intended for school use or to be available to parties outside the school system'. In spite of the efforts of a handful of individuals there has so far been no move to introduce similar legislation in this country.

Religion in Schools

The right of parents to choose a religious education for their child has always been given a high priority in Britain. The *Manual of Guidance* issued by the DES to explain when parents should be allowed their choice of school puts religious reasons at the top of the list.

Assembly

The 1944 Education Act not only says that there should be 'collective worship on the part of all pupils in attendance' but also specifies that this should be the first activity of the school day. It is stressed that unless it is physically impossible to fit everyone into the hall at the same time it should be 'a single act of worship'. Even if their child is at a church school all parents have a right to ask for their child to be exempted from assembly but the child cannot decide to exempt himself.

Religious Instruction

Since 1944 religious instruction (RI) – now usually known as religious education (RE) – according to an agreed syllabus has been part of the compulsory curriculum of every county and controlled school. The historians' explanation of the extraordinary fact that RE is the only compulsory subject on the curriculum is that at the time the Education Act of 1944 was being prepared the survival of goodness in the world seemed to be at risk. There was a widespread conviction that the Second World War – still in progress – was in some profound way a fight between good and evil and that religious teaching in schools was necessary to guarantee the victory of goodness. Compulsory RE was possible only because in the previous twenty years Free Churchmen and Anglicans had finally found it possible to collaborate on an 'agreed syllabus' for religious education in schools. This achievement solved for the first time the bitter rivalry between different sectors of the Protestant church but no one yet asked the question whether a specifically Christian religious education could truthfully be called 'non-denominational' in the context of a multi-racial society. So for thirty years the 'non-denominational' teaching provided by state schools has been entirely Christian. In 1974 the Birmingham education committee produced a new syllabus based on four years work by a group of forty churchmen, academics and politicians. It included a one-page section entitled 'Non-religious stances for life' which included Communism and Humanism as topics for discussion. The chairman of the education committee commented that 'It was the unanimous view of the conference that a wide variety of philosophies and beliefs should be included as part of religious studies. Communism was included as an example of a non-religious approach to life.' A legal battle raged which was really about whether or not non-religious topics should be discussed as part of RE as understood by the 1944 Education Act. The fears that without compulsory RE goodness will vanish is obviously still powerful in Birmingham.

Religious Education in Voluntary Schools

The religious education in church schools is in accordance with the teaching of that particular church. In all voluntary schools the governing body decides the character of collective worship according to the Trust Deed or as previously given in the school. In controlled schools RI must be in accordance with the agreed syllabus, though parents can insist that the school provide instruction according to the Trust Deed or previous practice for up to two periods a week. In aided and special agreement schools the emphasis is the other way round: RI is in accordance with the Trust Deed but parents can insist on the agreed syllabus. The governors make arrangements for inspection of religious instruction other than that according to the agreed syllabus. What about parents who want a non-religious education for their child? They will not be able to choose a state school which does not officially provide RE and a daily act of worship. Irrespective of what is provided by the school their children are attending, the law allows parents the

right to have no religious education for their child, to have RE
taught in a school according to the agreed syllabus, or to have RE
taught in school according to the teaching of their own church.
The precise details of who has to make a room available and who
has to arrange the teachers for special classes is all set out in Section 25 of the Education Act, but may not prove very practical. A
group of parents from a religious community who could provide
their own teacher ought to be allowed the use of a room and
facilities at some convenient time – while assembly is being held or
in the lunch hour. However, special treatment for individual children may cause a lot of problems and parents would have to prove
that there was no possibility of a place in a school which already
had their brand of RE as part of its curriculum before they could
expect much cooperation.

In practice, parents who want a denominational education for
their child in an area where there are no church schools of the right
denomination can always make up for lack of religious instruction
out of school hours. Those who want a secular education for their
child may not find it so easy to arrange. Some people are given no
choice. In rural areas there is often only one state school and that
may well be a church school. The whole atmosphere of a church
school may be palpably religious. Not only is the head bound to be
a practising church member, but the chances are that many of the
staff are too. An advertisement for the head of the English department of an RC comprehensive school makes this perfectly clear:

The St — School is a Roman Catholic voluntary aided school with a
deep concern for the spiritual as well as the academic development of
its pupils and the governors would welcome applicants for this senior
post who are prepared to assist in some aspect of the religious education
programme.

The British Humanist Association, in its pamphlet *The Case
against Church Schools* by Patricia Knight quotes from the Wheat-
hampstead parish magazine: 'The unwritten purpose behind the
existence of every church school is that every activity of the school
shall be informed with the Christian spirit. It applies to everything
from learning numbers to playing football.' A conscientious ag-
nostic or non-Christian parent may be strong-minded enough to

withdraw a child from assembly and religious instruction. But how can they withdraw him from maths and football?

Teachers of Religious Instruction (including Reserved Teachers)

Teachers selected to give RI according to the terms of the original foundation are called 'reserved teachers'. At county schools no teacher can be required to give RI or be disqualified because of religious beliefs. At controlled and special agreement schools reserved teachers are appointed by the LEA but approved by the governing body. The governors may call for the dismissal of reserved teachers for religious reasons. Non-reserved teachers cannot be required to give RI. The number of reserved teachers at a controlled school may not be more than one in five of the staff and the head cannot be a reserved teacher. At special agreement schools the number is decided by a special agreement between the LEA and the school and the head can be a reserved teacher. At aided schools the governing body can insist on all teachers' fitness to give religious instruction.

Reports

Every autumn brings a crop of 'schoolboy howlers' to the letters pages of the press gleaned by examiners from public examination papers. But every summer brings a crop of less well publicized 'teacher howlers' gleaned by parents from their children's school reports. What *was* the teacher thinking of when she wrote 'rather childish' on the school report of a five year old?

Although there is no law which makes school reports obligatory, the practice is well established. Circular 151 issued by the DES in 1947, the only statement they have ever made on the subject, says that 'parents should be given periodical reports, based on the records, on the progress of their children'. So a school, other than an infant or first school, which decided to do without reports could probably be found to be acting unreasonably.

The form a report takes, how often it is issued, when and how parents get it vary from one school to another. Schools are usually free to devise their own form of reports, if they choose to, even if the LEA provides a standard form. Reports are the property of the school and parents are not entitled to keep them if the school asks for them back immediately, although all reports may be given to parents by the school when the child leaves. Reports should be a private communication between the teacher and the parents, not disclosed to other people without the parents' permission. (This does not apply to confidential records – see Records.) If the school gives the reports to the children to bring home – sometimes economizing by not putting them into an envelope – half the children in the playground may have taken a look before it arrives home, muddy and smudged. Parents have every right to ask for the report to be sent in such a way that they are the people to see it first. If the school thinks it is helpful for reports to be discussed with children they should set up some official way of encouraging this rather than relying on the children's natural curiosity and reading ability. Many secondary schools have found that posting reports is the only reliable way of ensuring that parents receive them at all. Whether or not the report allows a space for parents' comments, parents should correct a report if they think it is damaging, in case it is used as a reference.

Report evenings are arranged by some secondary schools in which the parents are sent the normal school report and then have an opportunity to discuss it with the teachers. The head of first year of one comprehensive school organized a modest and very helpful version when he arranged for a personal letter from the class teacher of each child to be sent home after half a term in their new school. The following week parents were invited in to meet the teachers and discuss how the child was settling in.

The Plowden report said 'Written reports have often been a waste of time since they were so conventional that they conveyed nothing to parents.' One writer who did a survey for *Where**
magazine on several hundred secondary school reports found it a depressing experience. 'Surely no other aspect of school life has changed so little over 20 – or should it be 50 – years?' she asked and concluded '90% of school reports are bureaucratic form filling of the most pointless kind.' She defined the true purpose of an ideal

* *Where*, 54, February 1971.

school report: assessment, diagnosis, plan. There is no shortage of good ideas and experiments as to how this could be achieved.

Rules and Discipline

The Model Articles give the headteacher control over discipline in his school. So even if there is no explicit legal basis for his actions, the headteacher has only to claim that a rule is reasonable and necessary for maintaining discipline in the school to get the full backing of the law and the courts.

The courts have always supported the head's right to decide what rules he needs to maintain good discipline in his school. The password 'prejudicial to discipline' carries all before it in the courts – whether the threat to it arises from blue socks, long hair, trousers, a petition presented to the headteacher by the senior pupils, school pupils patronizing a particular local shop or smoking in the street on Saturday. These are actual cases. It does not matter how bizarre or arbitrary they sound. Provided that the head claims that something is essential for maintaining discipline in his school then his word is, in the literal sense, law. Or, at least, always has been in the past. This is underlined still further by the fact that even when the DES makes regulations in the form of Statutory Instruments they may include a clause subordinating their recommendations to the head's authority over discipline in his school. For example, 'The Provision of Milk and Meals Regulations 1969' (as amended) set out the requirements for providing milk and meals in schools. But Clause 6.2 states 'These regulations shall be without prejudice to the exercise by the headteacher of a school, under the articles of government . . . for the school, of any function relating to the internal discipline of the school.'

The law assumes that parents implicitly accept reasonable school rules whether or not they have ever seen them or been told of their existence. Some schools ask parents to sign the rules because, according to the NUT, 'this measure sometimes obviates difficulties which would otherwise arise subsequently'. So if the rules provide for detention after school as a means of punishment, and a parent has signed them, the parents cannot object later if their child is

188 The Parent's Schoolbook

given a detention. However, a parent's signature does not condone
unreasonable school rules.

In order to be reasonable in the eyes of the law, school rules do
not have to have a self-evident purpose such as the safety and con-
venience of the people who share the building. More than sixty
years ago a Lord Justice in the Court of Appeal proclaimed that
'education includes the inculcation of habits of order, obedience
and courtesy'. So school rules are not regarded as unreasonable in
law even if they serve no useful purpose except to make the pupils
conform (Smith v. Martin and Hull Corporation).

Out of School

There is a powerful argument that what a pupil does in his own
time is his own affair. However, the law allows schools to make
rules about what pupils may or may not do out of school as well as
in school.

Most parents take it for granted that schools have rules about
things like not running in the corridors. But they may not realize
that the legal principle has been established since 1893 (Cleary v.
Booth) that 'the authority delegated to the schoolmaster is not
limited to the four walls of the school' and that he can punish a
pupil for offences committed on his way to and from school as well.
What is more, a school rule can be enforced which 'contemplates
acts done, not indeed beyond the school term, but beyond the pre-
cincts of the school and in public'. In 1929 (R v. Newport (Salop)
Justices *ex parte* Wright) the court held that the school was within
its rights to beat a boy for breaking the school rules by smoking in
the street in his own free time even though his father allowed it.
G. R. Barrell (*Teachers and the Law*) has interpreted this principle
to mean that 'the teacher's jurisdiction extends to all matters
which may affect the welfare of the school'. For instance, a teacher
should intervene to stop fighting in the street between his pupils
and those from another school. However, that same argument
might be extended to cover rules by the school forbidding almost
any activity from going to see *Danish Dentist on the Job* (X certificate) to serving in the local fish and chip shop and, as the judge explained in 1893, the right of the school to do this would have to be

decided on the facts of each case. However one interprets 'the welfare of the school', the school's right to exercise control applies to almost anything a pupil does while wearing school uniform. Joining a political party and attending meetings wearing 'mufti' is any citizen's normal right and it would be unreasonable for the school to interfere. But the school may argue that it is their business if pupils are at a demonstration wearing school uniform or carrying a banner with the name of the school on it and that it is therefore reasonable for them to make rules about it.

It is a basic principle of English law that no one should be twice in jeopardy for the same offence. If a school student is fined for an offence committed outside school there is no possible justification for the school to impose its own punishment for the same thing. Too many school governors accept 'long history of disruptive and anti-social behaviour' as sufficient grounds for a suspension without asking whether that meant kicking in the doors, throwing bricks through the windows or going to the NUSS rally on Sunday afternoon. Unfortunately, punishment may not always be explicit. A nudge is as good as a wink to a university vice-chancellor or the personnel officer of the best local firm. (See **Pupils' rights**.)

Safety

Parents want to know that their children will be safe in school: that accidents will not happen, that someone will cope if they do, and that they will have some legal redress if there has been negligence.

Prevention of Accidents in School Time

There is no doubt that safety standards in some schools are well below what could be achieved. A government survey found that the accident rate – in terms of bones broken or injuries involving at least half a day's absence – was over three times higher in one local authority area than in another. So if the average accident rate in schools was brought down to the lowest rate actually achieved, some 17,000 children might be saved every year from this kind of serious accident.

Schools Regulations state that adequate arrangements shall be made for the health and safety of the pupils and staff in case of danger from fire and other causes, and that the fire resistance of the structure and materials should be sufficient to ensure the occupants' safety. It is up to the LEA to make specific regulations about safety and fire precautions in their schools. Most authorities insist that schools have a proper fire drill at least once a term and it is usual for the headteacher to report to the governors on how long it took to evacuate the building.

The Health and Safety at Work, etc., Act which came into force on 1 April 1975 affected some five million people, including teachers, who were not previously protected by health and safety legislation. Schoolchildren are not included in the category of persons 'at work' as defined in Section 52(1) of the Act, but come within the category of persons other than employees liable to be affected. Under the Act LEAs, as employers, are to prepare written statements of their safety policies for each school. These statements should explain the steps they are taking to protect pupils as well as employees. A staff HMI for science is reported as saying 'There is a deal of concern amongst science teachers at all levels about the implications of the Act.' Soon after the Health and Safety Executive was set up to be responsible for enforcing health and safety legislation, the DES started discussions with the Executive on how the new Act would affect schools. Schools are fourth in a list of five classes of premises which are to be designated as requiring a fire certificate under the Fire Precautions Act and it will be years before it applies to them. Even school buses do not have to conform to the same standards for drivers or vehicles as 'public service vehicles' because the passengers do not pay fares. The Department of Education and Science seems to think it has done its duty by giving good advice: when the Under-Secretary of State was asked in the House of Commons in 1974 to do something more positive about safety in schools, he replied, 'I see no need to seek powers in this matter.'

How Far are Individual Teachers Responsible for the Safety of the Children in their Charge?

The standard common law definition of a teacher's duty towards his charges derives from Mr Justice Cave's dictum in 1893: 'The duty of a school master is to take such care of his boys as a careful father would take of his boys' (Williams v. Eady, 1893). Judges have made it clear that they do not think parents, however careful, ought to mollycoddle their boys. Parents may not agree with Mr Justice Vaisey who declared 'It is better that a boy should break his neck than allow other people to break his spirit' (Suckling v. Essex County Council, 1955). Especially as, in this particular case, the issue was whether four-inch scoring knives should have been locked in a cupboard while a class of forty-eight eleven-year-olds were left on their own. It is difficult to understand how locking the cupboard door could break a boy's spirit; only too easy to understand how leaving it unlocked resulted in one boy losing an eye.

The courts take it for granted that 'accidents will happen'. Mr Justice Hilbery went so far as to say 'If boys were kept in cotton-wool some of them would choke themselves with it' (Hudson v. Governors of Rotherham Grammar School, 1938). Parents cannot necessarily rely on the school's view of the proper standard of care (upheld by the courts) being the same as theirs. In any case, what a careful parent would think reasonable at home may not be reasonable at all in school. So Mr Justice Hilbery's summing up sounds quite unrealistic when he suggests that the jury should imagine 'a boy of yours has some other little boys, who are friends of his, coming to tea on a Saturday afternoon, and you see them all playing in the garden'. As Mr Justice Edmund Davies commented in 1962, 'School life happily differs from home life . . . the standard is that of a reasonable prudent parent judged not in the context of his own home but in that of a school . . .' (Lyes v. Middlesex County Council, 1962). This judgement was made in the Queen's Bench Division and until it is tested in the Court of Appeal parents cannot rely on it.

Prevention of Accidents before and after School

The NUT's legal department has advised its members that the school's responsibility for the safety of children 'extends to a reasonable period before and after school when the children are either arriving or are awaiting school conveyance or parents after being dismissed in the afternoon'. The LEA can make regulations about how long teachers or other staff should be in school before the actual school day begins and when the gates should be opened to allow children into the playground. Nevertheless, when a five-year-old boy died from a fall through the glass roof of a school lavatory adjoining the playground within a few minutes of school being dismissed, the parents not only lost the case in which they claimed that 'the school authority should have had some person in authority until the children left the premises', but a member of the Bench objected to the family having been given legal aid to bring such a 'wholly artificial' case. (See also **School meals service, Break** and **Transport**.)

Prevention of Accidents outside School

If children are taken swimming or to sports or a visit during school hours, the teacher is clearly responsible for their safety until they are dismissed from school in the normal manner at the usual time or their parents agree to them being dismissed from some other point. There will be occasions when individual children have to leave school during the day, for medical treatment, for instance. The 'prudent parent' criterion applies here also. The National Association of Head Teachers suggests

that no child under the age of 8 should be allowed to leave the school premises, during school time, to attend a school clinic unaccompanied by a parent, teacher or other responsible person. Wherever possible the best person is the parent.

If the child is over eight and the headteacher still feels that he or she ought to be accompanied they see no reason why an appropriately older and responsible person should not be sent to accompany the younger child.

SCHOOL CROSSING PATROLS

The safety of children crossing the road at the beginning or end of the school day is not the responsibility of the school or the education committee. The Road Traffic Regulations Act 1967 (Section 24) gives responsibility to the local authority for the safety of children when they cross the road on their way to and from school. The Act says that crossing patrols may be employed 'during periods between the hours of eight in the morning and half past five in the afternoon when children are so on their way'. In some areas the police have made an agreement with the local authority that they will organize the recruitment and training of the road crossing patrols. Within the London Metropolitan Police area the statutory responsibility was given to the Commissioner of Police. If a crossing patrol is needed at a busy road crossed by schoolchildren the authority responsible should be approached. Any request will carry more weight if it comes with the support of the head, the governors, the PTA, or, better still, all three.

Who Will Cope after an Accident?

A factory with nearly 2,000 employees would be required by law to have about fourteen first aid boxes, with someone in charge of each one, and at least one person qualified to administer first aid. Electrical gadgets of all sorts and sizes are found in the classrooms of even the smallest infant school. Secondary schools are likely to have lathes and furnaces, chemicals and kilns: as much equipment as a small factory, but with greater potential hazards since there are many more people on the premises, and they are younger. That children are at risk is recognized by the DES. They have said

That as schools are not subject to the Factories Acts they are therefore not inspected under those Acts, nevertheless pupils ought to have at least the measure of protection afforded by measures which have proved satisfactory in the prevention of accidents in Industry.

Their safety booklets say:

All teachers should have a simple working knowledge of first aid and it is important for them to be able to recognize a situation where medical advice is necessary. It is also very desirable that teachers on the staff of every school should have attended a course of training and taken a certificate in first aid issued by the British Red Cross and the St John Ambulance Association. The names of those so qualified should be made known both to teachers and to pupils in order that, in the event of an accident, first aid may be applied without delay.

It is doubtful if this happens in practice.

TEACHING FIRST AID

The St John Ambulance Association have said that 'What is required is that a sufficient number of qualified people is available to provide convenient coverage in the school with the minimum interruption of the teaching . . .' They suggest that the answer is to train the schoolchildren themselves in first aid. Although only a few will show sufficient interest to take a course leading to a first aid certificate, elementary information and essential techniques, such as the recovery position, mitigation of shock and resuscitation, can be easily and quickly taught. They have produced books in basic first aid procedures designed for children from the age of eight upwards.

MEDICAL TREATMENT

The school would be guilty of negligence if they failed to get proper medical attention for a child who had been injured. Once it has been decided that a doctor should be called in or an ambulance sent for, a member of staff should get in touch with parents immediately. Someone from the school should stay with the child until a parent arrives or the doctor says the child may go home. No child should ever be sent home during the day without reliable information that there will be someone at home.

TEETH

Children are quite liable to knock their teeth out. Even when a tooth has come right out a dentist may be able to rescue it if he can be reached within half an hour and the correct procedures are followed in the meantime. The tooth must be kept warm and moist. The best place to do this is in the child's mouth in the 'pocket' between the lip and the bottom jaw. If the child cannot be trusted not to swallow it or lose it from there, it should be put in a small jar of warm water. Never wrap it in a cloth. If it has bits of playground all over it and must be cleaned before it can be popped into the child's mouth, hold it by the crown, never by the root, and wash it gently in warm water. Get the child to a dentist as fast as possible. Casualty departments of hospitals may have no knowledge or experience of rescuing teeth. There is a very good chance indeed of teeth taking root again in the jaw if the dentist treats it in time and the right procedures have been followed.

Negligence

It is a basic principle of English law that the master is responsible for the negligence of his servant if the servant is acting in the course of his employment. So it is the LEA which has legal responsibility for the safety of school pupils in county schools because the headteacher and staff are employees of the authority. In the case of voluntary schools, the governors are responsible for pupils' safety. There is a question of negligence only if

(1) the child was in the care of the school at the time of the accident: that is to say it took place within normal school hours (including the dinner hour if parents have made it clear that the child is expected to stay in school during that time) or during the time that it was reasonable to expect pupils to be going into or leaving school, or that the child was on a school outing;
(2) there was failure to provide the supervision which a careful parent could reasonably be expected to provide, or that the school premises were unsafe;
(3) the accident was a direct result of the school's failure to fulfil these conditions, not the result of the child's extraordinary wilfulness in outwitting the school;
(4) the school building failed to conform to the Regulations issued under Section 10 of the 1944 Education Act establishing national standards for school premises ('Standards for School Premises Regulations 1972', SI 2051). The Education Act does

not lay down any penalty for a breach of these regulations but in the case of Reffell v. Surrey County Council in 1964 the judge ruled that an authority which failed to maintain a school to the standard prescribed, in addition to being in breach of their duties under Section 10 of the Education Act, could also be found negligent in common law by someone who brought a case because they were hurt as a result. It would make no difference to the liability of the LEA that the Secretary of State had directed that the school should be 'deemed to conform' with the prescribed standards.

A parent's difficulties in establishing a claim for negligence are magnified by the fact that, while they are alone, the teachers are backed by their unions. In fact, it is the NUT's claim that 'Experience has proved that it is a matter of the greatest difficulty to establish liability against a teacher in claims based on negligence to a scholar if the teacher is adequately defended.' There is, to a parent's eyes, something distasteful about the advice to members printed in capital letters in their *Handbook*

'ANY MEMBER OF THE NATIONAL UNION OF TEACHERS UN-FORTUNATE ENOUGH TO BE INVOLVED, OR LIKELY TO BE INVOLVED, IN A CASE ARISING OUT OF AN ACCIDENT TO A SCHOLAR, SHOULD IMMEDIATELY GET IN TOUCH WITH THE UNION SO THAT THE NECESSARY STEPS IN THE DEFENCE OF PROFESSIONAL INTERESTS CAN BE TAKEN IMMEDIATELY.'

It certainly gives the impression that professional interests have a higher priority than the fate of the pupil.

A child is not entitled to compensation for a serious disability caused by an accident in school unless someone – the teacher, the governors, or the LEA – was legally responsible for the accident. In other words, if the injury was the result of negligence or defective equipment or a sub-standard building as set out in the conditions above. The only way to get compensation for an accident for which no one could be legally blamed is to take out a Personal Accident Insurance policy. Although the usual purpose of these policies is to provide for loss of earnings as a result of an accident or disability, most insurance companies can arrange cover for children of school age at a reasonable cost. The policy would produce a lump sum, according to the size of the premium, in the event of a serious accident.

School Fund

The education authority provides resources for running and equipping schools, but many schools raise money for extras on their own initiative. Extras usually include things like kits for school teams, costumes for plays, extra outings and so on. The money may be raised by the PTA and administered by their treasurer. But schools often have a school fund which is wholly controlled by the headteacher as well as, or instead of, money belonging to the PTA.

School funds may benefit from fund-raising activities like the inevitable summer fête or get a commission on school photographs or sales in the tuck shop. The basic income is normally supplied by straightforward donations from parents. Where the parents are not approached direct for an annual donation, children may be asked to bring a few pence each week and the school may try to stimulate rivalry between classes to see which can collect the most. More questionable is the practice of schools running a savings bank under the national schools savings bank scheme and using the compound interest earned on the children's deposits to bolster school funds. Parents may be happy to donate their interest to the school in this way, but they are not always given the choice.

In law, school funds are a form of trust fund which can be spent only on the object for which they were raised. Unless a particular target (such as a swimming pool) has been named the money must be used for activities which benefit the pupils of the school. Within this framework the head, as part of his control over the internal organization and management of the school, has final responsibility for approving how the school fund is to be spent and for supervising the accounting arrangements. The LEA has no say at all in how voluntary school funds are to be spent. However, running the school fund is part of the headteacher's job as an employee of the education authority, so they may insist on the funds being audited by LEA staff and also lay down regulations as to how the accounts are to be kept and to whom they must be presented. The Articles of Government may require the headteacher to show the governors the annual accounts of the school fund or any other funds raised for the school by voluntary efforts.

In spite of the fact that fund-raising has traditionally been a point of contact between parents and schools, welcomed even by schools which are opposed to any other form of parent participation, the money is often spent without any consultation with the donors or even giving them any idea as to what it has been used for. This is, at the very least, a basic lack of courtesy. One parents' group which attempted to persuade its LEA to introduce regulations allowing parents to see school fund accounts were told that 'Heads are very touchy about revealing information to parents.' One reason given for not publishing accounts is that funds are used to help individual cases of hardship. Naturally, details of this kind of help should not be shown in any published accounts, but they could be grouped under a general heading of 'welfare'.

The NUT recommends procedures to safeguard against misuse of funds. These include a separate bank or post office account for each private fund and separate account books; an annual statement of all receipts and payments; an audit conducted by someone outside the school. An acceptable procedure for administering voluntary school funds should also include:

(1) any cash collected to be taken by at least two people, the total to be entered in an account book and signed by them;
(2) a receipt issued for every payment made individually; this could be a ticket where the payment is in the form of an admission charge to a school event;
(3) advance notice of any admission charge whenever parents are invited to plays, concerts, swimming galas, etc.;
(4) information about what the money is needed for when it is first asked for;
(5) parents to be shown the annual accounts of the school fund;
(6) an explicit statement that contributions to the school fund are absolutely voluntary to be sent with every appeal.

Even if a school follows all these procedures parents still have no say at all as to how the school fund is spent. Parents who want to influence how the funds they have raised for the school by their own efforts are to be spent should be sure that the PTA has its own account or should collect the money in the name of a fund set up for a particular purpose, the trustees of which are appointed by a procedure agreed with the parents.

School Journey

'Travel in the younger sort is a part of education; in the elder a part of experience.' – Francis Bacon's thoughts on school journeys when he was writing his *Essays* in 1597. And there are still two kinds of school journeys: one kind whose purpose is educational, with direct relevance to the curriculum, like a geography field-trip; the other kind is just for the experience – a chance for school-children to see and do things which would not normally come their way.

In principle this difference is important to both teachers and parents. Teachers have a legal obligation to undertake duties connected with the work of the school and cannot refuse to go on a journey which forms part of a course (Schools Regulations, 1959). However, if the journey is a holiday, teachers do not have to take part unless they want to. So schools cannot sponsor journeys which are holidays unless teachers are prepared to go on them. This may explain the popularity of trips to the Continent and the unpopularity of camping holidays in Britain.

In practice the distinction can be quite difficult to make. Most schools base projects on their school journeys so any journey can be integrated into the curriculum after it is booked even if it did not start that way. And how do you decide whether an 'adventure' holiday with mountaineering, sailing and canoeing is for education or experience?

There are no special national regulations dealing with the legal aspects of school journeys. The teacher has to exercise the same quality of care for the children's safety as he would do in school – the standard of care exercised by a reasonable parent. He is on duty for twenty-four hours a day throughout the journey. The DES has published a booklet called *Safety in Outdoor Pursuits* which sets out a code of good practice for adventure holidays. This is simply an advisory document and has no legal force. Nevertheless, it could presumably be used as evidence if anything did go wrong: it would be relevant to the defence against a charge of negligence to demonstrate that the advice had been followed or it could form part of a proof of negligence to show that the advice had been ignored. Parents who are worried because their child wants to go with the school on a mountaineering expedition may feel happier about it if they read the booklet for themselves and make sure that the suggestions in it are going to be followed.

Headteachers are responsible for choosing school journeys and for making sure that they are properly run, although in secondary schools senior staff members will often take the initiative in planning journeys.

The LEA can have a powerful, though indirect, influence on school journeys. They can make their own regulations covering every aspect of the administration: the ratio of adults to children, the kind of insurance cover required, the financial arrangements and medical inspections. They could make it compulsory to conform to safety codes issued by expert bodies such as the Central Council for Physical Recreation or the British Mountaineering Council. Grants for school journeys are discretionary so the LEA can encourage journeys by making generous grants or discourage them with stingy ones. The LEA's preference can be expressed in tangible forms. They may purchase field study or rural centres to encourage their schools to choose this kind of visit by making it cheaper, easier and more convenient than private enterprise. At the other extreme, some LEAs take block bookings on 'educational' cruises so that their schools are tempted by the luxury life. More modest and practical kinds of help include a central stock of good camping equipment available on free loan.

School journeys present many families with a problem: they want their child to have the best of what is going and they certainly do not want him to miss anything which is necessary for school work. On the other hand, even one child's school journey abroad may cost as much as taking the whole family camping in England. Whether or not a school journey is part of the school curriculum, parents ought to be consulted before any plans are made. It is not fair to put them in a situation where they are under pressure to let their child do something which they cannot afford or do not approve of, unless they have had a chance to say so before the tickets are booked. They should be invited to hear what the purpose of the journey is to be and have an opportunity to ask questions or make suggestions about the most suitable plans for achieving it. Parents may have more experience of journeys with children than teachers have and could offer practical advice. If the school frankly tells parents that the journey is to be a holiday, many of them will welcome the opportunity for their child. But at least those who want to opt out can do so without worrying about the child losing ground and if they have had a chance to put their point of view at this stage, they will discover whether they are in a minority and may be more likely to accept the journey with good grace.

School Meals Service

The 1944 Education Act said that there should be a school meals service but left all the details to the Provision of Milk and Meals Regulations. These state that 'on every school day there shall be provided and on every other day there may be provided for every pupil as a mid-day dinner a meal suitable in all respects as the main meal of the day'. So LEAs are obliged to set up a school meals service capable of providing dinners for all its school pupils. If the head says that a child cannot stay for school dinners parents should ask the reason. It may be the headteacher's personal opinion that young infants settle into school better if they go home for dinner at least for the first few weeks. In that case, the head cannot legally refuse to allow any child to have dinner in school if the parents want it. However, if the head's reason is that there is physically no room for all the children at the school to have dinner then the only recourse is to the LEA and the governors. They may claim that it is not reasonable or practicable to make enough room available for every child to have dinners. If they can make a good enough case the DES will support them. It would not be reasonable for any school to refuse to supply a school meal if it caused hardship to the family.

In some LEAs the senior cook in each school is responsible to the headteacher but in others the school meals service may have its own administrative structure. In that case, the cook in school will not be answerable to the head but to the LEA school meals organizer and the head may not be able to deal with problems about the food and how it is served, but will have to refer them to the appropriate officers. The governors' oversight of what goes on in school includes school meals and they are responsible for seeing that suitable facilities are available for dinners. The Building Regulations lay down the amount of space which should be allowed for each child eating dinner: nine square feet for a primary school child, ten square feet for a secondary school child. The regulations allow LEAs to provide, in addition to school dinner, 'such other refreshments as the authority consider appropriate'. Some authorities have made use of this clause to provide breakfast for children in special schools. In Aberdeen two centres were set up for children who qualified for free dinner to be given breakfast – porridge, of course.

The DES has catering advisers available to give advice to LEA meals organizers. From time to time they set up working parties to report on every aspect of the schools meals service.

The main control over the school meals service by the DES is its standards for nutrition. These standards go into very precise details about what is meant by the 'main meal of the day'. In general terms this is taken to mean that the meal should provide one third of the child's calory and protein requirements for the day. LEAs are given a recommended pattern of menus with types and quantities of food needed to meet the requirements. A project conducted by the Department of Nutrition, Queen Elizabeth College, London, suggests that the average meal consumed in senior schools falls well below these targets. A report on the food value of school dinners, *Nutrition in Schools*, was published by HMSO in November 1975.

The standard of hygiene for school dinners has to conform to the highest public health standards as laid down in Food Hygiene (General) Regulations 1960. It is probably observed more strictly than in many public restaurants. If parents suspect that their child has any kind of food poisoning infection they should always tell the school immediately. The LEA organizer may ask for a portion of every meal served to be saved in the refrigerator for several days, so that it can be examined for any kind of contamination and the authority can trace the source of infection.

What Price School Dinners?

The LEA has discretion over how much it spends on school dinners, but none over what they charge for them, except in special schools. The charge is set nationally by the DES and was raised from 12p to 15p a dinner in April 1975. The official estimate was that this charge covered only 40 per cent of the actual cost of the meal. On 19 February 1976 the government's White Paper 'Public Expenditure to 1979–80' included a policy statement on charges for school meals: the government subsidy is to be reduced so that by 1980 parents will be paying 70 per cent of the true cost of the meals.

The LEA decides how much of its education budget it will spend on school meals. In 1972–3, there were LEAs spending as little as 5·70p (Wakefield) or as much as 9·08p (Birkenhead and Cardigan) on food for each dinner. The national average was 7·12p. (The total cost includes overheads as well as food.)

The headteacher has complete discretion over how dinner money is collected and children may be allowed to bring money every day, once a week or even once a term. However, he could not introduce an unreasonable system, and the head who stopped twins from having school dinners because their mother had not paid for them at the end of the previous term was ruled 'out of order' by the DES.

Free Dinner

The DES sets the level of income which gives the right to free school dinners. Many LEAs have a leaflet telling parents about this right and how to apply. (See **Grants for schoolchildren**.) In November 1967 when Patrick Gordon-Walker was Secretary of State for Education and Science he sent a personal message home with every schoolchild in the country inviting parents to apply for free dinners. The effect was dramatic: over the country as a whole the number getting free meals went up by 25 per cent and in some places the increase was as much as 60 per cent. It is up to the individual school to make sure that parents know their rights and are not embarrassed to ask for them. Even when parents realize that their children are entitled to free dinners they may prefer not to claim them if the children are labelled 'different' in some way. In Circular 3/71 the Secretary of State, Mrs Margaret Thatcher, made the DES's position perfectly clear:

... every effort should be made to ensure that the remission of the charge and the dining arrangements are so organized that those who receive free meals cannot be identified by other pupils. The Secretary of State knows that authorities accept the need for measures to avoid embarrassment to pupils and have instructed schools accordingly. She is grateful for the efforts that have been made but her attention has been drawn to practices at individual schools where arrangements are less than satisfactory ... she hopes that authorities will take whatever further steps are needed to ensure that satisfactory arrangements are made and observed in all schools.

The need for LEAs to monitor the arrangements was reinforced in Circular 1/75. A report by the Child Poverty Action Group, *School Holidays, a Crisis for Poor Families*, by Jane Streather and Sheila Woolfson, shows how important it is for poor families who get free meals in term time to continue to get school meals during the holidays and how few LEAs provide adequately for this need, in spite of the power given them by the regulations.

Supervision

The regulations state that 'The authority shall ensure that suitable arrangements are made for the supervision and social training of pupils during meals.' Since 1968 teachers are not obliged to undertake any duties connected with school meals from collecting the money to teaching table manners. However, a number of teachers do volunteer for dinner duty. The head remains responsible for the welfare of the children in school throughout the dinner break. Many teachers claim that 'duties connected with school meals' extend to all supervision of children on the school premises during the dinner hour and that, therefore, this too can only be voluntary. It is convincingly argued by G. R. Barrell in *Teachers and the Law* that the common-law duty of the teacher *in loco parentis* to take care of the pupils is binding as long as there are pupils on the school premises. The duty to supervise meals was imposed on teachers by regulations in the first place in 1945 and could therefore be removed by regulations in 1968. The duty of care is based on common law, not on regulations, and cannot be varied except by the courts or by Act of Parliament. Whether or not teachers could be shown to have a legal duty in principle, in practice most authorities employ part-time staff during the dinner hour to supervise the children. (See **Non-teaching staff** and **Break**.)

The Quality of School Meals

The National Association of Education Meals Advisers has commented that 'food only nourishes when it is eaten'. In September 1973 the *Sunday Times* colour supplement did a survey of school dinners. Their reporter sampled twenty-four dinners at schools of every type from nursery schools in Deptford in the East End of London to Roedean girls' boarding school. A comprehensive school in an LEA which spent 5·90p per meal on food rated two stars for a 'most impressive and imaginative lunch, a wide choice, efficient cafeteria service'. A comprehensive school in another LEA spending almost the same – 6·10p – rated no stars at all and the children called the food monotonous. Where self-service cafeterias have been introduced they are very popular with the children. However, there are complicated administrative problems in subsidizing them in the way that the standard meal is subsidized by the LEA and parents may have to pay the full cost of the food. There are particular difficulties where children should be having a free dinner.

Children Who Don't Eat School Dinners

The Chartered Institute of Public Finance and Accountancy publishes annual statistics which show the percentage of pupils in each

LEA who eat school dinners. Across the country in 1972–3 there was a range from 34·8 per cent in South Shields to 88·4 per cent in Westmorland. A report, *Catering in Schools*, published by HMSO in November 1975 says that school dinners are being 'virtually boycotted by pupils in the upper forms of secondary schools'.

PACKED LUNCH

Whether or not children who do not eat school dinners are allowed to bring their own food to eat in school depends entirely on the headteacher. In reply to a letter in 1975 asking him whether children had a legal right to eat their own food in school during the dinner hour the Secretary of State replied 'LEAs have no duty to make any provision for pupils to bring their own food to school. A parent cannot demand that his child shall be allowed to eat his sandwiches on the school premises or that anything in the way of facilities shall be provided.' However, Circular 3/71 recommends that

authorities and schools should make all reasonable efforts, within the resources available, to ensure that children who bring sandwiches are enabled to eat them in suitable conditions, including such supervision as may be necessary, with adequate provision of tables and chairs, and glassware and cutlery where these are required.

Mr Reg Prentice added, in January 1975, that

It is certainly my view that schools should wherever possible provide accommodation and facilities for these pupils.

Nevertheless, the experts on nutrition from Queen Elizabeth College discovered that in some schools heads do *not* allow children to bring sandwich lunches. They asked 'Why not?' One reason often put forward by teachers is that a packed lunch is not a good enough meal. But the nutritionists found that school meals could well be 'nutritionally inferior to a couple of respectably filled sandwiches'. A second reason for the ban on packed lunches is the need to provide official supervision. LEAs are bound to employ helpers to supervise children while teachers are off-duty during the dinner hour. It is up to the LEA whether they are prepared to employ enough helpers to supervise children eating their own food as well as those eating school dinners. Headteachers claim that they are forced to ban children who are not eating school dinners from the school throughout the dinner hour. (See **Parents *can* do something,** p. 249.) A row in Leicestershire in October 1975, as a result of a report by the Child Poverty Action Group, provoked this comment from the leader column of the *TES* under the headline 'Storm in a Dinner-Plate':

> The LEAs will have their work cut out to convince ordinary people that they are so narrowly confined that they can only take this line. In fact, Leicestershire LEA probably never took any conscious line at all, and were corporately unaware that that, as a result of wooden administration, children were being sent home across busy roads to empty homes and conscientious mothers were being forced to go without employment to look after them.

Schools, Types of

Independent

Independent schools (also known as 'private' or 'public' schools) are not maintained by LEAs. They all charge fees, except for the small number of urban 'free schools'. (See **Free schools.**) Any independent school providing full-time education for five or more pupils of compulsory school age must be registered with the DES and conform to certain standards. The DES also keeps a register of schools they recognize as efficient after inspection. Most independent schools likely to achieve recognition apply for it. DES List 70 (published by HMSO) is the complete register of schools which have been recognized as efficient, listed under their county.

Direct Grant Schools

Direct grant schools are part of the independent sector of the education system. They receive a grant from the Secretary of State under Section 100 (1) (b) of the 1944 Education Act. This says that the Secretary of State should issue regulations to allow grants to be paid to 'persons other than LEAs' for educational services.

The grant is basically a capitation allowance on every pupil over the age of eleven, with a supplement for sixth formers. In addition, the government pays the difference between the standard school fees and the fees paid by parents who are eligible for a subsidy on the basis of a means test.

Schools do not qualify for a 'direct grant' from the Secretary of State unless they were grant-aided in some way before 1944. They are now subject to Direct Grant Schools Regulations 1959 which prescribe the conditions relating to the grant and the administration of direct grant schools. At least 25 per cent of the places must be offered by the governors free to children who have at some time spent two years in a maintained school. The LEA has the first option on a further 25 per cent which it may pay for and use to give free places as part of its secondary school provision. The parents' income is not taken into account in allocating these free places. The governors allocate the remaining places for which fees are charged although the government grant ensures that these are below the level charged by other unsubsidized independent schools. Parents may apply for remission of part of the fees on the basis of a means test.

In 1973 there were 303 schools classified as direct grant, of which 176 were grammar schools, 114 were special schools, ten were nursery schools and three were technical schools. Direct grant grammar schools are equivalent to only 1 per cent of the total number of maintained schools. However, they amount to 21·5 per cent of the grammar schools in England and Wales and cater for 24 per cent of all pupils who go to grammar schools. The Public Schools Commission of 1970 characterized the direct grant grammar schools as 'predominantly middle class'. Although the 25 per cent free places provided by the governors are intended for working class children (which is why children are not eligible for a free place unless they have spent two years in an ordinary state school), 77 per cent of these places are given to pupils classified as coming from upper or middle class families by the Registrar General. It is therefore not surprising that governments pledged to end the selective system of secondary education in the maintained sector feel that it would be anomalous for the DES to continue making grants out of public money to these grammar schools. So in 1975 new regulations were published which said that the grant to direct grant grammar schools (under Regulation 4 of the existing regulations) would cease to be payable unless they declared to the DES by the end of 1975 that they intended to become comprehensive. Those which did not want to become comprehensive would no longer receive a grant and would have to become completely self-supporting. The schools which decide to become comprehensive will, in due course, issue Section 13 notices in the usual way (see Appendix). The Secretary of State has said that he will review progress at the end of each year and any schools which are evidently not putting their statement of intention into practice run the risk of having their grant withdrawn.

Maintained Schools

Section 9 of the 1944 Education Act defined the categories of schools which were to be maintained by the LEA. These are often known as 'state schools'. The information in this book applies only to maintained/state schools.

Nursery schools for pupils from the ages of two to five.

Primary schools for pupils from five, who stay there until they are at least ten years six months but must leave before they are twelve. Primary schools are often divided up into different departments or separate schools. These may be infants and juniors; first and middle; first tier and second tier.

Secondary schools for pupils older than ten years and six months.

Middle schools were legally recognized only in 1964 when an Education Act made it possible for new schools to be established with age limits which do not coincide with the age limits laid down for primary and secondary schools in Section 8 of the Education Act. However, these schools, which are generally known as middle schools, have to be 'deemed' either primary or secondary for official purposes. So statistics now show the number of schools which are 'middle deemed primary' and 'middle deemed secondary' separately from ordinary primary and secondary schools.

Sixth form colleges have been introduced largely as a result of reorganization of secondary schools as a way of rationalizing local resources for sixth form teaching.

T–H

All schools which are classified as primary or secondary have *county* or *voluntary* status. *County schools* are those which are owned and fully maintained and governed by the LEA according to their regulations. *Voluntary schools* are those which were established by charities and churches. These are maintained by the LEA but the foundation still has considerable legal rights. (See **Voluntary schools.**)

Special Schools

Special schools cater for children who have some handicap or disability which needs special educational treatment. (See **Handicapped children.**) They may be maintained and run by the LEA; non-maintained – established and run by a voluntary organization but catering only for pupils whose fees are paid by the LEA; independent, including direct grant.

Search

A shopkeeper who rushed after your child in the street, accused him of stealing and searched him for proof would be guilty of assault. The police are subject to Judges' Rules and if they want to search a child under seventeen years old in their custody, there must be present a parent or guardian or someone who is not a police officer and is of the same sex as the child. A teacher wanting to search a child is not bound by any formal legal procedures. Since he is *in loco parentis*, the only limitation on his rights is that he must act as a *reasonable* parent would. So, if a child has been searched personally or has been made to turn out his bag or pockets, parents must unravel the question posed by Chief Justice Cockburn in 1865

whether, supposing a parent had reason to believe that a child was doing something that was wrong, and the evidence of it was in a book in his pocket, the parent would not, and rightly, think himself justified in demanding it, and if it were withheld, then (supposing the child under the age of an adult) taking it from him . . . (Fitzgerald v. Northcote).

Put more simply, if it would be reasonable for a child to be searched by his parent, then the teacher is within his legal rights. Whether or not it makes sense to put the teacher *in loco parentis* in securing the safety of the child in school, it does not make sense to pretend that a teacher making a personal search of every child in the class is the same thing as a parent searching his own child.

Searching children is an infringement of their personal liberty and ought to be subject to control in the same way that corporal punishment in schools is subject to regulations – those of the DES and of the particular LEA. Parents should urge their own LEAs to make regulations governing the conditions under which children may be searched in school. The following conditions are, we suggest, those in which it would be reasonable for a teacher to search a child:

(1) The teacher must have good grounds for suspecting that the particular pupil has what he is looking for. A Home Office circular to chief constables says that particular modes of dress and hair should never be regarded as reasonable grounds to search anyone. The same ought to apply in schools. In some third tier schools in the Wirral it used to be the practice to search only the 'secondary modern' stream pupils when anything was missing. The pupils in the academic stream went unmolested.

(2) That the issue is sufficiently grave. Suspicion of having hard drugs or a weapon is grave; suspicion of stealing a pencil sharpener or of having cigarettes is not. The difficult ones to deal with are 'lost' fountain pens and small sums of money, etc. – too valuable to be written off, too trivial to justify a search.

(3) That the procedures are not degrading or open to abuse. No pupil should be required even to turn out their pockets in public. No pupil should be searched by a teacher of the opposite sex. A third person should always be present when a teacher physically searches a pupil. The NUT legal department advises its members to avoid physical searches wherever possible. They suggest that while teachers may sometimes ask pupils to turn out their pockets, the teacher should not do the turning out.

If the conduct of a teacher was sufficiently arbitrary to be judged unreasonable in law, he would forfeit the protection of having

acted *in loco parentis* (since in law parents are always reasonable!).
He could then be found guilty of assault. There are few circumstances in which parents would want to go to these lengths. However, it is worthwhile writing to the school to ask for an explanation
and justification of a search.

Summer-born Children

Young couples are amused when the best advice offered to them
by older friends experienced in the ways of education is 'Be sure
to have your babies in the autumn.' It is sound advice. The rigid
administrative timetable according to which children move
through the state education system puts summer-born children at a
disadvantage throughout their school career.

Starting School

Legally a child is entitled to a school place at the beginning of the
term *after* his fifth birthday. But in most education authorities
children stand a good chance of a place at the beginning of the
term in which they have their fifth birthday. So children are usually
admitted to infant/first schools at the beginning of all three terms.
However, by the summer term, after two intakes, the reception
classes get full up and the last group – the children who will be five
during the summer term – often have to wait till September for a
place. The chance of a summer-born child getting a school place
for the term of his fifth birthday has been calculated at one in three,
whereas all the children with autumn birthdays and three quarters
of those with spring birthdays are likely to get a place for their
birthday term. The result of this type of admissions policy is that
autumn-born children go to school when they are four years and
nine months while summer-born children who start with them are
already nearly five and a half. The age of transfer to junior (or
middle) schools is usually fixed by the L E A. For instance, all those
who are seven years old by 1 September start the new school year in
the juniors. The child who started school while he was still four
will not have his seventh birthday until December and therefore

has another whole year in the infant school. The child who was five in May is already seven and has to move into the juniors after only two years in the infant school. (Somewhere in between will be those with spring birthdays who often get two years plus one or two terms in the infants.) Children who have just had their seventh birthdays are in the same class in the junior school as children who will be eight within a week or two. They are younger and consequently may well be less mature both physically and mentally, and they have had a whole year less of schooling. They are never given back that 'lost' year.

The consequences have been measured. Not only was it found that the potential ability of summer-born children, even when equal to that of older children, was constantly underestimated, but their actual achievement suffered. A literacy survey in London in 1971 showed a clear correlation between reading age and how long children had spent in infant school. A child who moves into the junior school unable to read may find that none of his new teachers had any initial training in the teaching of reading. Even where teachers are equipped to teach reading, a junior school with a separate head may well use an entirely different system. For a child in a muddle that may be the final straw. A child who has had a shorter time in the school than his classmates, as well as being younger than them, is at a marked disadvantage if he is then in competition with them for a place in the A stream. Evidence from the National Foundation for Educational Research demonstrated that where schools are streamed the younger children in any school year-group tend to be in the lower streams of both primary and secondary schools.

What can be done for summer-born children? A number of different proposals have been put forward to remove the bias against them. The problem would not arise were it not for the rigidity of the present system. Flexible schemes are needed which allow for less discrepancy in the age at which children start school in the first place and the age at which they move on to the next stage, so that the length of infant schooling is determined by the needs of the individual child and not the date of his birthday.

Suspension

The purpose of suspension is to provide a cooling-off period if a crisis has blown up with a pupil in school; the pupil remains on the school register but is 'excluded' from school temporarily. It ought therefore to be used constructively as an opportunity to resolve conflicts, not just as a punishment.

Following the practice of the majority of schools, the term 'suspension' is used here in the way it is used in the Articles of Government, to mean excluding a child from school temporarily because of his unacceptable behaviour. (See **Exclusion** and **Expulsion**.) Schools Regulations state that a pupil shall not be excluded from a school on other than reasonable grounds, and LEAs have an obligation to establish procedures which ensure that Schools Regulations are complied with. The LEA's own regulations may, for example, set a time limit on how long a suspension may last. For instance, Northumberland Education Authority state that a suspension must be ended within seven days unless the Director of Education has confirmed it. The LEA may set out the proper method of informing parents of their right of appeal, including details like giving them the name and address of the person to whom they should send their appeal. They may give guidance to heads as to when suspension is appropriate.

What, in practice, are the reasonable grounds on which pupils are suspended? These quotations from letters to parents explaining the circumstances in which headteachers suspended pupils tell their own story:

C has been closely associated with, and possibly responsible for, two fires in the school during the last fortnight.

G was involved in a fight in which he inflicted stab wounds on another pupil.

L attacked Miss G using a window pole with a steel fitting.

T has been particularly disruptive of other pupils' work . . . he wanders in and out of classrooms ... I have been unable to get from him an assurance that he will not disrupt lessons or that he will apologize to the members of staff whose lessons he has been sabotaging ...

It would be unreasonable NOT to remove pupils who are a potential danger to other pupils and staff or who are seriously disrupting the life and work of the school. However, not all suspensions are like this.

In March 1974 *The Times Educational Supplement* reported the case of a five-year-old boy who had already been suspended for six weeks. The episode began when a dinner lady told him to wash his hands and he refused. After having a row with his mother over this, the headteacher suspended the child on the grounds that 'when people gain a reputation such as she had got it could make my staff unwilling to have their child in class'. Is it reasonable to suspend a five-year-old from school because the staff do not like his mother?

At the other end of the age range, two boys of seventeen and eighteen, sufficiently respectable to be prefects at a grammar school, were suspended for playing a joke on April Fool's Day. One of them walked on to the platform at assembly in fancy dress and announced to the pupils and staff 'I have a special presentation for brightening up morning assemblies.' He then presented his friend with a light bulb. Unfortunately the headmaster did not share their sense of humour and, although they were working for their A levels, they were suspended for the rest of term. Few parents would concede that episodes like these provide 'reasonable grounds' for their children being excluded from school.

Who Can Suspend a Pupil?

The procedure for suspension is outlined in the Articles of Government of every school and they may differ from one authority to the next. But the majority of LEAs still conform to the Model Articles of Government which state that the headteacher 'shall have the power of suspending pupils from attendance for any cause which he considers adequate, but on suspending any pupil he shall forthwith report the case to the governors, who shall consult the LEA'. No other teacher has the authority to suspend a pupil. One or two LEAs require the headteacher to get the consent of the governors *before* he can suspend a pupil.

So the governors of the school must be involved in the suspensions procedure. What can they do? A handful of LEAs give parents a legal right of appeal to the governors against a suspension, written into the Articles of Government. When parents make an appeal, the governors must listen to the account of events leading to the suspension given by both the headteacher and the pupil and then decide whether or not the suspension should be confirmed. In that situation, it is quite clear that the legal power to suspend a pupil or to reverse a suspension lies with the governors. Not every suspension leads to an appeal: many authorities do not incorporate a formal right of appeal into the Articles of Government and parents who have this right of appeal do not always exercise it. The Model Articles give the governors 'general oversight of the conduct and curriculum of the school'. They could, therefore, claim that they had the right to investigate all suspensions reported to them by the head and pass judgement upon them. How likely they are to do this will partly depend on how fully they are kept informed of what is going on. One survey of heads found that proposed suspension was the most frequent reason for heads consulting the chairman of governors between meetings. A chairman who felt that an April Fool's Day joke was not a reasonable cause for suspending a pupil could bring pressure to bear on the head to allow the child back immediately and could, if necessary, call a special meeting to discuss the case. However, governors could not do this effectively in Leeds, for instance, where the Articles of Government state that the governors should be informed at the *next* governors' meeting, which could be more than three months away.

What Happens During a Suspension?

DES regulations have nothing to say about how long a suspension should last, but no child ought to be out of school, for whatever cause, for more than a few days without some arrangements being made for his education. If a pupil is *expelled* from a maintained school the LEA has to find a place for him at another school.

LEAs which ignore the fact that schools are suspending pupils for long periods are therefore evading the legal responsibilities which they would incur by expelling them. The device of leaving a child's name on the register while not allowing him into school does not amount to providing an education. LEAs which do this are, in effect, failing to discharge their duty under the 1944 Act, and they have a legal obligation to make provision for the care and education of the child who is suspended – for example, by arranging for home teaching. Too often there are no facilities at all for suspended children. One youth worker commented in the *Observer*:

Perhaps headteachers think the children will receive special help or attend a special school. They should be clearly told that such facilities don't exist and the kids end up on the streets all day. Their suspension may have made a teacher's life easier but it may have turned a discipline problem into a crime problem.

Code of Good Practice

Evidence collected from several LEAs suggests that the number of pupils suspended from secondary schools is increasing substantially every year. As a result a number of organizations have drawn up recommendations about suspension, which is, at best, a short-term expedient for coping with many intractable problems.

The following code of good practice is based partly on the policy paper on Suspensions produced by the National Association of Governors and Managers.

1. No child should be suspended for a first offence unless he is a danger to the school.

2. Parents should be consulted when problems begin to develop, before they have time to build up to a level at which suspension is thought to be necessary. This is done routinely in Sheffield, for instance, where an education official holds a meeting every Friday with educational psychologists and welfare workers to go through reports on difficult pupils. They encourage teachers to send in a report before trouble appears. They discuss the case and try and provide practical classroom advice. In Avon there is a graduated system for dealing with difficult pupils of which the first step is to

tell the parents about the trouble and ask for their support. If this does not work, heads may impose up to ten days suspension but they must then see the parents again.

3. In all other than emergency cases, if the head is considering suspending a pupil he should inform the parents and give them up to seven days to discuss the situation. A common practice is to do it the other way round and suspend the child first 'until parents come to see the head'. This has been described as a somewhat heavy-handed way of getting the family to come to the school and will be effective only if three conditions are guaranteed: that the parents receive the message; that the parents are prepared to come; that the head is available when they do come. Children can be out of school for months on end because at least one of these conditions is not fulfilled.

4. When a child has been suspended by the school, a formal procedure should be specified by which parents are informed and governors are consulted. For instance, since 1973 the following procedure has been spelt out in the Articles of Government of County schools in Liverpool:

> The headmaster shall also have power to suspend pupils from attendance for any cause which he considers adequate, but on suspending any pupil for a period exceeding three days he shall forthwith report the case to the Director who will convene a special meeting of the Governors to consider the suspension. The parents of the pupil shall be notified that they have a right to be heard by the Governors and shall be invited to the meeting of the Governors which is to consider the suspension.

5. It should be open to the pupil or his parents to bring a 'friend' to any proceedings to consider the suspension. A friend should be anyone the pupil or his parents wish to bring to help them present their case. This is absolutely essential because, although the governors may well have no legal qualifications, the hearing may resemble a legal trial, with evidence being produced on both sides and cross-examinations. One parent, herself a primary school teacher, described her appeal to the governors as 'just like an inquisition'. She was given permission to bring a friend to the hearing – but when the governors were told that he was the edu-

cation officer of the National Council for Civil Liberties, he was not allowed to take part.

6. Parents must be present when the head states his case so that they know what they have to answer. He will be there to hear the reply. However, whether or not the head is a member of the governing board he should withdraw while it reaches a decision. No one should act as 'prosecutor' and judge in the same case.

7. Any suspension should be for a limited period. If there is no set limit on the duration of the suspension the pupil is being made into a compulsory truant, while other truants are being chased back into school.

What Should Parents Do if Their Child is Suspended?

If the suspension is the first hint of trouble, parents should contact the school immediately for an appointment. However, if the school has talked the problem over and has warned them that suspension will be the next step, there is not much point in arguing, *provided proper procedures are carried out*.

1. If parents are given a verbal message about their child being suspended, they should write to the school immediately, with copies to the chairman of governors and the education officer, asking for full details of why the child is to be suspended, when he will be allowed back to school and any right of appeal.

2. It is important for parents to know if the Articles give them a formal right of appeal because it puts them in a stronger position. But whether or not this right is written into the Articles, they should make an appeal in the same way by writing to the chairman of governors immediately, stating that they want to appeal to the governors before the suspension is confirmed. On no account should parents set out their case in a letter, or they may receive a reply which says that their points have been considered, a decision has been reached and no further appeal is called for.

If a request for a proper hearing is turned down, the threat of publicity may embarrass the school and the authority, as long as the family does not mind the whole neighbourhood knowing what their child has been up to. A fifteen-year-old pupil was suspended from school for three months after he threw a dishcloth at a prefect who had ordered him to wipe the dining room tables. His cause was enthusiastically adopted by the victimization department of the National Union of School Students who protested in the press, wrote to MPs and councillors and held a demonstration. Two days after the demonstration the boy was readmitted to school. This could, of course, have been pure coincidence, but there was a slip-up in the Education Office and a letter intended for the head-master was sent to the boy's parents. They were most edified to read what the Education Officer had to say: '. . . I am anxious that he should be readmitted to the school without any further delay, but I would not wish this to happen in such a way as to give the impression that this was a result of the action which the National Union of School Students is attempting to take . . .' LEAs do not like to be exposed as acting contrary to 'natural justice' in their treatment of suspended pupils.

Parents have a right of appeal direct to the Secretary of State if they consider that their child has been suspended by the governors on other than reasonable grounds. This appeal would be made under Section 68 of the 1944 Education Act.

Teachers

'When children are asked what class they are in, they usually give their teacher's name in reply.' This observation from the Plowden Report highlights the crucial nature of the relationship between each child and his or her class teacher. In primary schools, most class teachers still spend the greater part of each day in their own class with the same group of children. But even in secondary schools, the class teacher, or tutor, will be the adult who has most immediate concern for the welfare of individual children.

Employment

HEADTEACHER

In county, controlled and special agreement schools the LEA employs and pays the salary of the head. Governors are normally consulted over appointments, but the extent to which they are actively involved varies widely. The arrangements are described in the Articles of Government. In aided schools the governing body alone appoints and employs the head, subject to confirmation of his educational qualifications by the LEA which pays his salary.

Only the LEA may dismiss the head of a county, controlled or special agreement school although the governors may take the initiative in recommending his dismissal. It may withhold consent to the dismissal of the head of an aided school.

ASSISTANT TEACHERS

In county, controlled and special agreement schools assistant teachers are appointed, employed and dismissed by the LEA. Interviewing of staff may be delegated to the governing body in consultation with the head and they then recommend to the LEA which candidate should be appointed.

In aided schools the LEA determines the number and pays the salaries of teachers but the governing body makes the appointments and employs them. The LEA may require or refuse the dismissal of a teacher (except teachers of denominational religious instruction). The Articles may give the LEA power to insist on certain educational qualifications for teachers of secular instruction and make their appointment subject to LEA approval. In spite of the 'conscience clauses' in the Education Act (Section 30), voluntary aided schools can in practice choose active church members for every job in the school if they can find enough of them.

In spite of the nice legal distinctions, whoever has control of appointments is, in practice, often ready to delegate the whole thing to the headteacher possibly with the help of the chairman of the governors.

Qualifications

The DES has regulations about teachers' qualifications which apply to every teacher in the country. In addition to any degree or diploma they may have in their own subject, teachers must also have a specific professional qualification in teaching. Where there is a serious shortage of teachers in particular subjects, as there has been in maths and science, this requirement may be waived. Student teachers are allowed to practise on real classes before they qualify, and instructors who have special skills may act as teachers if no qualified teachers are available. The Education Act allows LEAs to insist on special qualifications for teachers employed in their area. This does not apply to reserved teachers.

Supply

There is not a free market for teachers. The DES determines the number of qualified teachers by its control over the number of places available for teacher training. It can cut back on places but it cannot compel people to apply to fill them. The Schools Regulations 1959 allow the Secretary of State to allocate a quota of teachers to each LEA if it seems to be the best way of making sure that there is a 'fair distribution' among areas. The reasoning behind the quota is that it will force teachers to go where there are jobs. When the most congenial areas have filled their quota, teachers are expected to go to less immediately attractive districts. Since part-time teachers and married women returning to work as their families grow up are not able to move house to get a job, LEAs are allowed to recruit them without counting them towards their quota. Some LEAs are more energetic at this than others and can achieve a much better ratio of teachers to pupils than the quota alone would allow. The quota is a gentlemen's agreement which relies on good faith to operate effectively. In September 1973 when LEAs were panicking about all the extra children to be provided for because of the raising of the school-leaving age, sixty-six authorities in the North and the Midlands were reported to have exceeded their allotted quota of teachers. In spite of the fact that other areas, notably Greater London, were in critical difficulties in trying to fill staff vacancies and children were able to have only part-time schooling, the DES did not take any formal action to enforce its quota system. In 1974, when LEAs cut back on staffing to save money, the DES allowed class sizes to rise without insisting that LEAs recruit the minimum number of teachers allowed by their quota. So the LEA decides whether or not it will try to recruit its full quota and when it has decided the overall total of teachers to employ it tells each school how many it can have to complete its 'establishment'. (In April 1976 Mr Fred Mulley, the Education Secretary, announced that the quota would be discontinued because there was no longer a need for any rationing device.)

Salaries

Teachers' salaries have always been paid by the LEA, their employers. But their salary scale is negotiated and fixed nationally. The structure of teachers' salaries is settled by the Burnham committee, which is composed of an independent chairman and representatives of teachers, LEAs and the Secretary of State. Teachers start on a basic scale with annual increments and a step up to a higher scale post is worth a percentage salary increase. The school has a total pool of points which are allocated for scale posts. The total in the pool is calculated on the basis of the number of children in the school, with children in different age groups counting for a different number of units, but older children always counting for considerably more than younger ones. A school belongs to a group according to the total number of units it has. Senior teachers, deputy heads and heads are paid according to the group the school is in and can get a salary increase by moving. For instance, a large 11–16 school may be in a low group because it has no sixth form, but a smaller 11–18 school may be in a higher group because of all the extra units produced by the sixth form. So the pupils produce units; the units produce the group; the group produces the points. And it is at this last stage that the LEA can exercise its discretion: the number of points to be allocated to a school within a particular group is not fixed absolutely and the LEA can choose to allocate from the minimum to the maximum. This means that although they cannot choose to pay individual teachers a different salary from what they would earn on the same scale anywhere else, they can offer incentives to staff to go to a school by providing the school with more points to allocate to scale posts and, therefore, better promotion prospects. It has been recognized as a serious problem that teachers often have to move to another school in order to move onto a higher scale.

In 1974, the Houghton committee reported on teachers' pay

structure. A significant conclusion of the committee was that 'the salary levels we recommend justify expectation of professional standards of performance in return. As in other professions, these salary levels are in part recognition of the fact that the job cannot be compressed within a rigid structure of prescribed duties, hours or days.'

Dismissal

Teachers are notoriously secure in their jobs and general incompetence has never been a ground for dismissing them. The problem of how to prove incompetence has never been solved since the last attempt – the payment-by-results scheme in the nineteenth century – resulted in children being trained to jump through the hoops of the elementary school grades. When it comes to dismissing teachers, the voluntary aided school governors have no more power than the governors of any other type of school. The exception is a teacher who has been specifically employed to teach religious instruction as laid down by the original trust deed who can be dismissed by the governors alone. Only the LEA may dismiss any other teacher or headteacher. But as one Chief Education Officer is quoted as saying:

I have no doubt that every CEO can point to at least one head, and not only in the smallest schools, whose mismanagement teeters on the edge of public scandal. Unless the offender is a proven thief, pederast or goes indisputably mad, it is remarkably difficult – nay usually impossible – to relieve him of the burden of command. (British Educational Administration Society Conference)

It is legally possible to get rid of bad teachers, but the cumbersome procedure is so weighted in their favour that, with the additional protection afforded by their unions, LEAs have in practice found it almost impossible, unless a criminal offence is involved. The result has been, in the words of another Chief Education Officer, that 'teachers have nearly as much security of tenure as a parson . . .' It is hard when a child gets the dud teacher in primary school for a year. It is even harder when there is a dud head and all the children in the family each have him for six years. Dismissals are sufficiently rare to attract a vast amount of publicity, of a kind which is damaging to the school and the children in it and embarrassing to the authority. Often these cases are about unconventional, rather than incompetent, heads at odds with the powers that be.

The discussion on whether or not headteachers should have contracts to serve for a fixed number of years achieved sufficient currency to lead to a Private Member's Bill. It failed, but the discussion goes on. Whether or not a fixed contract system made any appreciable difference would depend on the tough-mindedness of the people who vetted the applications for renewing contracts which had run their course.

Transport

LEAs must provide free transport for taking children to and from school if they live more than the statutory distance away by the shortest possible route – even if that route is no more than a cart-track. For children under the age of eight the statutory distance is two miles; for children over eight it is three miles. The LEA has to make sure only that the transport is free, so it may provide a pass for the child to use on public transport, or run its own school bus service. It makes no difference whether the pupils are of compulsory school age or not in order to qualify for free transport.

The LEA's duty is to get the child to the nearest suitable school which has a vacancy, so if parents choose a school which is more than two or three miles away in preference to one round the corner, strictly speaking, they are not legally entitled to have free transport. Over and above their legal duty, under Section 55 of the Education Act, the authority has discretion to decide whether or not to help any other children with free passes or places on the school bus to get them to a suitable school. Transport is provided for handicapped children under this section. Some authorities use their discretionary powers to provide free travel for journeys to school where the walk would be particularly dangerous. But in 1954 the courts decided that LEAs were not obliged to take account of how dangerous it might be for a child to walk to school by the shortest route (Shaxted v. Ward).

As long as they are not on a public transport route, children who live on the route taken by the school bus may be allowed to pay for a seat on it if there are spare places, even if they do not qualify for a free place. Wherever you draw a boundary line, someone will live just the wrong side of it. Some children who go to school by bus may qualify for free travel while others who go from the same bus stop have to pay because their home is a few doors nearer to the school. As one witness told the DES working party on school transport (report published in 1973) 'It can be a very expensive hundred yards.'

If the LEA decides that the only suitable place for a child is at boarding school, they must pay the fares at the beginning and end of each term and official half-term holidays.

School Buses

Children often have a lot of hanging about at the beginning and end of the school day because of the timing of the school bus service. Teachers may be around for the first quarter of an hour or so, but parents ought to make sure that their children do not have a long wait outside in all weathers with no one to keep an eye on them. The LEA, not the individual teacher, is responsible for seeing they are properly looked after if they are waiting for an LEA bus. The LEA is responsible for the safety of children travelling on their own buses whether or not they are paying fares. They must make sure there is adequate supervision and can be sued for negligence if someone gets hurt because of lack of supervision. It seems likely that the courts would count buses hired from private contractors by the LEA as school buses.

The way in which schools are exempted from safety provisions thought essential for the general public extends to school buses. Because the passengers are not paying fares school buses are not 'public service vehicles' and do not have to conform to their rigorous standards for drivers and the maintenance of vehicles. So LEAs can buy somewhat questionable secondhand buses and hire drivers who do not have to have the training and experience necessary for work on public transport.

School transport cost £75 million in 1975. At that time about a quarter of the LEAs economized as much as they could by providing free transport only when they were obliged to by law. As transport costs increase more LEAs may be less generous with the free transport which they provide at their discretion. The DES working party on school transport, having considered all the problems created by the present system, came out with a proposal for a fundamental change in the law involving a maximum flat rate charge for anyone who did not want to walk to school. In October 1975 the DES started consultations with LEAs based on the working party's report. The DES accepted that there was no consensus about an acceptable alternative to the present scheme. Their aim was to go some way towards meeting the problems of both parents and authorities. In particular, it was hoped to find a way of providing 'equality of treatment' for all pupils regardless of age or where they lived. (See also **Grants for schoolchildren.**)

Truancy

Truancy is not a new problem. We all recognize Shakespeare's

> ... whining school-boy, with his satchell
> And shining morning face, creeping like snail
> Unwillingly to school.

Truants are children who are registered as pupils at a school but who are frequently absent. Different surveys produce different figures but it seems possible that at least 10 per cent of the school population is away from school without good reason on any day. The legal proceedings for dealing with truancy are summarized in Chart 1 in the section on **Attendance** (p. 28).

Who is Responsible for Detecting it and how?

Schools are supposed to keep records of attendance and to follow up any unexplained absences, whether a child is off school for a long period or very frequently misses some sessions with only flimsy explanations. This is one of the functions of the school register. Any determined truant understands this perfectly and will be sure to 'get a mark' before slipping over the wall. A pupil who constantly fails to register will be spotted by the staff and referred to the welfare service far sooner than one who evaporates between lessons. Some schools try to cope with this undetected truancy by asking the teacher of each lesson to take a register or by making spot checks.

Once the school becomes concerned about a truant they will contact the Education Welfare Service, one of whose functions is to carry out the work which used to be done by school attendance officers. (See **Welfare**.) The education welfare officer should then call on the family to find out what is wrong.

The traditional attitude of turning an indulgent blind eye to a likely lad 'playing hookey' on a sunny day still persists. But it is no longer a joke. One inquiry conducted by education welfare officers in Manchester investigated 77,000 cases of absence. In 40 per cent of these – 30,800 – the parents knew that their child was playing truant but had done nothing about it. The parents were, of course, legally as well as morally responsible since it is their legal duty to make sure that their child is educated. Everyone knows that you cannot take a six-foot fifteen-year-old by the hand and drag him to school, but this is no excuse in law.

The Police and Truancy

Truancy has reached such proportions in some areas that the Education Welfare Service are unable to cope. Although the police have no direct responsibility for seeing that children attend school, their help is occasionally enlisted by LEAs in, for example, carrying out a 'truancy sweep' in a specific area and returning all the truants to school. A child who is truanting is not, as such, committing any offence. But as a policeman from one Juvenile Bureau has said 'Truancy is the kindergarten of crime.' Some police divisions have reported as much as a 95 per cent drop in day-time crime following a truancy sweep. So any policeman is quite likely to take a child of school age back to school when he sees them loitering with or without intent.

The proper legal course is to take him home since it is his parents who are responsible for seeing that he goes to school. However, many parents will not object to the child being taken back to school, especially if they are out at work and there is no one at home.

Official Sanctions for Truancy

Whatever punishment the school may devise for truants, the law is concerned with the parents, not the children. Under Section 39 of the 1944 Education Act parents may be prosecuted in a magistrates court for failing to see that a child registered as a pupil at a school goes to that school regularly. Only the LEA can bring this kind of prosecution and the penalties rise from a nominal fine to a maximum of one month's imprisonment. Because truancy has come to be regarded as a symptom of trouble within the family, which fines and imprisonment can generally only make worse, it is nowadays much more likely that LEAs will bring care proceedings in a juvenile court under the Children and Young Persons Act 1969. In that case the LEA has to prove *both* that the child is a persistent truant *and* that he is in need of care and control that his parents cannot or will not provide. This 'care and control' test can usually be proved only by showing that strenuous efforts have already been made to get the child back to school. Only the hardcore cases reach the juvenile court. The chances are that the local Social Services Department will already have been informed about the family and the court always insists on their being consulted. The most probable outcome of the proceedings will be that a supervision order or a care order will be made giving the Social Services responsibility for the child and for making sure that he gets an education.

Theoretically, the Social Services Department can select the most suitable placement from a range of possibilities – from foster homes to community homes. In practice, many children subject to a care order are sent back to live in their own home, the only difference being that a social worker should be keeping an eye on them.

Both the schools and the Education Welfare Service have often been highly critical of the way in which this has worked out. One education welfare officer went so far as to suggest that the Education Department should prosecute the Social Services Department for failing in its responsibility *in loco parentis* to ensure that a child attends school regularly.

Commentary

Truancy is not a problem: it is a contagious disease and if allowed to take its course, will in the long term need even more drastic surgery. (Letter from three education welfare officers to the magazine *Social Services*, 17 August 1974.)

A great deal of time and money is at present being spent on diagnosing the patients suffering from this disease and in devising treatments for it. Unfortunately, treatment such as sanctuary units, alternative centres, educational psychology or child guidance clinics reaches only a small proportion of the whole.

David Reynolds did a survey of the contagious disease of truancy for the Medical Research Council's Epidemology Unit. This was reported in *The Times Educational Supplement*. He compared truancy rates over a period of seven years for nine similar schools whose pupils were made up from the same ability range and came from similar social backgrounds. He found that their rates of absenteeism varied widely and this could not be explained by differences in the amount of illness. 'Year after year it is the same schools which appear to be dealing well with truancy for girls as well as boys.' His conclusion was that 'To argue that because children do not want to go to school there must be something wrong with them and not with their schools is unconvincing.' This was endorsed by Professor Tizard, Research Professor of Child Development at the University of London Institute of Education. He wrote that those who are responsible for helping children with problems should look carefully at the routines of particular schools and at the classroom to discover if the environment there, where children are expected to spend such long periods of time, gave any clues as to what was causing stress to vulnerable children. David Reynolds offered a practical line of investigation: 'If some of our schools are preventing the development of these problems in the first place should they not tell the rest of the teaching profession how they are doing it?'

Tuck Shops

As far as sweets are concerned, schools seem to take the line 'If you can't beat 'em join 'em.' So many schools sell food during break times. In primary schools it may be just biscuits or apples; in secondary schools a more elaborate range of confectionery in a tuck shop. This private enterprise normally makes the same percentage profit as an ordinary shop and puts it into school funds. For instance, the funds of one secondary school benefited by £763·78 in one year from the profits made by the tuck shop. It would be entirely up to the headteacher whether or not there was a tuck shop in school.

Parents and dentists sometimes campaign for a policy of selling only fresh fruit, nuts and raisins, etc., in tuck shops. But schools believe that if they give up selling sweets altogether the profits will go to the corner shop instead.

One curse of parents who worry about tooth decay, overweight children and road safety are the ice-cream vans which haunt school gates. One secondary school head solved the danger problem at any rate by inviting a cooperative van driver to take up an exclusive pitch inside the playground of the school on payment of a contribution to the school fund.

Uniform

Pupils at a maintained school cannot legally be compelled to wear school uniform because the law recognizes a parent's natural right to choose their children's clothes: state schools may not infringe that right by imposing a compulsory uniform. But, when it comes to the point, the head can impose school uniform by making it a matter of school discipline, on the grounds that there is a close association between appearance and attitude and, if uniform was not compulsory, troublemakers would challenge the discipline of the school. When the head has ruled that uniform is necessary, he can refuse to allow into the school children who are not wearing uniform or whose appearance does not conform to the rules. Heads are not accountable to anyone to prove in what way blue socks in school, a blue shirt in the examination hall, or boys with long hair are prejudicial to discipline. The courts have ruled (Spiers v. Warrington Corporation, 1954) that 'sending a child to school dressed in such a way that it is known that admission will be refused as a matter of discipline, constitutes failure to attend school'. So parents can end up in court on the charge that they failed in a parent's statutory duty to see that his child gets a proper education. In fact, the NUT's *Handbook of School Administration* says:

In some instances an infringement of a reasonable school rule relating to dress may be more the fault of the parent than of the child. If it is, and as a result the child is suspended from, or denied entry to the school . . . . a prosecution of the parent under the appropriate sections of the Education Acts should be seriously considered . . .

This was why the parents of a fifteen-year-old Sunderland schoolgirl were fined £10 in December 1975. She had repeatedly been barred from school because she was wearing gold 'sleeper' rings in her ears.

However, parents can appeal to the DES if they feel that the school was acting unreasonably in excluding the child (Schools Regulations, 1959). The National Council for Civil Liberties appealed to the Secretary of State, Mrs Thatcher, on behalf of a ten-year-old boy who was suspended from a primary school in Worthing because his hair was too long. The acting borough education officer had written to the parents to say: 'I must ask you to arrange for David's hair to be shortened to the collar level indicated by the school as acceptable. If you feel unable to accept the school's ruling in this instance arrangements will be made for David to be transferred.' Although the DES specifically pointed out that each individual case was different their conclusion was that 'there can be no question of a boy being excluded from a particular school simply because he wears long hair.' An LEA can also take a strong line in the way that Staffordshire did in 1974. The authority sent out a circular saying that no child should be debarred from participating in school activities because its parents were unable to provide uniform. If an authority adheres to this policy and refuses to confirm suspensions of pupils or to prosecute parents in uniform cases, the schools would have difficulty in the rigid enforcement of a compulsory uniform. In February 1976 the *TES* reported that Staffordshire education department overruled a headteacher who twice sent home fifteen-year-old twin girls because they wore trousers in school during the cold weather.

Heads, pupils and parents may differ on school uniform. Those who are in favour say that it is a status symbol, a social equalizer, a boost to morale, a sign of loyalty to the school. Those who are against argue that schools destroy good relationships with pupils by forcing constant emotional confrontations over trivialities like the colour of their socks; that modern education preaches thinking for yourself, and learning to dress appropriately is part of that process; that uniform is often more expensive and less practical than ordinary clothes. Parents who disagree with the policy of their children's school should ask not for a personal preference, but for a democratic decision. The head of one north London school who personally preferred uniform sent a questionnaire to all pupils and parents suggesting a range of options: uniform for all pupils, for none, for all except the sixth form and so on. A substantial majority wanted uniform made optional for all pupils and the head accepted the verdict.

Schools find modern life a quicksand of moral dilemmas. It was 1974 when the headmistress of a Birmingham comprehensive asked a *TES* reporter, a woman, 'Well, would you visit a school wearing trousers?' and added that she and her staff had to 'walk a tightrope of public opinion'. Circumstances alter cases. Some schools found it did not prejudice discipline for children to wear warmer clothes such as tights or long trousers during a fuel crisis, but that discipline was threatened as soon as normal heating was resumed. A letter from a Surrey school tells parents 'girls may wear trousers *after* the half-term break in October/November and the whole of the spring term . . .' But can anyone seriously maintain the argument that trousers are prejudicial to discipline only in the summer?

There are two real issues: one is whether a question of personal liberty should be allowed to become identified with the very proper concern of the school for its internal discipline. In no other

Western country do schools feel that they can maintain discipline only by interfering in what pupils choose to wear. It is no doubt the persistent rebels who get sent home to change their socks. Why give them such an easy opportunity for making trouble? The other issue is that of democracy in schools. Once uniform is no longer seen as the manifestation of law and order, the decision whether or not to have it can be shared by the people who are expected to wear the uniform or to pay for it.

Voluntary Schools

When they send their daughter to Roedean, parents certainly know they have chosen an independent school. When they send their son to Droop Street School, parents certainly know they have chosen a council school – or, to give it its proper name, a county school. But what about All Saints, the local village school? On the one hand it is free; on the other hand parents are always being asked to contribute to the building fund. The library books come from the Education Office but the hymn books come from the church next door. The answer is that it is a voluntary school. Like a county school, it is fully maintained out of public money: all the staff salaries, equipment and upkeep of the interior of the building are paid for by the LEA. But in return for what it *does* pay for a voluntary school buys a good deal of independence.

Any parent who wants to query anything which is happening to the school itself or to a child in school must first find out whether it is a county or a voluntary school. It may make a difference as to whom they have to talk to and how they can appeal against any decision. Unless the Articles of Government for a voluntary school specifically state that it should be subject to LEA regulations these apply to county schools only. *The Parent's Schoolbook* always points out any difference in the procedures for county and voluntary schools.

There are three kinds of voluntary schools: controlled, aided and special agreement. The more they needed state money in order to bring their facilities up to the standards laid down by the Education Acts, the more control voluntary schools had to relinquish. *Con-*

trolled schools are those which became unable to raise the money needed to maintain or improve the school building. *Aided* schools are those which can manage to raise the proportion of funds needed for capital expenditure and maintenance. They often have an income from the foundation which first endowed them and from later bequests which enables them to pay their costs. *Special agreement* schools are a hybrid anomaly left over from an attempt made in 1936 to raise the standard of existing non-provided secondary schools. The proposals were overtaken first by the war and then by the provisions of the 1944 Act, but outstanding agreements were kept.

The biggest of these three categories is that of aided schools, which make up over half the total.

Because the Church of England is the established church, there are statutory Diocesan Education Committees for almost every diocese in England. They plan and organize the funds and resources available for the churches and church schools as a whole throughout the diocese. They have powers of supervision over the schools generally. They also promote religious education in co-operation with churches of other denominations within the LEA.

Other religions have their own committees and coordinating bodies. These religious organizations and their regional officers are all listed in the *Education Committees Year Book*.

Some changes of status are possible for schools in each of the voluntary categories. Any voluntary school can become a county school if the governors reach agreement with the LEA and the Secretary of State gives approval to the proposals. If the governors of aided or special agreement schools cannot fulfil their obligations as regards finance the aided status lapses and the school becomes a controlled school.

Why Does the State Support Voluntary Schools?

By 1870 the need for a national system of elementary education became overpowering, and voluntary effort alone could no longer cope. William Edward Forster found the formula which would do the trick: it was 'to complete the present voluntary system, to fill up gaps, sparing the public money where it can be done without,

procuring as much as we can the assistance of parents . . .' Seventy
years later R. A. Butler, too, was searching for a formula – one
which would meet the demand for a national system of secondary
education. The same pressures were at work : although the churches
and charities had already established a number of their own
schools, their resources were totally inadequate. So, for all the
differences in detail, the 'dual system' of county and voluntary
elementary schools – now to be called primary schools – established by the 1870 Act was extended by the 1944 Act to a dual
system of county and voluntary secondary schools.

Where Does the Money Come From?

The financial situation of the voluntary schools has been eased
progressively since 1944, although rising costs have brought their
own problems. They have now to pay 15 per cent of costs where
previously they had to find 50 per cent. To give some idea of the
commitment involved, the Westminster Archdiocesan Commission of the Catholic Church has to find an income of approxi-
mately £¾ million a year : not only to finance new schools and pay
interest on loans, but to repay the loans which have to be returned
over a set period. They are still financing and repaying loans from
earlier schemes where they had to pay a higher proportion. Voluntary schools have to rely on the unpredictable generosity of individuals to fund their percentage of the total cost, while county
schools have had access to the rates from the moment they were
established. Although voluntary schools are now fully maintained
by the LEA, they still inherit the legacy of poverty of provision.
Their buildings are often appallingly sub-standard.

Significantly, less than half the total of all voluntary schools
have controlled status, although controlled schools have complete
relief from all their financial liabilities while retaining the right to
give denominational religious instruction according to the terms of
the original foundation. A voluntary school can opt for controlled
status at any time. So it is clear that the voluntary schools put a
high value on the temporal independence given to them by aided
status.

It is considerably cheaper for an LEA to build a new voluntary school than a new county school. If it sets out to build a new county school it must find the capital from its own resources. If a voluntary body puts up a new school as part of the LEA building programme, not only does the voluntary body find 15 per cent from its own funds, but the grant of 85 per cent from public funds is paid direct by the Secretary of State. The LEA does not have to pay anything towards the school buildings. So, although the substantial cost of ancillary buildings has to be met by the LEA, it still gets a new school for its area at about half the capital cost of a new county school.

Who Can Tell the Voluntary Schools What to Do?

1. GOVERNORS

The independence enjoyed by voluntary aided and special agreement schools comes from two sources. Firstly the Articles of Government give the governing bodies of these schools wider powers than is the case with county or controlled schools. Secondly the foundation concerned appoints two thirds of the governors at each aided or special agreement school. This combination allows the foundation governors a powerful influence over the ethos of the school and will normally give them control over admission of pupils, appointment of staff and headteacher and the power of veto on plans for reorganizing the school in any way.

This is reinforced by the sort of people likely to be chosen as foundation governors to represent the trustees. In one convent, a girls' comprehensive school, there are eight foundation governors. One of these is the priest, one the Mother Superior of the convent to which the headmistress belongs and there are two other nuns from even higher in the hierarchy of the same Order. It is normal practice in a parish school for the priest or vicar to be elected as chairman of the governors. He is responsible for the pastoral care of the children, in the original sense of the word. He is intimately involved in the affairs of the school and has a positive function as an integral part of its life while even the most conscientious chairman of governors of a county school, a political appointee, must remain a visitor from outside however often he or she puts in an appearance.

2. INSPECTORS

The secular teaching in voluntary schools must be inspected by HMIs or LEA inspectors on the same basis as county schools. The foundation governors are responsible for the inspection of denominational religious instruction. The church authorities organize advisers to carry out this inspection. They act in a supervisory and advisory capacity in relation to church schools and 'they don't ignore academic standards'.

3. LOCAL AUTHORITIES

LEAs have an obligation under the 1944 Act, Section 8, 'to secure that there shall be available for their area sufficient schools . . . for all pupils . . .' The DES is not concerned about what kind of schools – voluntary or county – make up the total school provision. In accordance with the spirit of 1870, all that matters is that there should not be any gaps. This can cause difficulties. The University of Liverpool has published a report* which includes a description of the kind of planning problems faced by LEAs on Merseyside (before local government reorganization) in trying to meet the needs of the whole area in the face of non-cooperation from the voluntary schools:

> There is overcrowding in Catholic schools, while some county schools do not fill their quota . . . The Archdiocesan commission insists on Catholic children being educated in Catholic schools. The situation where county schools have 300 *places* too many and the Catholics 360 *pupils* too many, simply continues.

The fact that LEAs cannot tell the voluntary schools what to do in planning provision becomes a highly sensitive issue where the LEA wants to reorganize on comprehensive lines and the voluntary schools will not go along with this. In 1974 the government increased its contribution towards the building cost of voluntary schools to the present level of 85 per cent. This was in answer to their plea that they could not cooperate in comprehensive reorganization schemes because they could not afford the necessary buildings. They got their money with no strings attached. A num-

*M. H. Parkinson, *Politics of Urban Education*, University of Liverpool.

ber of them used the additional aid to adapt their buildings and become comprehensive; many of them have been able to claim their money while they continue to run an active campaign of opposition to LEA policy.

The ultimate weapon of the authority faced with recalcitrant voluntary schools is to cease to maintain them; that is to say, to stop paying all the staff salaries, supplying all the equipment, meeting all the running expenses and so on. They have to follow the procedure set out in Section 13 of the 1944 Act and the final say rests with the Secretary of State.

Welfare

The 1944 Act directed LEAs to take an interest in the welfare of the children whose education they provide. They have to enforce attendance at school, to provide medical inspections and treatment and to regulate the employment of schoolchildren. Nevertheless, the Plowden Report found it necessary to justify schools' more personal concern in the welfare of their pupils by the 'need to identify and help families with difficulties that lead to poor performance and behaviour in school'. Since Plowden, a whole range of confusing and sometimes conflicting agencies have become involved in the social and individual aspects of a child's school life. A persistent truant, for example, may be the concern of the education welfare officer, a local social worker from the Social Services Department, the Child Guidance Clinic, a voluntary social work agency such as the Family Service Unit or the Family Welfare Association and the police.

Education Welfare Service (EWS)

Most LEAs have some kind of Education Welfare Service. The first detailed report on the working of the Education Welfare Service, published in 1974, showed that the structure and organization of the service differed widely between LEAs. One of the main duties of education welfare officers (EWOs) has always been the enforcement of school attendance, but the title of 'school attendance officer' with its punitive associations has generally been dropped. Nowadays they see themselves as providing a link between the family and the education service as a whole, so as to help children in some kind of difficulty or hardship at school. In the words of one voluntary worker 'I have found them exceptionally ready to turn blind eyes and wangle things to help distressing cases, in marked contrast to social security officials.'

Education welfare officers seem to inhabit an uneasy realm somewhere between the social workers proper and the administrator who has access to services and can arrange to provide them. Only a small percentage of them have any social work training. Where the service is well organized, the EWO will have a whole range of functions related to the child's direct needs, such as free dinners and clothing grants, and to less easily identifiable problems relating to suspected family difficulties, moral welfare, including pregnancy, behaviour causing concern at school, suspensions and the possible need for special education. Any head or assistant teacher who has reason to suspect that a child needs help ought to be able to call on the EWO to try to find out exactly what the problem is and what can be done about it. Parents can find out whether they have a local EWS and how to contact it from the school or from the Education Office. They can often take the initiative and approach the EWO themselves if they want help.

In fact, even where the EWS is highly organized and generously staffed by average standards, the case load carried by each individual officer is often too heavy to allow him to carry out his functions properly. The case load in most LEAs is one EWO to 4,000 children. This leads to disillusionment with the service and angry frustration on the part of teachers who find it difficult to get help in time for children at risk. Their frustration may be increased by the fact that 50 per cent of headteachers in one survey refused to allow the assistant teachers directly concerned with the child to have any contact with the EWO.

Pastoral Care

The concept of pastoral care – the relationship of the teacher shepherd to his pupil flock – is another manifestation of the way in which schools have found it more and more important to try to cope with pupils' emotional difficulties in order to be able to educate them at all. Most large schools have developed a formal structure of responsibility for pastoral care, starting with the class tutor and developing through year or house head to the ultimate responsibility of the head for every aspect of school life. (See **Organization and structure.**) The extent to which staff members are given extensive responsibility for pastoral work combined with a very light teaching load varies from school to school. On the one hand, it is impossible to carry out the many administrative and pastoral responsibilities of a head of house properly if every problem is an interruption of someone's history lesson. On the other hand, the complete separation of 'pastoral' work from teaching in the classroom has been rejected as artificial.

Teacher/Social Worker

Some schools have tried to cope with the problems of liaison with outside agencies by the creation of a special post on the staff of the school which may be variously known as teacher/counsellor, education social worker, school counsellor, etc. Ideally, such a person would have teaching experience as well as social work training and would make sure that all the various agencies and individuals concerned with the welfare of a particular child are working in co-operation with one another and with full knowledge of what the others are doing. Even where the EWS is well organized, an EWO will be responsible for a number of schools in his district and cannot have the intimate knowledge of schools and pupils that is possible for someone permanently based in the school.

Counselling Service

Some secondary schools provide a more specialized individual counselling service for their pupils to help them with personal and work problems. LEAs may set up young peoples' advisory services to give help to adolescents outside the schools, or they may support with practical help voluntary organizations such as the Young Peoples' Counselling Centre. This was set up in Hampstead

to enable young people to come and discuss their problems –
whether about work, health, personal relations, contraception,
etc. – with sympathetic and qualified people. Others are being
established in other parts of the country and the local Citizens'
Advice Bureau should know if there is one in the area.

Welsh in Schools

The Welsh language is a distinguishing feature of education in
Wales which – though it is subject to the same statutory provisions
as education in England – is the responsibility of y Swyddfa Gym-
reig (the Welsh Office) in the primary and secondary sectors.
Almost every child at school in Wales will have some experience of
Welsh, whether he learns it as a second or modern language or
attends a school in which the ethos is Welsh and the Welsh language is the main medium both for teaching and for all school
administration. As a result, many monoglot English children
(those speaking only English) will be able to recite and sing in
Welsh while, at the other end of the scale, there will be children
who are genuinely bilingual.

A report, *The Welsh Language in Nursery Education*, published
by Cyngor yr Iaith Gymraeg (Council for the Welsh Language)
in 1975 claims that 'given vision and a pioneering spirit on the part
of Government and local authorities alike . . . Wales can be in the
forefront of the nations of the world in developing bilingualism in
education'. This policy is encouraged by a number of government
and other organizations, each with its own proposals and projects.
One example is the Schools Council project, Bilingual Education in
Anglicized Areas of Wales, in which infant and later junior schools
in some areas where pupils were monoglot English-speaking,
switched their medium of instruction for everyone to Welsh for
substantial parts of the day.

The Legal Situation

Secular instruction in schools is the responsibility of the LEA and
school governors in consultation with headteachers. The language

to be used as the medium of instruction in the schools is determined by the LEA as part of the general character of the school. Commenting on this in July 1971, the Secretary of State for Wales said 'This is as it should be, and on the teaching of Welsh in schools I do not propose to take any action that would restrict the freedom of LEAs in formulating bilingual policies which are in keeping with the linguistic characteristics of their areas.' In the same speech, he made a clear reference to Section 76 of the Education Act, saying that it was his firm belief 'that parents should be free to choose whether or not their children should learn Welsh in school provided this is compatible with the efficient organization of the curriculum and the avoidance of unreasonable public expenditure'.

The DES *Manual of Guidance* on choice of schools says that 'It would be reasonable for authorities so to organize their schools as to make it possible to meet a demand for instruction in either Welsh or English.' In other words, irrespective of the policy of their LEA, parents ought to have some say in the matter. According to the *Manual*, the wishes of parents who want a particular school because of the language used for instruction could 'properly be taken into account by authorities'. Nevertheless, the same limitations apply in this situation as in any other question about choice of school: if the kind of school place a parent wants does not exist in their area, they cannot be given it without unreasonable public expenditure. Especially in rural areas, there will often be only one school.

What Can Parents Do?

Parents who feel that the governors of the school or the LEA have made unreasonable arrangements for the teaching, or non-teaching, of Welsh can complain to the Secretary of State under Section 68. If every parent in a class objected to their child being taught in either English or Welsh or even to lessons in Welsh as a second language, it is probable that the authority would be acting unreasonably in the meaning of Section 68 if they persisted in making this compulsory.

Since the medium of instruction is part of the general educational character of a school, a change in this – even for a Schools Council project – would probably amount to the kind of 'significant change' which ought to be subject to a Section 13 notice and parents would have the right to submit objections to the Secretary of State. If an LEA does make a significant change in the general educational character of a school and fails to issue a Section 13 notice, the Secretary of State can direct the LEA to restore the *status quo* until proper procedures have been carried out by using his powers under Section 99. (See Appendix, p. 304.) After all, in the words of the Secretary of State for Wales, 'In the long run we cannot in a democratic society compel anyone to learn anything.'

Work Experience

Work experience for schoolchildren is not intended to be a series of visits to watch other people at work but rather a new dimension in the school curriculum which gives pupils an understanding, based on their own experience, of working life and of how the skills they are learning at school will be of use to them.

Although it is illegal for a child of compulsory school age to do paid work in school hours, work experience arranged or approved by the LEA as part of his education is allowed during the last year at school under the Education (Work Experience) Act 1973. A DES circular (7/74) sets out general guidelines as to how work experience projects should be planned and carried out. Pupils are not paid for taking part in the schemes although LEAs or employers may meet the cost of fares and meals. There should be insurance cover against accidents and certain kinds of employment are prohibited. The teacher in charge is responsible for seeing that proper arrangements are made for the safety and welfare of the pupils while they are at work. The firm will have the same responsibility for the safety of the pupils as they would have for their employees.

The NUT suggests that parents should always be consulted in advance when work experience schemes are being set up and that they should be given full details of the firm where the children will be working, the job to be done, the hours of work, the arrangements regarding travel, safety, welfare and insurance.

Since 1971, a voluntary organization, the Trident Trust, representing school, voluntary associations and industry, has been successfully organizing work experience schemes for schools in cooperation with LEAs in six different parts of the country.

Part Two

How to get things changed

Parents *Can* Do Something

In 1975 a polytechnic advertised a six-day course. Called 'Pressure groups and the educational organization', its aim was to help education officers to decide how much they should take the views of active pressure groups into account when they made decisions. So, however daunted parents feel at the immense power of the head and the apparently impenetrable bureaucracy of the LEA, it seems that they *can* have an influence on policy and practice.

Parents are always warned not to expect an immediate response, that although they will rarely have the satisfaction of seeing that justice is done, any complaint will create a lot of activity behind the scenes. Some true case histories show that it does sometimes work that way:

Case 1: A mother wrote to complain that her son was hit by the PE master in a secondary school which had officially abolished corporal punishment. The only visible response was a bland reply from the headmaster defending the teacher. But he had sent for the teacher and given both him and the head of department a 'rocket'. The mother heard all this from the teachers themselves when she met them at a local Christmas party. They gave a graphic description of the head saying 'It's always *your* department that gets the school into trouble with the parents.'

Case 2: A mother asked a primary school head to allow children to bring sandwiches for school dinner. He refused on the grounds that he would lose some of his dinner ladies if fewer school dinners were eaten. The mother sent copies of her letters to the education officer and he contacted the school and assured the head that the helpers depended on the number of children in school during the dinner hour irrespective of what they were eating. The head had to look for a new excuse.

Case 3: In her book *Policy-making in Secondary Education,** Rene

* Oxford University Press, 1973.

Saran described an education authority which was considering proposals to *reduce* by about 50 per cent the number of free places bought by the authority in private selective schools because there were vacant places in the authority's maintained schools. After three years of protracted discussions, the chairman of the education committee received a deputation from a Roman Catholic lobby whose schools were seriously affected by the proposed cuts. On the following day he asked his Chief Education Officer to investigate the implications of taking *additional* free places in the schools concerned instead of reducing them. One powerful lobby of constituents cut more ice with the councillor than all the facts and all the weighty arguments of his official advisers.

Starting at the Right Place

Before you can try to change anything you need to know who made it what it is in the first place and how and why. *The Parent's Schoolbook* has told you the legal framework within which decisions are made. This section of the book sets out to tell you about the people who make them. It is not enough to know where the legal responsibility lies – with the school, the LEA or the DES. You need to know how those machines operate if you want to put a spanner in the works.

This section describes the machines and gives some tips on the best way to wield the spanner.

When to Go it Alone and When to Look for Support

If a request is contrary to some general policy but parents want to plead a special case which will get a concession for their child, they must conduct the whole affair on their own. Allowing one child to have an extra year in the infant school shows that administrators are human after all. Faced with a general campaigning group of twenty or thirty parents all wanting a place at the 'wrong' school, the authority can concede only by abandoning a respectable policy.

If the aim is to get an official policy changed, then the more supporters a cause can muster the greater its chance of making an impression.

The Basis of the School's Power

Headteachers in Britain have more independence and freedom than in any other country in the world. Enterprising and creative headteachers are able to experiment and innovate, unhampered by a cumbersome process of official endorsement. But giving people freedom to choose how they do things means that they may choose to do them very badly or to let them go by default. So the official supervision which might have hampered an enlightened and eager head is lacking when it comes to restraining or chivvying a bad or incompetent one.

Where Does This Independence Come From?

In the first place, the Articles of Government of the school (see **Governors**) are likely to give the head control of 'the internal organization, management and discipline of the school'. However democratically he runs his school, he will have the last word on and has to bear the final responsibility for everything that happens there including the safety of all the children. Secondly, all teachers are regarded in common law as taking the place of the parent in relation to the child while the child is in school and having the same rights over the child as a parent would. This is the concept of *in loco parentis*. Thirdly, headteachers have virtually absolute security of tenure and while teachers, children, parents, councillors and even education officers come and go, the head can go on and on until retirement. Fourthly, the precise relationships between the headteacher, the LEA, the inspectorate and the governors have never been well defined. Most LEAs are far too large for the councillors who make the political decisions, or for the officers who carry them out, to know the schools well enough to see what is going on. Where a school has its own governing body, this vacuum should be filled. However, until recently it has not been common for schools to have their own governors and for any governors to take an active role in school affairs. By default, heads have been left to get on with it on their own.

In Loco Parentis

In 1865 Chief Justice Cockburn said 'a parent, when he places his child with a schoolmaster, delegates to him all his own authority, so far as it is necessary for the welfare of the child' (Fitzgerald v. Northcote). Court cases since then have made it clear that the teacher has to act as a 'wise', 'careful' and 'reasonable' parent would. A wise, careful and reasonable parent will be concerned about almost everything a child might do, and consequently the powers of teachers *in loco parentis* extend over almost all the child's activities in school. Parents have a right to expect that teachers will intervene to prevent a child from hurting himself whether or not he is breaking the law.

The sad irony is that the whole relationship of the school with the child – its duty to protect his safety, its authority to insist on good behaviour and to use any form of punishment for bad behaviour – is based on assumptions about what the law considers a parent would want for his child. It has nothing to do with what real parents want for their own children and may in fact be opposed to it. The most obvious example is corporal punishment; the law assumes that a reasonable parent will beat a naughty child. So whether or not the parents of a particular child have ever raised their hand to him, the teacher has the legal right to cane him. A parent may feel very strongly that adults, whatever their relationship with the child, ought not to make a physical search of children, except in dire circumstances. But it is not the parent's opinion that will count, however reasonable he may be. And if a court would rule that it was reasonable for a *parent* to search a child for stolen sweets, then the teacher is within his legal rights to do so.

The concept of *in loco parentis* reflected a Victorian view of the relationship between children and their parents. We would argue that it is no longer good enough to justify corporal or any other punishment in terms of what a reasonable parent might do. The school must be able to produce a justification related to the psychological effect of the punishment and to the fundamental right of protection against assault extended to everyone else in the community. Family relationships have changed since the court cases of the late nineteenth century embalmed the status of *in loco parentis*. It is time that the law recognized that relationships in schools have also moved on. Moreover, however conscientious teachers may be, the standard of care of a prudent parent is out of date and inadequate as a means of securing the safety of children in school. They need statutory protection, such as the Acts to protect people from hazards at work.

Who Can Tell the Head What to Do?

The headteacher is not above the law, even though the law is on his side. He has to accept the educational character of the school: if he is head of a grammar school and responsibility for admissions has been delegated to him, he cannot decide to start accepting children of all ranges of attainment. He must conform with DES regulations in so far as they affect schools. He is also subject to LEA regulations: for instance, if the authority makes a regulation stating that children in primary schools must not be caned, this limits his power over school discipline. He would have to justify ignoring recommendations from the DES, the LEA or the inspectorate. He has no legal right to take action on matters over which the governors have control according to the Articles of Government, although they may choose to delegate some of these matters to him or may habitually use their powers to rubber-stamp any actions he takes.

Education law and common law are based on the assumption that everyone should behave reasonably. Anyone who thinks the headteacher has behaved unreasonably and fails to enlist the support of the governors and/or the LEA can appeal to the Secretary of State to use his powers under Section 68 of the 1944 Education Act against them. (See Appendix.) Section 68 makes no mention of the headteacher. As an employee of the LEA (or of the governors of a voluntary school) he is their agent and they must accept responsibility if they condone or support any unreasonable actions he may take. This is why a complaint about the head must first be made to them, and why an appeal to the Secretary of State has to be made on the devious grounds that it was unreasonable of them to support the head's unreasonable actions. Since the Articles of Government give the head control over the day-to-day running of the school, the DES would hesitate to intervene however misguided or unreasonable a particular course of action taken by a headteacher appeared to be.

A cat may look at a king, and a number of people may talk to a headteacher. How much notice he takes of what they have to say is entirely up to him, irrespective of how prestigious they are or of how convincingly they argue their case. Whether or not he is going to take any notice, the head has to let some people have their say: the LEA, the governors and the inspectors.

There are others who have no legal claim but who may be difficult to ignore. The people who live in the streets surrounding the school, the shopkeepers near by, the conductors on the buses which serve the school can all apply their own sanctions which ensure that their view of the school is taken into account. So even though a head may run a school in his own style and plan a curriculum which reflects his own interests, a primary school head would not get away with a scheme by which none of his children had been taught to read. And a secondary school head who did not believe in exams could not send his sixth-formers into the world without any qualifications which would enable them to get a job or go on into further education. A head's freedom is curtailed by the need to see that his pupils have the right educational equipment when they leave his school and progress to the next stage.

Whatever a headteacher wants to do with a school, he has to have the support of the teachers. One head told research workers 'It's terribly tempting to expect members of staff to take on the general ethos of the school. But one also wants one's staff to be as individual in their approach as the children are in theirs ... I think that, fundamentally, a person can only teach in a style which he himself feels to be right for him.' The head may have the power to compel the staff to do things his way, but their reluctance may poison the teaching and in due course drive them away. Losing one or two dissidents and replacing them with teachers with the 'right' philosophy may help a new head to build the team he wants, but a mass exodus will disrupt the running of the school altogether. So one of the constraints on the headteacher is the need to carry his staff with him.

The difference that the goodwill of parents and pupils makes to a school is almost palpable; it can create more 'team spirit' than all the school uniforms and prize-givings put together. A head who has the emotional support of pupils and parents may convert them to changes which they would never have contemplated; a head who rides roughshod over their prejudices does so at his peril.

In spite of these constraints on his authority, the headteacher of a school is more of an absolute than a constitutional ruler. The same was true of the monarchy 300 years ago. Then kings claimed to sit on the throne by Divine Right and when parliament presumed to encroach upon the king's prerogative, Charles I – sounding like a headmaster confronted with a petition from the school council – abolished it for eleven years, complaining of the vipers who cast a mist of undutifulness over the sincerer and better part of the House. Now kings have learnt the hard way: they sign the Bills when parliament tells them to and the government writes their speeches for the state opening of parliament. An absolute ruler can be transformed into a constitutional one if the people concerned are sufficiently determined to hold them accountable.

Taking Things up with the School

What Sort of Thing to Take up with the School

How much a parent feels like telling the school will depend on what the school is like and on other factors such as whether a very young mother with her first child is talking to an experienced teacher, or an experienced mother with the youngest child of a large family is talking to a very young teacher in her first job. There are a number of problems (many of them discussed in Part One) which a teacher could help parents and children to understand and cope with provided they are handled with tact and sensitivity. In general, the best advice would be to nip any problem in the bud by discussing it with the school at an early stage.

However private parents feel their domestic problems are, they are not being fair to the school or to their child if they do not tell the school when parents split up or there is a bereavement or serious illness in the family circle. Where a brother or sister or other relative who lives with the family is handicapped or disabled, children who cope admirably at home may react when they get to school. Any class teacher ought to know if a child has this kind of stress to go home to.

Messages about medical and emotional problems do not always reach everyone who has dealings with the child. If a teacher or helper appears to be disregarding the sensitive area, assume it is by accident and approach them personally before taking further action.

Heads may become cynical about pleas of children being 'specially sensitive' since they may hear that story too often. But they should not ignore clear evidence of a child being unhappy – not wanting to come to school, stress symptoms like bed-wetting. They will certainly want to discuss it with the class teacher, who may not have noticed anything was wrong, before they decide how to deal with it.

There are heads who will refuse to listen to anything a parent has to say about how a child is getting on in school no matter how much evidence may be produced to show that the child is too distressed to benefit from his education. In that case, parents must decide whether it is worth enduring the rest of that year in the hope that things will sort themselves out or that next year's teacher will be more congenial. Parents could not appeal to anyone against the head's decision on this kind of question unless the circumstances were exceptional. In that case, as it is a professional matter, they should write to the local inspector.

How to Contact the School

Problems which affect only one child – refusing to do his homework, losing his raincoat, worrying about whether he has the right kind of sports kit, or something personal about family circumstances – are best taken to the class teacher. However the school is organized for lessons, a child's teacher or tutor is the person who takes the register.

Problems which involve other children or are a question of school policy will be the concern of a senior staff member. It is often quite clear if a worry concerns something which happens in the house or year group or is so general that the deputy or head needs to be involved. A question about a school subject would be dealt with by the particular teacher who takes the child's class for that subject or the head of the department.

If in doubt the best plan is to write to the headteacher briefly stating the problem so that he can make the necessary arrangements.

If the school has not told parents how to get in touch with teachers, the best procedure is to write a note asking for an appointment, explaining which times could be convenient. Teachers cannot leave a class of thirty children unattended while they go to the telephone, but parents can ask for a message to be given to them.

Parents who turn up without an appointment, even at the end of the day, cannot assume that the teacher will be free to stay behind after school.

You cannot do worse than rush up to school in a fury when something goes wrong. You may be left kicking your heels in the corridor until someone is free and, too upset to argue a rational or coherent case, in the heat of the moment you may say or do things which are damaging. The stronger the case, the more important this is; if you start off with right on your side it is madness to throw away the advantage. Everyone defends themselves when they are attacked and an aggressive antagonistic approach is the one least likely to succeed in getting a frank discussion about problems.

Although parents have a moral right to call in at school they are technically on LEA property while they are there and have no legal claim to stay on the premises whatsoever. So anyone who becomes aggressive or awkward, whatever the provocation, can certainly be made to leave.

Primary schools which put a high value on contacts with parents make special efforts to be available to talk to them when they take their children to school or collect them. One primary school head, for instance, moved the time of assembly to after morning break because he found that a lot of parents liked to pop in when they brought their children to school, before they went on to work. He knew that many of them would not be free to come back again later in the day and made sure he had time to talk first thing without having to worry about being late for assembly.

You can always write to the PTA or the school governors at the school but you should mark the letters personal and confidential. The Education Office will send letters on to the governors and is less likely to open them first.

Getting a Subject Aired in School

One way of getting any topic aired is to get it discussed at a public meeting. It is harder for those in authority to refuse to answer and gives you an opportunity to assess how much support you have from other people.

It is worth warning sympathizers in advance, so that they are prepared to steel themselves to support you. It is heartbreaking when you have a good cause which you know is privately supported by a considerable body of people and they all lose their nerve when it comes to 'standing up to be counted'. At one school in north London a head who had resisted requests for a parent–teacher organization for years took everyone by surprise by suddenly giving way and calling a meeting. He took the chair and from this vantage point he forcefully and persuasively explained to the assembled parents why a vote for a PTA would be a vote of 'no confidence' in the school. Most people were very happy with the education the school was giving their children. The group of parents who had worked for so many years to get a PTA with the conviction that all the parents were behind them now waited for their supporters to declare themselves. There was silence. Five years later there was still no parent–teacher association in that school.

Let us suppose that you and a group of other parents are concerned about school journeys. Ask the chairman or secretary in advance to put school journeys on the agenda of the next PTA meeting unless there is always some standard general item such as

'headmaster's report' on which you could hang your question. Do
not be put off by the fact that this opportunity has never previously
been taken to ask questions about school policy. However nervous
the PTA may be about overstepping the mark and moving away
from jumble sales, the head may welcome the chance to answer
questions he is constantly being asked and may turn out to be an
unexpected ally. At one PTA meeting every attempt to ask a question about the procedure for collecting dinner money, or what to
do about wet blazers was firmly ruled out of order by the Chairman – 'This is not the place to discuss that kind of thing.' But the
headmistress intervened to say 'Madam Chairman, if you have no
objection I should be quite happy to answer the questions.'

If you do not succeed in getting your topic onto the agenda raise
it under Any Other Business which is a standard item on every
agenda. This is not quite so satisfactory because everyone has
usually had enough by the tail end of the meeting and it may not
get the popular support it deserves. Never attack the school with a
question like 'Why does the school expect parents to pay £70 for
four days in Sorrento especially as none of those going learn
Italian?' A better approach is: 'Could the headteacher possibly
tell us something about the school's policy on school journeys,
their relationship to the curriculum and how children are selected
to go on them?'

This assumes that there is a convenient public meeting. A PTA
often welcomes suggestions for meetings if they do not look obviously controversial or critical and they could be asked to hold
one on school journeys.

If there seems to be no prospect of airing the subject at a meeting
at which you can personally be present, you may have to settle for a
meeting which discusses it in your absence, such as a meeting of the
PTA committee or the school governors. When you are not going
to be there to make the right points, having 'School journeys' on
the agenda will not be enough. So write to the clerk to the governors
or the secretary to the PTA and their respective chairmen setting
out your questions in the same neutral and general form and ask
for your letter to be discussed. Always send a copy of letters of this
kind to the parent governor if you have one. The governors are
probably the best bet because the clerk has to administer the com-

mittee according to formal rules and ought to report to the meeting on any correspondence he has received. The head does not have the authority to rule anything out of order at a governors' meeting, although a question can drag on for the best part of a year before he produces a satisfactory answer since governors normally meet only once each term. A parent-governor ought to be a great help in making sure that the matter does not lapse through oversight, inertia or diffidence on the part of the governing body.

Failure

So you have run the gamut of possible approaches to the school about a question which is wholly within their authority such as whether or not your thirteen-year-old is put into the stream which will be allowed to take O level. You have established how local and national policy impinges on the school's authority in this matter and to what extent the inspector is prepared to impose the LEA's publicly stated dislike of early streaming on a recalcitrant school. You have produced a doctor's certificate at an interview which showed that the child was suffering from hay fever during the test which settled which stream children would be put into. You have subsequently had a second try when you offered to arrange for extra help at home and have quoted research evidence showing that 12 per cent of children selected on this type of test were found on their subsequent performance to have been selected wrongly. The school is adamant. There is a point in parents' dealings with schools at which the only possible honest advice is that if you cannot tolerate what is happening you must try and find another school. Find a better new one and make sure of a place there before you do anything irrevocable about the old one. Legally, you could probably get your place back but it would be humiliating to have to ask.

Local Education Authorities

While other countries have had state schools, in Britain we have had 'council schools'. Our educational system has always been a local one and the 1944 Act confirmed LEAs as the main providers of the education service.

Since 1974 there have been 104 LEAs:

- 39 counties (old-style counties now called non-metropolitan counties);
- 8 new enlarged Welsh counties;
- 20 Greater London boroughs, in the outer London areas of the GLC;
- 1 ILEA – the 12 inner London boroughs and the City of London (the councillors elected to the GLC for these boroughs all sit on the Education Committee);
- 36 Metropolitan districts. These are sub-divisions of the 6 large Metropolitan counties: Greater Manchester, Merseyside, South Yorkshire, West Yorkshire, West Midlands, Tyne and Wear. Councillors are specifically elected to serve as district councillors and have responsibility for social services, libraries, housing, etc., as well as education.

One major preoccupation of the 1944 Act was to ensure that local initiative and expertise were fully exploited. The importance attached to this is shown in the elaborate provision for LEAs to establish Divisional Executives with wide powers over schools in their areas. Although the reorganization of 1974 generally increased the size of LEAs it put an end to Divisional Executives other than in an advisory or purely administrative capacity.

Education Committee

Every LEA must have an education committee to formulate their policy and to carry out their functions as local purveyors of education. The majority of members are elected councillors. (Being a councillor is still a part-time, unpaid job, and serving on the Education Committee is only one part of it. Most councillors have to serve on more than one council committee and have many other duties to carry out as councillors.) Representatives of local interests – churches, teachers' organizations, community groups and employers – may serve on the Education Committee. The majority party on the council will make sure that their party is in a majority on all committees and subcommittees so even co-options are usually done on a party political basis. It is provided by law that the minutes of the Education Committee must be open to inspection by any local elector.

The committee may appoint subcommittees to carry out functions on their behalf. A large authority will have separate subcommittees for schools, finance, staffing, buildings, further education, etc. In some authorities important decisions are taken by these subcommittees and endorsed formally later by the full Education Committee. A controversial decision, such as the ending of selection, will always be taken by the full committee, who might overturn the recommendations of the specialist subcommittee or substantially amend them. All Education Committee decisions are subject to the approval of the full council (except in the ILEA) which has been known to reject them. Subcommittee meetings do not have to be open to the public, although many authorities now allow this.

In any case, in both the Education Committee and subcommittees the majority party will have held a group meeting beforehand at which the party line will have been hammered out, and members instructed how to vote by the party whips. Needless to say, these meetings will not have been open to the public.

Caroline Benn has described how difficult it is for members to retain control of an education service the size of ILEA when so much committee time is taken up with the essential practical day-to-day problems of keeping the machine going at all. She wrote in *New Society*:

When so much time is spent responding to the administrators' prepared suggestions, little is left to talk about carrying into practice new decisions arising out of the political objectives for which members were all directly or indirectly elected.

Staff

Every LEA has to appoint a Chief Education Officer (sometimes called Director of Education, or, in Cornwall, a Secretary) as head of their administrative staff of local government officials. The 1944 Act gave the Secretary of State a power of veto over unsuitable appointments, to ensure that people with real educational knowledge and appropriate experience were appointed. This veto was withdrawn in the Local Government Reorganization Act of 1972. In 1974 only one woman was a Chief Education Officer.

Depending on the size of the authority the Chief Education Officer will be assisted by deputies and assistant education officers who would normally be in charge of different sections of the service. All senior staff will have had some kind of experience in teaching as well as in administration. Other staff will be local government officials who may stay permanently in the education service or may transfer to and from other departments in the course of their career.

Duties and Powers

It shall be the duty of the LEA for every area so far as its powers extend, to contribute towards the spiritual, moral, mental and physical development of the community by securing that efficient education shall be available to meet the needs of the population of the area. (Section 7 of the 1944 Act)

This gives the LEA very wide scope in providing not only schools and colleges, but also playing fields and swimming baths, play-centres and youth clubs, libraries and career services. In addition, they must make sure that there is adequate further education, whether for vocational or cultural and leisure needs.

In Part One we have set out in detail the various responsibilities of the LEA in the particular exercise of this general duty. There is, however, one very important distinction always to be kept in mind: the LEA has duties which it *must* perform, and powers which can be exercised according to its own discretion, limited only by the need for the Secretary of State's approval, or by DES regulations. This area of discretion is where the LEA has most influence on the quality of the local education service, and where, theoretically, it can best respond to the needs of the local population. But the converse of the freedom to use discretion as to what support services are to be provided or what grants are to be made is the freedom to do nothing at all.

Taking Things up with the LEA

What Sort of Things to Take up with the LEA

To find out whether the LEA is the right place to take something up, start by looking it up in Part One to see if it is their responsibility. There are different kinds of issues which would involve the LEA. For instance, the question may be about something which only the LEA has the authority to change, such as how the boundaries are drawn for a school's catchment area. Or you may want to persuade the LEA to act in a matter in which they have discretionary powers; the headteacher may have said that the parents cannot hold a jumble sale in the school hall one Saturday and you want the LEA to overrule him. You may want information about the LEA's performance on a recommendation made by the DES, such as the need to make sure that children having free school dinners are not publicly identified.

If you want to get an objective view of how the level of local provision compares with similar authorities look at the education statistics published annually by the Chartered Institute of Public Finance and Accountancy.* They are normally published early in the new year for the previous year. These give very detailed figures on every aspect of LEA provision from pupil–teacher ratios in each type of school to the number of dinners supplied per pupil day and the cost of each dinner divided into food and overheads. There are about ninety columns of figures for each authority, which sounds daunting but it is clearly set out and no one needs to be a statistician to gain valuable information from them about an LEA and how it compares with others.

How to Contact the LEA

You need to know the names and titles of the permanent officers employed in the relevant departments, their status and responsi-

* 1 Buckingham Gate, London SW1E 6HS.

bilities, and which councillors are on the Education Committee and its subcommittees, especially the chairman and leading opposition member of each one. The basic information is in the *Education Committees Year Book* or a similar publication, in your local reference library. Your own councillor should help you, but if he is elusive, the offices of local political parties should have lists of all council committee members.

It is a hard and time-consuming job to get on to the right person at the Education Offices, the County/Town/Shire Hall. You have to be prepared to tell your story all over again to the person on the end of six different extensions. But once you do get the right one be sure to ask for their correct name, the name of their department, and their telephone extension number. Always make it clear where you live before you launch into your story so that you don't waste time with the wrong divisional officer or the wrong councillor. Telephone calls have the particular disadvantage that you have no evidence to show that the conversation ever took place or that you really have asked them eight times for a reply to your request. So you may sometimes need to chase things up with a letter or postcard as well.

Local Ombudsman

The commissioner for local administration – the local ombudsman – can investigate complaints about maladministration on the part of LEAs. This does not include the actual teaching or curriculum of a school or its internal organization, management and discipline. Cases which can be taken up in the courts are normally excluded but it is possible to appeal both to the Secretary of State and the ombudsman about the same matter.

The ombudsman does not consider the rights and wrongs of a decision nor whether the authority was acting reasonably or unreasonably. He considers only the way in which the matter has been handled: arbitrariness or bias, neglect or delay, undue haste, incompetence, faulty systems. So the Secretary of State may find that an LEA has acted unreasonably but the ombudsman may find that there was no maladministration involved or, on the other hand, they may have acted reasonably but have proceeded in an improper way and incurred a charge of maladministration.

You may not address your complaint direct to the commissioner unless you can show that you have previously brought it to the attention of the authority and they have had a reasonable time to reply and have not removed your grievance. A pamphlet giving a full description of the powers of the local ombudsman and a form for submitting complaints should be available in any public library or from Citizens' Advice Bureaux.*

A summary of the work of the commission during its first year of operation issued in June 1975 showed that twenty-three complaints had been received about education out of a total of 473. Reports on two of these had been published and in both cases maladministration had been found. Unlike the Secretary of State, the ombudsman has no powers to direct LEAs to put things right, he can only require information about what action it proposes to take and, if necessary, make a further report. In practice, an adverse report can be as effective as a direction.

The Department of Education and Science

'Students of the 1944 Education Act can be in no doubt as to who is the senior partner in the educational system.' This is what Taylor and Saunders' *New Law of Education* has to say about the power of the DES.

The political head of the DES is the Secretary of State who is a senior member of the government with a seat in the Cabinet. Other MPs are assigned to the DES as Ministers of State and Parliamentary Under-Secretaries. A publication called *Her Majesty's Ministers and Senior Staff in Public Departments* (HMSO) can be assumed to be up to date unless there was a Cabinet reshuffle last week. This publication (or a comparable one with the same information) should be in any public reference library.

* It can also be obtained direct from: The Commission for Local Administration in England, 21 Queen Anne's Gate, London SW1H 9BU (tel: 01-930-3333); or, in Wales, The Commission for Local Administration in Wales, Portland House, 22 Newport Road, Cardiff CF21 DB (tel: 0222-371073).

From 1 April 1964 the Secretary of State for Education and Science has had the functions of both the former Minister of Education and the former Minister of Science and Technology. He has been responsible for all aspects of education in England in addition to other functions in the fields of science and art. The Secretary of State for Wales, who is also a member of the government, has the responsibility for all schools in Wales and these are administered from the Welsh Education Office. The Secretary of State for Scotland oversees the entire Scottish education system. Universities throughout Great Britain come within the sphere of the Secretary of State for Education and Science.

The Department is staffed by civil servants who are, of course, permanent and non-political; the title of the Head of the Department is the Permanent Under-Secretary of State. The Department has territorial teams who each deal with all matters relating to the LEAs in their territory as well as departments specializing in different aspects, such as special schools or the school meals service. Senior officials will have been in the Department longer than their political masters. Delay alone can solve problems for civil servants about policies they do not like; if they hang on, the government or the individual Secretary of State who wanted that policy may well go the way of all politicians, out of office altogether or moved on in a Cabinet reshuffle. It may not be sufficient for a Secretary of State to win a vote in the Cabinet or even in the House of Commons for him to be sure of getting his policy through – he has to win over the civil servants, if it is to be carried out energetically.

The Education Act of 1944 gives the Secretary of State the duty 'to promote the education of the people of England and Wales'. But the central government does not build, own or administer any schools or colleges; it does not employ any teachers; it does not say what the schools should teach (except that they must provide religious education). So the Department has the responsibility for the education system but it does not actually provide it – that is done by the local education authorities. Therefore, in the very first section of the 1944 Education Act, the Secretary of State is explicitly given the duty of taking active steps to ensure that LEAs effectively carry out the national educational policy of the government. Nevertheless, when questioned by a parents' group about the striking inequality of provision between one area and another, one Secretary of State replied: 'You want me to be a dictator.' In practice the DES imposes its policy in two ways: first of all through its control of resources: finance, buildings, teachers. (All of these are discussed in detail under their own heading in Part One.)

Regulations, Circulars, Administrative Memoranda

The other means used by the DES for controlling and directing the education service (in addition to Acts of Parliament) is the issuing of regulations, circulars and administrative memoranda.

Regulations issued by the DES have the force of law and are properly called Statutory Instruments. They normally lay down in detail the conditions which are necessary to fulfil a general clause in an Act of Parliament. For instance, Section 36 of the 1944 Education Act says that every child must have efficient full-time education; Schools Regulations 1959 explain how many hours of how many days schools must be open so that this can be possible. Copies of all Regulations can be bought from HMSO.

Circulars are statements of policy; for example, the well-known series of contradictory circulars issued by successive governments on the subject of comprehensive reorganization. Circular 10/65 was pro-comprehensive, issued by a Labour government; Circular 10/70 was in effect and intention anti-comprehensive and was issued by a Conservative government; Circular 4/74 was to all intents and purposes a reinstatement of 10/65. The last figures in these circulars give you the year in which they were published. Although they state DES policy they are not necessarily party political; Circular 3/71, for example, issued by a Conservative government on the subject of school meals was accepted as a policy statement by the following Labour administration.

Administrative memoranda give advice to LEAs. For instance, Section 61 of the 1944 Education Act says that education shall be free; an administrative memorandum was issued to give advice as to when it would be legal for schools to charge pupils for activities in school. Copies of circulars and administrative memoranda are available free of charge on request to the DES direct. DES List 10, published by HMSO, is an index of all current circulars and administrative memoranda.

Keeping Up to Date

The Appendix (p. 291) is a brief guide to the 1944 Education Act. Although there has been no major legislation since then, there has been a considerable volume of amendments, minor acts, regulations and circulars. To find out the up-to-date legal position the first step is to look it up in the latest edition of *The New Law of Education* by Taylor and Saunders. You can phone or write to the DES and ask the information department if there have been any changes which have not yet found their way into Taylor and Saunders.

For a day-to-day commentary on the national education scene, in addition to the daily papers, there are a number of specialist educational publications, of which *The Times Educational Supplement* (weekly) covers the widest general range of current topics and *Where* magazine (monthly) gives serious informative coverage of general educational issues. When you see from the daily or education press that there has been a debate relevant to your concerns you may want to see precisely who said what. Any good reference library subscribes to *Hansard*. You can always buy the particular issue of *Hansard* from an HMSO shop or their mail order service.

Reports and Inquiries

Under the 1944 Education Act the Secretary of State is required to have two Central Advisory Councils – one for England and the other for Wales – and an annual report of their activities is to be presented to Parliament. These councils could advise the Secretary of State on any matters connected with education theory and practice as they thought fit, as well as giving advice on matters referred to them by the Secretary of State. In the past, the Councils have been responsible for major contributions to educational thought. They have focused attention on areas with a need for more resources and new resources have been allocated to them as a result. The Crowther Report considered 'the education of boys and girls between fifteen and eighteen'; the Newsom Report considered 'the education between the ages of thirteen and sixteen of pupils of average and less than average ability'; the Plowden Report considered 'primary education in all its aspects'. Since Plowden reported in 1967 the activities of the Central Advisory Councils have been allowed to lapse. Nevertheless, there have continued to be official reports on aspects of education. Both the James committee on teacher education and training and the Russell committee on adult education were set up by the Secretary of State. The Robbins committee on higher education was set up by the Prime Minister of the day, Mr Harold Macmillan.

The Bullock committee of inquiry into language and reading gives some idea of the kind of procedures involved in producing a major report. The committee was appointed in June 1972 and published its report in February 1975. In the course of their inquiries they asked more than 2,000 schools to fill in detailed questionnaires. The report listed 332 conclusions and recommendations and seventeen principal recommendations. But anyone who thought they could take a short cut was warned that 'it would be altogether misleading to take these seventeen as a distillation of what we have to say'. Mr Prentice, the Education Secretary, said in his preface to the report that recommendations needing extra money would have to be shelved.

It is established practice for members of committees of inquiry to be appointed in a personal capacity and not as representatives of particular interests. However, they are usually people who are in touch with the views of those who are especially concerned with the field of the inquiry. Although committees send a specific invitation to submit evidence to certain organizations only, a general invitation is often published in the press. Whether or not you see such an invitation you may always write in to a committee of inquiry. Since the procedure favours the weighty evidence of large associations, an individual or small group writing in might find it helpful also to make contact with any members of the committee who are likely to take a sympathetic interest and ensure that significant points are not overlooked. Ask first if there is any briefing so that you can cover important points, in the right order (essential for a committee which may have to compare thousands of submissions) and not write too much. Any information about the membership of a committee or about the evidence can be obtained simply by writing to The Secretary, — Committee, at the appropriate government department.*

The question has been posed just how different might education have been if the reports had carried all before them? And the conclusion was reached by a writer who made a critical survey of the fate of the major educational reports† that

Effective as they may be in digging out facts and creating a climate for change, there are points at which they come up against political priorities – or ought to. Many of their recommendations imply political decisions . . . these reports have laid the foundations for reform even if others now have to finish the building.

Taking Things up with the DES

You might need to approach the DES in various situations. To take three examples:

1. To clarify the law or DES policy. You may want to reinforce a case by citing the official DES opinion. Or you may want to check that the justification produced by the opposition – 'It would never be allowed by the DES' – is strictly accurate. Camden CASE (Confederation for the Advancement of State Education) was told by the ILEA that as the school population fell, schools would have to be closed down. To admit only 180 pupils a year to a school built to take 240 pupils would be an uneconomic use of school buildings and the DES would never allow it. They decided to confirm this for themselves and a deputation went to see senior officials at the DES, who came up with a legal way of allowing a reduction in the number of pupils in a school.

2. Your aim may be to change the political policy of the government or to persuade them to give higher priority to a special need, such as further education for handicapped school-leavers. The

* Usually the DES, Elizabeth House, York Road, London SE1 7PH.

† Corbett, Anne, *Much To Do About Education*, 3rd edn, Council for Educational Advance, 1973.

campaign for nursery education has succeeded in enlisting the support of both Tory and Labour governments for giving national priority to programmes to increase nursery provision. One outstanding example of an attempt to influence government policy occurred in 1944: the Catholic lobby tried to deflect the government's policy proposal to reorganize existing all-age schools into separate establishments for primary and secondary age pupils, since they could never afford to do it without financial support from the government and that would mean giving up their independence and accepting aided status with some measure of control by the LEA. This was way removed from any local pressure group – it was lobbying at the very top levels. But the 1944 Education Act went through with this provision intact, although the lobby won a series of vital concessions for voluntary schools.

3. In spite of the independence given to LEAs to run their own education service and control their own educational policies, the law does allow people direct access to the Secretary of State as an ultimate appeal against the LEA or the school. All you need to do is write a letter to the Secretary of State. Your MP may be prepared to write on your behalf and to support your case.

The Ombudsman

The full title of the ombudsman is the Parliamentary Commissioner for Administration.* His job is to investigate complaints about maladministration on the part of government departments, including the Department of Education and Science and the Welsh Office. 'Maladministration' has never been given a precise legal definition but a likely case is a department dismissing a case cursorily or acting with such haste that proper procedures are skimped. On the other hand, it could also be a result of acting so slowly that a grievance is unnecessarily prolonged.

Complaints must always be referred to the ombudsman by an MP. Where he reports that maladministration has occurred the

* Information about the ombudsman can be obtained from: Office of the Parliamentary Commissioner for Administration, Church House, Great Smith Street, London SW1 P3 BW (tel: 01-212-6271).

assumption is that the injustice caused by it will normally be remedied. Where it appears that the injustice has not been or will not be remedied, the ombudsman may make a special report to Parliament on the case.

Useful Arts

Fact Finding

Whether you are persuading the head to let a child take O level history or undertaking a major campaign to change the education system, you must start with the facts. The facts must be above and beyond reproach in being full, accurate in every detail, and up-to-date to the last minute. Part One has given you enough information to take up most questions, together with the legal basis of who takes decisions about them. If you need more details and statistics to back up your case, always start by writing to ask for the information. But you may still end up having to do some research of your own.

Letters

Correspondence – the chosen weapon of civilized government, as Antony Jay called it – can be aimed at any target. You may simply want to ask for information, or to make a request or a complaint. On the other hand, you may be conducting a long-term campaign to get a new school building or to persuade your LEA, or even the government, to change its policy. Campaigns can be won or lost at the typewriter.

WHOM TO WRITE TO

Unless you know to whom to write, it is always proper to address letters to the person at the top, however trivial the question: the headteacher, the Chief Education Officer (or Director of Education), the Secretary of State. Address them by name in preference to writing 'Dear Sir'. This will not guarantee that they ever see the letter but entitles you to make the assumption that they have.

If you do not know the name you can always ring the school or the Town Hall and ask. It is worth doing that to check the precise spelling of the surname or the school if you have any doubts – people can be very sensitive about their name always being slightly wrong. It should be given to you without question but the worst that can happen is that they insist on knowing why you want it; you then say it is because you want to write to him.

Even when they take their child to school every morning parents are not always certain of the correct postal address or the phone number of the school. The school may be in the telephone directory under its own name, but some authorities list their schools under the entry for the education authority which may, in turn, be under the heading for the Council. There are authorities which refuse to have any entry at all in the telephone directory for their schools. The *Education Committees Year Book* gives all these details for secondary schools, but a phone call to the LEA to ask for the information ought to save you a trip to the reference library.

There is a list of useful addresses on pp. 307–8.

The reply to your letter may have the Chief Education Officer's or Secretary of State's name typed under the signature with 'pp' (short for *per pro*) before the name. This means 'on behalf of' and shows that it was not signed by him at all. It can be quite difficult to track down the person who is dealing with your correspondence, although the reference on the top of the letter will certainly tell the officials in the office who is responsible. If you want to ask a question or follow up a point in the correspondence with the person who wrote the letter, you will have to use this clue to track them down through the jungle of the Education Office.

WHAT TO SAY

Antony Jay* has described the function and standards for an effective campaigning correspondence:

A steady stream of sensible and critical letters that demand careful replies has a powerful softening-up effect. Officials will begin to realize

* *The Householder's Guide to Community Defence Against Bureaucratic Aggression*, Jonathan Cape, 1972.

that it is going to be a very tough campaign, giving them a lot of extra work and plenty of opportunities for slipping up or getting caught out. After all, they have plenty of work to do without answering tricky correspondence . . . The worst sort of letter, from your point of view, is one that takes you an hour to compose, and is answered in two minutes. Conversely, the letter that you can dash off quickly, and that keeps the official busy for a long time concocting the answer is what you are aiming for.

A letter from the Secretary of the North London Dyslexia Association to the ILEA written in June 1973 is a classic example of an effective campaigning letter:

On behalf of the Association, may I seek an assurance that immediate steps will be taken to ensure that all heads of primary and secondary schools are made aware of the Authority's provisions which are considered relevant to dyslexia, perhaps on the lines stated in the Education Committee Minutes of Wednesday, 14 March 1973, page 81? In addition, could some procedure be advised until such time as the Authority's full diagnostic and treatment service comes into operation? I very much hope any such procedure will not entail referral of dyslexic children to child guidance clinics, since the unsuitability of these clinics is indicated not only by the experience of our members but also by Professor Jack Tizard in the *London Educational Review*, Vol. 2, No. 2, Summer 1973.

COPIES

The judicious sending of copies of your letters to the right people may increase their effectiveness. Always list in the bottom left-hand corner the people to whom copies have been sent. A copy of all letters concerning the school can usefully be sent to the chairman of governors, the parent-governor and the secretary of the PTA. If you want them to do more than take note of it, you must attach a covering letter asking them to take some form of action, such as discussing it at their next meeting. Similarly, letters to the Chief Education Officer can always include a copy to the chairman of the committee concerned, your own councillor and any friends at court. If the letter is about the school, it is tactful and courteous to send a copy to the head. It may be helpful to send copies of any letters to the DES, to your MP, and to the party education spokesmen. The Chairman or Leader of the Education Authority and

Chief Education Officer should have copies of correspondence which affects them.

This all sounds like a war of attrition and may the most indefatigable letter writer win. In fact, any correspondence is likely to peter out from bureaucratic inertia – yours as well as theirs – when you run out of energy and impetus or into the school holidays.

That may be the time for a campaign to move on from correspondence behind the scenes to personal appearances in the form of individual interviews or deputations and demonstrations.

Interviews

Moral support can make any interview less of an ordeal. You do not need to mention in advance if both parents are going along to discuss a child's case. But if only one parent is going, it is a good idea to take a friend. You should mention this in advance and say who it will be. The parent-governor, PTA secretary or your local councillor may be prepared to act in the capacity of 'friend' when there is a really serious issue at stake.

Before any discussion starts, check on whom you are talking to. For example, you may have written to the head in the first place, but the school may think it is more appropriate for you to discuss your problem with the deputy head or head of house. The person conducting the interview may not have the courtesy to introduce himself or to explain if he is standing in for his superior. This is very disconcerting for anyone who assumes that he is talking to the person with whom he made the appointment, so ask unless you are quite certain that you have got the name and title right.

Make notes beforehand of the points you want to raise – it is only too easy to forget half of what you wanted to say until you are out in the street again. Take a notebook and something to write with into the interview and make a brief note of the answers to your queries.

To avoid misunderstandings afterwards about any agreement reached at a meeting in school or in the Education Office, it is a good idea to send a note confirming what was discussed. This can be phrased as a formal memorandum or an ordinary letter. Make the point that you will assume this is correct unless you hear to the contrary within a reasonable period of time – say three weeks. Keep copies of all letters.

Appeals

If you do not get anywhere at the first attempt, it is sometimes worth having a second try with the person who turned you down the first time. Set out the substance of your complaint and the reasons, with their authority, for your appeal, and any additional background information that you think would be helpful – such as medical history.

Whether or not there is an official formal appeals procedure against a decision, the chain of responsibility means that anyone who is a step up in the same hierarchy has the power to overrule a decision taken lower down. So, in theory, you need only to know how the particular hierarchy is constructed to know where to go next. For example, a head of department can overrule a teacher but can, in turn, be overruled by the head. Even the Chief Education Officer can be overruled by the Chairman of the Education Committee and the Secretary of State may overrule the lot of them. In practice, those in authority are more likely to support their subordinates than to overrule them on behalf of a parent.

The more you know the people involved, the friendlier you are with them and the more you want to stay that way, the more you may feel you could not face them on the same terms again if you have made an appeal over their heads. In that case, a general policy ruling from above, rather than an individual appeal, has a better chance of keeping the whole thing impersonal. So instead of asking the Education Officer to overrule the head's decision to suspend your primary school son because his hair is too long, you could write a friendly letter direct to the head referring to some higher authority, such as an LEA statement of policy or a DES circular if there is an appropriate one.

Pressure Groups

Most pressure groups aim to change policy either nationally or locally: they exert pressure so that the political machine is deflected from its path in order to make something happen or to stop something from happening. Any group which aims to influence events is functioning as a pressure group and is fulfilling a recognized role within the British constitution. The simplest issues are the easiest to put over to potential supporters: schools with outside lavatories, tiny playgrounds, no teachers, authorities which give more than their fair share of resources to children in selective schools.

There are guidelines which apply to almost any campaign from ending selection to rebuilding a secondary school with Victorian buildings on five different sites or getting a new climbing frame for the school playground.

1. Do not align the cause with any political party. They will use it to make political points against their opponents. This will make it very difficult for any sympathizers in the other party to support you. You need to be able to show that you have support in all sections of the community. It is, for instance, a great mistake to have a well-known party politician as your chairman because it will be difficult to convince his opponents that you are not a political organization. You also want to be free to criticize the policies of any party.

2. Discover the opposition's vulnerable spots. If you organize all your information into a chart or timetable it will be easier to spot hidden implications. For instance, if a change of plan is announced a few days after your timetable reveals that the chairman of the committee received a particular deputation, think hard about that deputation's influence. What kind of pressure was that lobby exerting?

3. Think carefully how you frame the issue in the light of this – make it hard for people *not* to feel sympathetic towards you. It is very much better to say 'Stop the eleven-plus' than 'Destroy the grammar schools.' If you can put your opponents into the position of having to say 'Of course I am in favour of comprehensive schools *in principle* . . .' (with the clear implication of 'not for *my* child'), it does rather weaken their position.

4. Find out what other groups are doing both locally and nationally and cooperate with them if possible. This may provide an

opportunity of using fair means as well as foul. One group can concentrate its efforts on charm and diplomacy, sending polite deputations to discuss the matter and gain what concessions it can in that way. Another group can raise hell in the press at the same time – both groups working to achieve the same ends.

5. Do not just be obstructive. Show that you have something constructive to suggest, or, better still, *do* something constructive. A number of CASE groups, as well as campaigning for better state education, have provided a useful service – for example, running holiday play schemes or publishing guides to holiday activities – creating goodwill and a respectable image which all helps when it comes to campaigning.

How to Set up a Pressure Group

Whatever abuse you are agitating about or cause you are propagating, you will inevitably form some sort of committee. But a committee is not a device for doing things: it is for deciding what should be done and who should do it. So be sure you know how to run it effectively.

Do not have a formal constitution if you can possibly avoid it. It will not make any difference at all except to create a new dimension of legalistic obstacles to add to all the real practical ones. One frustrated parent wrote to the chairman after a typical PTA annual general meeting: 'Last year we spent the whole evening amending the constitution. This year we spent the whole evening amending the amendments. Can we look forward to amending the amendments to the amendments in a year's time?' An active group of people which cares about what it is doing does not need a written constitution. Britain has kept going perfectly well without one for several hundred years.

How to Run a Committee

Informality sounds friendly, but without officers to do specific jobs or proper procedures for meetings, you will keep talking round in circles without reaching any conclusions and never know how to get decisions carried out at all.

Books have been written listing the desirable qualities which any chairman or secretary ought to have. Real life is not like that. Most small groups know only too well that it is difficult to find people prepared to undertake the work voluntarily and quite out of the question to subject them to any detailed scrutiny.

More committees at every level founder because of clashes of personality than on clashes of policy. If you really want the thing to succeed aim for a sense of humour and a policy of positive thinking. Keep your eye on the cause and remember that you are all working for the same thing and you cannot afford to lose any support.

In theory a society selects its committee at the annual general meeting (AGM) from among its members. The committee may invite people to join it during the year – this is known as being co-opted. Some societies select the committee and leave them to decide who should do what. Other societies vote for individuals at the AGM to fill the jobs of chairman, secretary, treasurer and so on.

Unless you have a very strict constitution which limits the number of committee members, do not be too hasty to hold elections as this will eliminate people who are willing to help. No local group can afford to lose the goodwill and support of a potential committee member. People sometimes have to resign during the year, others simply fade away, so you are unlikely to end up with too many people.

When you are launching a new campaign one individual has probably been the prime instigator. In small local groups it is sometimes difficult to know what to call the leader: the choice seems to be between 'honorary secretary' or 'chairman'. The driving force who motivates and organizes the committee, bearing the brunt of the work and the responsibilities, is unlikely to be the classic sort of impartial chairman at committee meetings. This may not matter in a small committee (unless he keeps on ruling out of order anyone who disagrees with him) but in a big public campaign, it may be best *not* to have him as chairman. Ask some helpful local public figure to do that. The leader can do all the real work as organizing secretary.

The one officer no committee can do without is a treasurer.

However little money is involved the treasurer must have an infallible system which is above suspicion and confusion. Any amateur book-keeper can avoid getting in a muddle by keeping a 'day-book'. This involves listing every transaction *separately* when it is made, even if he immediately hands over cash from the subscriptions to pay the printing bill. As long as the day-book really is kept up to date the accounts will add up right when he comes to give a financial report at each committee meeting and the annual accounts which must be presented to the AGM should hold no terrors.

It is a good idea to analyse the other functions which need carrying out by the committee and to allocate them to different members while everyone is feeling enthusiastic enough to volunteer for things. No two committees are the same but you probably need to find people for: membership; production of newsletter; circulation of newsletter; publicity; press officer; minutes secretary; keeping press cuttings and minutes, agendas of council meetings, etc.; liaison with other organizations. Do not just say 'Will you do publicity?' and leave whoever it is to get on with it. Make quite sure people are properly briefed and know exactly what is expected of them. They must have all the records and information necessary for the job when they take it on, not six months later when the person who did the job before gets around to handing it all over.

COMMITTEE MEETINGS

All committee meetings have the same basic structure whether they are a high-powered government body or a local voluntary group. School governing bodies all conform to the same pattern, with their own minor variations. Part of the art of being an effective committee member is understanding how the whole thing works so that you can raise your points at the right time and in the right form. Valuable contributions can be lost altogether by being ruled out of order and you can end up leaving the meeting without ever having discovered when it would have been correct to raise it.

All properly run meetings have an agenda which lists all the issues requiring a decision. Ideally, every committee member gets a copy in advance, together with any accounts and other working papers. Then everyone comes primed with the relevant information, ready to get down to business. If it really is beyond the secretary's resources to produce a copy for each member, it can be written on a large sheet and pinned up in the room where everyone can see it.

Formal matters are taken at the beginning. *'Apologies for absence'* is always the first item. It is thoroughly bad form *not* to send apologies if you cannot get to a meeting.

'The minutes of the previous meeting' are taken next. Good minutes are the key to an efficient committee. They should be a reliable source of reference – a record of all basic facts, such as who was present, decisions taken and reports given. It does not matter who said what; only the outcome needs to be recorded. A useful tip is to type out the minutes with a margin headed 'Action' in which the name of whoever is responsible for anything can be listed beside that item. The minutes are circulated as soon as possible after the meeting, then members have no excuse for forgetting what they said they would do and absentees can catch up with what went on. If this is done, it will not be necessary to read out the minutes at the next meeting. You can go straight on to *'Matters arising from the minutes'* – feedback from decisions made at the last meeting.

Items that need careful thought should be high on the agenda: there is a ratio between the amount of time left before the pubs close and the amount of time taken to reach a decision. Anyone may have to give a report. Do not give an action replay. Keep in mind what will be useful for future reference. For instance, if you are reporting on a meeting, was the hall comfortable, was the speaker a dreadful bore?

Technically, a *'motion'* is any subject under discussion by the committee. But it can be difficult to pinpoint an issue. So, however pompous the wording may sound, if you formally *'put the motion'* at least everyone knows what they are voting about. A motion becomes a *'resolution'* when the committee has resolved by a vote how to act on it. The only person to whom anyone should speak directly is the chairman. You should interrupt another speaker only to make a *'point of order'*, drawing attention to a transgression of committee rules, or a *'point of information'*, which must be strictly relevant to what the speaker is saying and cast some light on his subject matter. There are three formal procedures for cutting short a long boring discussion. You may move that whatever you are discussing is '*referred back*'. If this is passed it goes back to whoever it came from without more ado. You may move '*next business*' which would mean dropping the subject and going on to the next item on the agenda forthwith. You may move '*that the question be now put*' and if this is agreed a vote is taken on the issue without any further argument.

Every meeting concludes with '*any other business*', known in the trade as '*A O B*'. Members can raise then any matter not already covered. But if it is something important, ask in advance for it to be included on the agenda so that it is not skimped over by a committee who have already had enough.

Exerting Pressure

Lobbying is effective. Officers and politicians, however impassive their public face, care about vocal public opinion. So make your opinions as vocal as possible. Officers may begin to have doubts about any course of action which is going to cause endless trouble. Politicians may have doubts about a course of action which causes so much public criticism that it may lose them votes.

WHAT TO DO WHEN THE PUBLIC IS CONSULTED

You should subscribe to the agendas and minutes of the Education Committee and any subcommittees, if that is possible. Ask the press officer of the council if you can be included on the mailing list for receiving their press releases. Remember that press relations are part of the council's public relations – they put over policy in the most favourable way. Let them see you in the public gallery for important debates, even if all the decisions have really been made by the party groups before the meeting.

Much of the information which you collect in this way will be too late because it will be about decisions which have already been made. You need to know what is in the pipeline. Somewhere on the Education Committee there must be a sympathetic councillor or a councillor who is married to your treasurer's mother-in-law's cousin. They may be prepared to tell you the kind of approaches which are under consideration before a policy is formulated. It is up to you to build up a composite picture from the jigsaw of pieces of information that come your way. Councillors, teachers, parents, children, officers and educational theorists may each have one piece of the picture. They will know how the changes will affect their part of the system and their interests. When you have put all these pieces together you may have the only complete picture of how the thing will work out – it may be the only one, for instance, which includes how parents see the changes as affecting them and their families and, at the same time, how teachers see the changes as affecting them and their interests.

In the course of garnering these grains of information you may well uncover crops of discontent in unexpected places. Discontented people are often ready to spill the beans about what is going wrong. If you start off by asking for support for your campaign you may be met by a rebuff; if you simply ask them to tell you what they think about the policy and the way it is carried out you may gain valuable ammunition.

Effort spent in tracking down a friendly and acknowledged expert is an investment: one hour with him may save weeks in the reference library. And his word may carry considerable weight in impressing the authority that you have a serious case and really know what you are up to.

Make sure you have someone at every meeting on the proposals, whoever organizes it. The organizations calling the meeting will often be willing to let you come along even if it is not intended for the general public. In fact, try to go to any meeting addressed by the officers or councillors concerned with your issue whatever the subject. You may get a chance to ask a leading question. Let them find a member of your pressure group wherever they turn up – preferably standing by a table piled up with a supply of your leaflets and copies of your campaign manifesto.

Do not disrupt other people's meetings. If you are rude or objectionable to a speaker at a meeting, however strongly you feel that he is being less than honest or fair, it is counter-productive. With a really strong case it is unnecessary anyway. The main thing is to be omnipresent, so that on every occasion they have to try and find an answer to your case, whatever they thought they were coming to do. If you have distributed your publicity around, and you have presented a good case, other members of the audience will support you.

When you are at a meeting be very sensitive to any changes in emphasis or tiny details in the official line. Any subtle alteration in the way in which the topic is presented may give you a hint as to the way the official mind is working.

DEPUTATIONS AND DEMONSTRATIONS

Deputations are to show the strength of your case; demonstrations are to show the strength of your support. Before you arrange a deputation make sure you are going to meet the right person – the one who is the real power behind the policy you are campaigning against or is responsible for vetoing the policy you are campaigning for. In theory, you would ask for a deputation to be received by the politicians – the chairman of the council committee or the Secretary of State at the DES. But occasionally the officers are enforcing a policy in spite of the politicians. This is likely to be the case, for instance, when there have been continual changes of political control and the only person who has been there throughout is the Chief Education Officer. When your local information network has found this to be the case, try and meet the Chief Education Officer or the officer at the DES, as well as, if not instead of, the politicians.

When you write and ask them to receive a deputation, it is courteous to tell them how many people want to come. You may be asked to send in their names a week or so before the meeting. If at the same time you give a list of headings of the topics you want to raise they will have no excuse for pleading that they cannot discuss a point because they do not have the information to hand. You should not spell out your arguments. Deputations must be carefully planned beforehand so that everyone does their homework, knows the order in which topics will be raised, who will raise them and what to say when it is their turn.

A formal agreement or even a tentative move in your direction may merit a press release the same day. You must check this with the Press Officer of the DES or the LEA before you publish it so that they do not repudiate it afterwards.

Every pressure group will probably find it necessary to hold a public meeting or demonstration at some stage. This may be on any scale from a meeting in a local school hall to a parliamentary lobby. They serve many purposes: they aim to muster support for your cause or to demonstrate how much support your cause has; they set out to give information or to collect it; they may discuss the pros and cons of an issue, or may choose to present only the pros or only the cons. Decide which is your particular purpose and plan your strategy accordingly. A demonstration can have mass support and still be a total failure if no one thought out clearly what it was supposed to achieve.

Do some research to avoid competing with a really glamorous counter attraction. The London Schools Campaign had the misfortune to hold a parliamentary lobby which coincided with a picturesque farmers' lobby. Their supporters saw several interviews with indignant farmers in front of the House of Commons on the TV newsreels that evening and recognized their friends in the long queue of anonymous people filing past into the House which formed a silent background to the picture.

Demonstrations outside County Hall or the Houses of Parliament are best timed to coincide with a relevant debate. Although you are entitled to arrive unannounced at the Central Lobby of the House of Commons and send in the green card provided by the attendant asking to see your MP, it is much better to write in advance. It is no use sending down two coachloads from Newcastle to lobby Parliament only to find that all your local MPs are on a mission to Yugoslavia. With the LEA you have to choose the day even more carefully. Either there will be no one there at all or else you may find yourself lobbying a meeting of the subcommittee on the Sewage Works.

ALLIES

Your own councillor and MP have a moral obligation and a vested interest in helping constituents. Each political party in Parliament has an education spokesman and there are often smaller groups for special interests within the parties. To work the system most effectively you need the help of at least one of these inside groups or individuals so that you get all the procedure right and adopt the tactics most likely to succeed. A member of the majority party can do a great deal to promote your cause because he will have 'friends at court'. A Grimsby parents' group (which was totally non-political in its aims) had the active support of their Conservative MP in their efforts to get a new primary school during the time that there was a Conservative government in office. One letter from him started: 'I have had informal discussions with the minister in the corridor about the primary school re-building programme.' You cannot expect this sort of support if the basis of your campaign is an attack on the party which is in power. It is quite different if your council member or MP is on the Opposition side. As long as you can stop him from making political capital out of the issue, he can ask questions in Parliament or in the council, which, as well as eliciting information, are a particularly prestigious form of publicity.

When you are thinking about your likely sources of support remember to take every section of your community into account. For example, a small experimental free school was set up in Camden by some teaching students. They made a house-to-house appeal for funds in the immediate neighbourhood and angled this to appeal to local community feeling. A personal approach was made on their behalf to a number of wealthy left-wing actors and artists, worded to appeal to their liberal progressive sentiments. The local council was hooked by the welfare aspect (many of the pupils were from problem families); the education authority cooperated because the pupils had been chronic truants. And a whole spectrum of local organizations of all types forked out help in money or in kind when contacted on their particular wavelength. You need to make a list of all possible allies. These may be local organizations like the Parish Council or the Women's Institute or a group with a special educational interest such as a local Association for the Advancement of State Education (CASE) or a school PTA. Try and get a personal contact in each one who will make it their job to keep your campaign on their agenda. National organizations like the National Council for

Civil Liberties have files of case histories to draw on. You can find out about national organizations which might help from the *Education Committees Year Book*, which lists all 'parents' organizations' in one section and 'education and allied organizations' in another. No one is better informed on rights, responsibilities and duties than the NUT, and support from local teachers' associations could be invaluable.

PUBLICITY

Hardly any pressure group has enough members or supporters to influence the seat of a single borough councillor, let alone an MP. But the more publicity you get, the more voters will know what is happening.

Press. Every group needs someone to act as press officer to talk to the press and radio and television reporters and to issue press releases about your activities. This enables you to put the story over with *your* angle and it is surprising how often you will read your own statement in the press reproduced word for word as you wrote it. News stories should always be circulated to all the papers on the same day. For national news you can do this by telephoning the Press Association and dictating it to them. They will issue only stories they think sufficiently newsworthy so if you are in any doubt as to whether or not the PA is going to put out your story over their tape, call them back. You can always circulate all the papers yourself if they have decided that it does not warrant a release from them. It is often difficult to resist the temptation to go for a sensational story which will have a good chance of getting printed but this may do more harm than good to your cause; it is better to stick to the more complex and serious angle which reflects your real aims. Always remember to put a date on the press release; it is sometimes helpful to weekly papers, who tend to go to press two or three days before they appear, if you can send it out early but put an 'embargo date' on it as well as the date of issue. This means that no paper should print it before the given date. You can even name a time of day in your embargo and if the really influential paper in your area is an evening one, a noon embargo is more likely to get a story into the paper as it will not have appeared in the morning papers already. Find out the press days of any papers which are important to you. Local papers can be the main platform for a campaign. Always give the name of a 'contact' and a phone number on every press release. This will usually be your press officer but it should be someone who is going to be around and can answer questions without putting their foot in it too often. When you write your press release type it out double spaced so that it is easy for the editor to mark it up for type-setting and send it straight down. Put the most important points first – the easiest way to shorten anything is just to cut off the end. If you are aiming for the local papers remember that they like specific local details about personalities, with their full names, local schools and so on.

You should put yourself out to be helpful to the press, even if you are fuming from the way you were misrepresented the week before. Be careful what you say and how you say it but never refuse to talk to them if you want to rely on good coverage when you need it. Make sure someone looks after reporters at any meetings and saves them a place near the speakers, with a table to write on if you can manage it.

Television and Radio. Local television and radio are often desperate for good news stories with a strong human and local interest. Listen to the programmes to find where your campaign would fit in most naturally and get to know the names of the producer, research assistant and reporter working on it. You are never given as much time on the air as you think your cause deserves and you will never be asked just the question you particularly want to answer. Go prepared with an absolute maximum of three points which you can put over in less than a minute and which can be understood without elaboration or qualification. Do not get drawn into a major row just because your meeting or discussion is being filmed and you know it is pedestrian and boring. It is better not to be on the telly than to damage your reputation as responsible and reasonable people. Everyone knows that the press sometimes gets facts or angles wrong and you can sometimes get away with blaming your thoughtless remarks on to them, but if you are on the air, you will be condemned out of your own mouth.

Appendix

Parents' Guide to 'An Act to Reform the Law Relating to Education in England and Wales' 3 August 1944 (As Amended)

When the 1944 Education Act became law in August of that year, Sir Winston Churchill sent a telegram to R. A. Butler, the President of the Board of Education (later to become the Department of Education and Science), who had spent four years in its creation. The telegram read:

Pray accept my congratulations. You have added a notable Act to the Statute Book and won a lasting place in the history of British Education. Winston S. Churchill.

According to Butler's own account the Act was driven on to the statute book by two forces: idealism and expediency. Churchill appointed him to his post with the injunction to 'introduce a note of patriotism into the schools' and Butler himself presented the Bill to the Cabinet decorated with a quotation from Disraeli: 'Upon the education of the people of this country the fate of this country depends.' From the beginning Butler relates that 'Educational problems were thus seen as an essential part of the social problem ... Educationally after the war Britain had to be one nation and not two.'

But in quite a different tone he explains that

Another decisive argument in favour of an early Bill was that no other Minister on the home front had been able to bring his plans to fruition ... I was also encouraged by the Whips' Office ... for whom the beauty of the Bill was that it would keep the parliamentary troops thoroughly occupied; providing endless opportunity for debate, without any fear of breaking up the government.

For the first time every child in the country was guaranteed a free secondary education. The children of those who owe their secondary education to the Act are now completing their own school careers. Yet the raising of the school leaving age to sixteen came into effect only in 1973. Many of the ideals of 1944 have not been achieved, some have become irrelevant. Some parts of what was once a major educational advance have now, in spite of numerous minor amendments, become obstacles to further progress. The three major criteria for the kind of education a child ought to receive – his age, ability and aptitude – still legally limit what parents have a right to expect from the education system. But until the major new education act, so long anticipated and so endlessly discussed, finally emerges, education in England and Wales will be decided within the framework constructed by the 1944 Act.

The Education Act 1944

PART I CENTRAL ADMINISTRATION

Sections 1–3 *Powers and duties of the Secretary of State*
   (See the section on the Department of Education and Science, p. 266.)
Section 4 *Central Advisory Councils*
   (See the section on the Department of Education and Science, p. 269.)
Section 5 *Annual Report to Parliament*
   The Secretary of State's annual report to Parliament on the work of the DES is presented and published in the late spring of the following year. Each department within the DES contributes to the report. It can be bought from HMSO. Six volumes of statistics are also published annually covering every aspect of the educational service and these cost around £3 each from HMSO.

PART II THE STATUTORY SYSTEM OF EDUCATION

Section 6 Which categories of authorities were to act as LEAs.
   This was superseded by the 1972 Reorganization of Local Government which came into operation on 1 April 1974. (See **Local Education Authorities**, p. 260.)
Section 7 The public education system was to be organized in three progressive stages to be known as primary, secondary

and further. The Education Act 1964 made it possible for middle schools to be established which straddled the age limits specified in section 8 although they still have to be classified according to the categories laid down in Section 7.

This section also states that the purpose of the education system is 'the spiritual, moral, mental and physical development of the community' to which the LEA must contribute.

Section 8   This spells out the LEA's duty to provide enough school places for children of primary and secondary age (and defines what these ages are) and to make sure that children under five, handicapped children and those who need boarding education also have the school places they need.

Section 9   Definition of maintained schools covered by the Act: primary and secondary schools may be county or voluntary. The other categories are nursery schools and special schools.

Section 10   This gives the Secretary of State the power to lay down national standards for school premises and to make LEAs conform to them. But if the nature of the site, the shortage of suitable sites or the lack of money for new buildings makes it 'unreasonable' for the Secretary of State to enforce these standards, he can direct that sub-standard buildings and sites 'be deemed to conform to the prescribed standards'. The Regulations issued under this section are the 'Standards for School Premises Regulations 1972' (SI 2051 available from HMSO).

Sections 11–12   LEAs had to prepare a development plan which took account of the immediate and prospective needs for schools of their area. This was so that one of the main purposes of the Act – to replace the many decrepit old elementary schools – could be planned and carried out coherently. The Secretary of State could then decide which schools should be maintained by the LEA.

Section 13   Section 13 of the Education Act deals with the procedure to be followed when a maintained school is to be set up, closed down or significantly changed in character or size. The 1968 Education Act which amended Section 13 set out what constituted a 'change in the character of a school':

this was a change from voluntary to county or vice versa; from maintained to non-maintained; taking in pupils within a different age range; changing from a single sex to a co-educational school; altering the arrangements for admitting pupils according to their aptitude. According to Section 13, any proposals to change a school have to be submitted to the Secretary of State. The LEA submits proposals for county schools but only the governors can take the initiative in putting forward proposals affecting the position of voluntary schools.

After the proposals have been submitted to the Secretary of State the authority or the governors must publish public notices 'forthwith'. This is what is meant by Section 13 notices. There is a whole set of Regulations devoted to public notices about schools (SI 1968 No. 615). These make it clear that sticking a notice on a lamp-post will not do although notices are supposed to be posted in some conspicuous place or places in the area and at or near any main entrance to the school. They also have to be published in at least one local newspaper.

After the notices have been published a period of two months is laid down in the Act during which any ten or more local government electors or the governors of local voluntary schools or the LEA can submit objections to the proposals to the Secretary of State.

Section 13 has become very much more important since 1965 when the government made the first official move towards requiring LEAs to reorganize all their existing secondary schools on comprehensive lines. At that date there were 5,863 secondary schools and although some were already comprehensive several thousand Section 13 notices would have to be issued before a fully comprehensive school system would be established throughout the country. Section 13 has proved to be controversial on a number of counts and to be exceptionally vulnerable to political manipulation.

1. *The time limit.* This has not always been strictly observed. The two months specified in Section 13 has not prevented the Secretary of State from receiving written objections and

even deputations months after the 'limit', but objectors should not rely on this, particularly if their objections go against government policy.

2. *Objections*. Section 13 appears to allow only for *objections* to proposals and in accordance with normal planning practice no provision appears to be made for receiving expressions of support. In fact, people campaigning for comprehensive schools have often been warned *not* to write in to the Secretary of State after a Section 13 notice has been posted as all letters received were automatically included in the total number of objections. People who wanted to support the overall proposals but objected to a minor detail were worried in case their submission would be registered as a complete objection. When this was raised with the DES, the civil servants gave a verbal assurance that letters and petitions of support were distinguished from objections. So it is worth writing in to support any proposals you would like to see going through.

3. *How many objections*. It has become clear that any individual may send in comments on a Section 13 notice without necessarily having to find nine other people to sign the letter although it may be as well to conform to the letter of the law to avoid being overruled on a 'point of order'. It is entirely up to the Secretary of State whether weight is given to the sheer volume of objections regardless of the reasoning behind them or of the dubious means used to collect them. The National Education Association – a save the grammar schools pressure group – set up a streamlined procedure for collecting thousands of signatures for dozens of petitions at a time. A report in the *Teacher* at the end of 1973 quoted their activities in Birmingham alone: caravans were parked on street corners and each objector could, if he had the time and the patience, sign 112 different petitions. One Secretary of State may count a serious constructive well-argued letter – whether in support or an objection – as worth more than a million names written by people who had very little idea of the implications of the piece of paper thrust under their nose on a street corner. Another may use the 'evidence' of mass support to justify

overruling proposals which were the outcome of years of careful planning and endorsed by local elections.

4. *What the proposals are about.* Section 13 lays down a procedure for proposals affecting individual schools. But in the context of a scheme for reorganizing every secondary school in an area on comprehensive lines it becomes questionable whether or not proposals for individual schools make sense at all unless they are looked at as part of the whole scheme taking the other schools into account as well. For example, a school which has been taking pupils up to sixteen years may have a Section 13 proposal to change its character by taking them up to fourteen years only. It could not make sense to look at this proposal without considering at the same time the accompanying proposal for the school next door to take pupils from fourteen years upwards. Where Mrs Thatcher refused to look at schemes as a whole, insisting that the Act required each Section 13 proposal to be considered individually, she left LEAs in an impossible position. For instance, Harrow was 500 places short in its high schools and had too many places in its junior colleges. One legal opinion was 'that the department's refusal to consider reorganization schemes as a whole and to approve or modify them as such, and its insistence on dealing with overall proposals item by item, are not merely unconstructive but are positively destructive of education authorities' ability to administer their systems'.

5. *Implementation.* The approval of Section 13 proposals by the Secretary of State does not mean that the changes will necessarily be carried out; it means only that the LEA (or the 'persons concerned' where it is a voluntary school) can go ahead if they decide to (Clause 6). When they do decide to proceed they have first to submit detailed plans and specifications of the buildings to the Secretary of State. Anyone who is submitting plans and specifications in this way for a voluntary school must consult the LEA. It is only after approval has been given to the building plans that there is a duty 'to give effect to the proposals' (Clause 7). Trafford Association for the Advancement of State Education appealed to the Secretary of State under Section 68 on the

grounds that their LEA was acting unreasonably in failing to implement proposals for reorganizing secondary schools which had been approved more than a year earlier. The reply was that since Section 13 did not require proposals to be carried out until building proposals had been approved, the authority was not acting unreasonably within the terms of the Act.

Section 14   This section limited the power of the governors of voluntary schools to close the school down without adequate notice thus creating an unexpected shortage of school places. The Secretary of State can impose conditions on the way in which the premises of voluntary schools are disposed of after they are closed – for instance they might be converted by the LEA into a valuable village community centre.

Section 15   Describes the three different kinds of voluntary schools. (See **Voluntary schools.**)

Section 16   Arrangements for schools which move to new sites. (See **Buildings.**)

Sections 17–21   Governors and Managers. (See **Governors.**)

Section 22   Use of voluntary school buildings. (See **Buildings.**)

Section 23   The education (secular instruction) given in schools is to be under the control of the LEA unless the Articles of Government say otherwise. The governors control the education given in voluntary aided schools. This is the section which gives the LEA power to make regulations about such matters as suspensions, corporal punishment in schools and school hours and holidays.

Section 24   Teachers in county schools are employed by the LEA and can be dismissed only by them. In voluntary aided schools the LEA decide how many teachers the school should have, what their qualifications should be and when they should be dismissed. Any other matters are settled by the Articles of Government. Women teachers cannot be disqualified or dismissed simply because they are married.

Sections 25–9   These sections set out the arrangements for assembly and religious education. (See **Religion in Schools.**)

Section 30   The teachers' conscience clause states that any ordinary teacher can choose to opt out of assembly and RE classes without jeopardizing their career in any way. This protection is not extended to teachers in voluntary aided schools.

Sections 31–2   Provisions for enforcing the 1944 Act – no longer relevant.

Sections 33–4   Arrangements for special schools and ascertainment procedure for sending children to them. (See **Handicapped children.**)

Section 35   Compulsory school age. (See **Compulsory school age.**)

Section 36   '*Duty of parents to secure the education of their children* – It shall be the duty of the parent of every child of compulsory school age to cause him to receive efficient full-time education suitable to his age, ability and aptitude, either by regular attendance at school or otherwise.' (See **Attendance.**)

Sections 37–40   It is these sections which set out the procedures by which education is made compulsory.

Sections 41–2   Duty of the LEA to make sure that adequate further education facilities are available.

Sections 43–7   County colleges – these have never been established.

Section 48   Medical. (See **Health.**)

Section 49   Milk and meals. (See **Milk** and **School meals service.**)

Section 50   Board and lodging other than at boarding school. (See **Boarding education.**)

Section 51   Repealed.

Section 52   This section was amended by Section 5 of the 1948 Education (Miscellaneous Provisions) Act. The basic principle is that parents who can afford it may be compelled to pay all or part of the cost of board and lodging or clothing provided by the LEA. This does not apply where the LEA arranged for the board and lodging because there was no other way in which they could provide the pupil with an education suitable to his age, ability and aptitude.

Section 53   It is the duty of the LEA to make sure that there are adequate facilities in their area for recreation and social and physical training. One of the discretionary powers given to the LEA by this section is the ability to offer a whole range of help to voluntary societies and individuals, such as paying the costs of handicapped children who go on holidays provided by voluntary societies.

Section 54 Cleansing. (See **Health.**)

Section 55 Transport. (See **Transport.**)

Section 56 LEA's power to provide primary and secondary education otherwise than at school in extraordinary circumstances. This is the section under which LEAs set up Truancy Centres, non-school projects such as adventure playgrounds, day care centres and sanctuary units, immigrant language centres and so on. It is this section which covers arrangements for home and hospital teaching.

Section 57 This was the section under which some severely handicapped children used to be classified as 'ineducable'. It was repealed by the Education (Handicapped Children) Act 1970.

Sections 58–60 Employment of schoolchildren. (See **Employment of schoolchildren.**)

Section 61 Education provided in schools maintained by the local education authority is to be free.

Section 62 Duties of the Secretary of State as to the training of teachers.

Section 63 On the Secretary of State's direction school buildings may be exempt from building bye-laws but not from planning permission.

Section 64 Voluntary schools used to be exempted from paying rates by this section, which has now been repealed. The question of rates for both county and voluntary schools is now settled between the local authority which levies them and the education authority which is one of its own committees. The LEA is responsible for paying the rates of all maintained schools.

Section 65 This determined what should happen to funds from existing endowments of voluntary schools.

Section 66 This section has now lapsed. It allowed LEAs to help voluntary schools with liabilities incurred before the 1944 Education Act came into force.

Section 67 This gives the Secretary of State power to settle disputes as follows (unless there are other specific provisions in
the Act):

1. Between the LEA and the governors of a school, for
example, about powers and duties under the Act or concerned
with the Articles of Government.

2. Disputes between two LEAs about payments.

3. Questions about religious instruction in a school in
accordance with the Trust Deed.

4. Whether or not a change in a school is sufficient to
require a Section 13 notice.

Section 68 This section gives the Secretary of State the power to
intervene if the LEA or the governors of any maintained
school have acted or are proposing to act unreasonably. This
applies whether or not they had discretionary powers in the
matter involved. The Secretary of State can take action on
receiving a complaint 'or otherwise'. In reply to a parliamentary question asked on our behalf in May 1975, Mr Reg
Prentice, the Secretary of State, said: 'The most common
subject of complaint is a local education authority's un-
willingness to admit a child to a school of his parent's choice.
Very many complaints of this kind are settled to the com-
plainant's satisfaction without formal determination, but
most of the relatively few directions I give under Section 68
relate to such cases.' This section does not refer directly to the
headteacher. (See 'Who Can Tell the Head What to Do?',p.
253.)

Section 69 Medical Inspections. (See **Health**.)

PART III INDEPENDENT SCHOOLS

Section 70 Registration.
Sections 71–2 Complaints.
Section 73 Taking them off the register.
Section 74 Putting them back on again.
Section 75 Tribunals.

PART IV GENERAL

Section 76   Section 76 says that in the exercise and performance of
all powers and duties conferred and imposed on them by the
1944 Education Act, the Secretary of State and the LEAs
shall have regard to the general principle that, so far as is
compatible with the provision of efficient instruction and the
avoidance of unreasonable expenditure, pupils are to be
educated in accordance with the wishes of their parents.
Claims have been made that this entitles parents to a choice
of school, a choice of curriculum, a choice of which language
should be used as the medium of instruction, a right to
determine whether or not their child should have corporal
punishment, and even that it is this section of the Act which
requires schools to send school reports to parents about their
child's progress. In fact it does not appear ever to have
guaranteed parents any real rights or choices at all. Parents
who feel that the LEA has acted unreasonably in denying
them their choice of school should appeal to the Secretary of
State to use his power to intervene under Section 68.

Section 77   Inspections of schools. (See **Inspectors**.)

Section 78   Children who are receiving their education from the
LEA otherwise than in a school can have medical and dental
inspections from the School Health Service. The LEA may
make financial arrangements to provide milk and meals and
medical and dental treatment to children at independent
schools in their area.

Section 79   Repealed.

Section 80   All schools must keep a register giving particulars
of every pupil. Being a registered pupil of a school is legally
significant. (See **Suspension** and **Exclusion**.)

Sections 81–4   Power of LEAs to give assistance to pupils by
means of scholarships and otherwise; to conduct or assist
educational research; to organize or participate in educational conferences; to make grants to universities.

Section 85   LEAs permitted to accept gifts for educational purposes.

Section 86   Arrangements for solving some legal problems which made it difficult for church schools to participate fully in the state system of education.

Section 87   Repealed.

Section 88   LEAs must appoint a Chief Education Officer. The veto of the Secretary of State over what he considered unsuitable appointments is now repealed by the Local Government Act 1972.

Section 89   Repealed.

Section 90   Arrangements for compulsory purchase orders of land and other dealings in land by LEAs.

Section 91   Repealed by Local Government Act 1972.

Section 92   Every LEA shall give the Secretary of State any reports, returns or information he requires in order to carry out his functions.

Section 93   Power of Secretary of State to direct local inquiries into any matter connected with the Act.

Section 94   In order to ascertain a child's exact age, the LEA has the right to apply to the registrar for particulars of entries in the register of births and deaths.

Section 95   A provision which puts the onus of proof on the parent of a child claiming to be of a certain age as long as the LEA has tried all reasonable means to get evidence about the age of the child. Provision about the status of documents to be brought in evidence in court.

Section 96   Spent (i.e. no longer relevant).

Section 97   Post-war arrangements for local authority staff and teachers.

Section 98   Spent.

Section 99   If LEAs or governors fail to carry out their duties under the Act or any regulations arising from it or under the Articles of Government, the Secretary of State is given the power to intervene by this section of the Act. Such directions may be given 'as appear to the Minister to be expedient' to enforce the execution of their duty. This section of the Act also gives the Secretary of State the power to appoint governors if this has not been done and to allow the governors of a voluntary school to arrange for the maintenance of the school if the LEA fails to do this, the DES to reimburse them and

recover the money from the LEA as 'a debt due to the crown'.
The Secretary of State exercises his powers under this section
'either upon complaint by any person interested or otherwise'.

When private individuals are caught contravening a
regulation, such as causing an obstruction by parking a car
on a double yellow line, not only do they have to pay the
penalty, but the obstruction is physically removed by the car
being towed away. When an LEA fails to comply with the
regulations, in spite of the powers given to the Secretary of
State by Section 99, there may be no penalty and they will not
necessarily be obliged to put things right. For instance, in
June 1967 the Nottingham LEA refused to continue to serve
2,000 children with school dinners because they argued that
they did not have enough space. The Child Poverty Action
Group appealed to the Secretary of State to intervene using
his powers under Section 99. He declined to take any action
against the LEA on the grounds that 'there is no point in
using statutory powers if the physical conditions obtaining
make it impossible for an authority to comply'. In answer to
a parliamentary question asked on our behalf in May 1975
Mr Reg Prentice, as Secretary of State, said that he had never
made any directions under this section. Nor is there any
record of any other Secretary of State having done so.

Section 100   Grants from the Secretary of State to reimburse
LEAs and other persons for certain expenses incurred in
providing education services. This includes payments to
direct grant schools.

Section 101   Repealed.

Sections 102–5 Grants and loans to voluntary schools from the
Secretary of State.

Section 106   Superseded.

Section 107   Expenses of Ministers to be paid by the government.

Sections 108–10 Spent.

Section 111   The Secretary of State has power to revoke any
orders and directions he has made under the Act.

Section 112   Parliamentary check on Regulations issued under
the Act.

Section 113   Legal statement of what constitutes delivery of a notice, e.g. of an attendance order.

Section 114   Legal definition of the terms used in the Act.

Section 115   Spent.

Section 116   Exemptions from the Act for people of unsound mind and young people detained under a court order. Gives LEAs power to provide education for people in prison.

Section 117   Repealed.

Section 118   Reference to Scilly Isles.

Sections 119–22   Legal formalities.

Schedules are attached to the Act elaborating various aspects of sections of the Act, e.g. the constitution of conferences for setting up the agreed syllabus for religious education in county schools.

Address List

We have selected the addresses we thought you would find most useful.

Advisory Centre for Education, 32 Trumpington Street, Cambridge. Tel: Cambridge (0223) 51456

Confederation for the Advancement of State Education, 1 Windermere Avenue, Wembley, Middx. Tel: 01-904-1722

Campaign against Secret Records on Schoolchildren, 10 Argyle Road, Swanage, Dorset. Tel: Swanage (092-92) 2861

Campaign for Comprehensive Education, 17 Granard Avenue, London SW15. Tel: 01-788-5931

Child Poverty Action Group, 1 Macklin Street, London WC2. Tel: 01-242-3225

Children's Rights Workshop, 73 Balfour Street, London SE17. Tel: 01-703-7217

Department of Education and Science, Elizabeth House, York Road, London SE1. Tel: 01-928-9222

HMSO (mail order), PO Box 569, London SE1; (retail) 49 High Holborn, London WC1, and branches

National Association of Governors and Managers, Holbrook Centre, Holbrook Road, London E15

National Confederation of Parent Teacher Associations, 1 White Avenue, Gravesend, Kent. Tel: (0747) 606-18

National Council for Civil Liberties, 186 Kings Cross Road, London WC1. Tel: 01-278-4575

National Union of School Students, 3 Endsleigh Street, London WC1. Tel: 01-387-1277

Pre-school Playgroups Association, Alford House, Aveline Street, London SE11. Tel: 01-582-8871

Society of Teachers Opposed to Physical Punishment, 12 Lawn Road, London NW3

Welsh Education Office, 31 Cathedral Road, Cardiff. Tel: 0222-42661

Book List

This list does not include all the books we have used in our research. We have given here the titles we would recommend to parents who want to pursue the subject further.

Barrell, G. R., *Legal Cases for Teachers*, Methuen, 1970. The law in relation to education as demonstrated in nearly 150 court cases.

Barrell, G. R., *Teachers and the Law*, 4th edn, Methuen, 1975. A comprehensive guide to the education system from the teacher's viewpoint which does for teachers what we hope *The Parent's Schoolbook* will do for parents.

Benn, Caroline, and Simon, Brian, *Half Way There*, 2nd edn, Penguin Books, 1972. Survey and report on British comprehensive school organization and structure.

Burgess, Tyrrell, *A Guide to English Schools*, 3rd edn, Penguin Books, 1972. A guide to schools of all kinds – including private schools – together with an outline of the administration and structure of the education system.

Corbett, Anne, *Much To Do About Education*, 3rd edn, Council for Educational Advance (Hamilton House, Mabledon Place, London WC1H 9BD), 1973. A critical survey of the fate of the major educational reports.

Duncan, Ann, compiler, *Where to Look Things Up*, Advisory Centre for Education (32 Trumpington Street, Cambridge), 1974. An A–Z of the sources of information on all major educational topics.

Education Committees Year Book, Councils and Education Press (annual). We have referred to this reference book throughout the text. The thirty-six sections in the book cover every specialist and general interest in the field of education. It is worth trying it first whatever organization you are looking for from examining bodies to sports centres and parents' organizations. It is important to use the current edition.

Kogan, Maurice, and others, *County Hall*, Penguin Books, 1973. Conversations with three Chief Education Officers on their role.

Newell, Peter, ed., *A Last Resort?*, Penguin Books, 1972. The case and the evidence against corporal punishment in schools.

Pratt, John, and others, *Your Local Education*, Penguin Books, 1973. The local finance of education with detailed information of facilities and services provided by every LEA (this was compiled before the reorganization of local government).

Taylor, George, and Saunders, John Beecroft, *New Law of Education*, 7th edn, Butterworth, 1971. The present legal framework of the education system with the text of all relevant government documents and an authoritative commentary.

Index

Page numbers in bold type indicate a major discussion of a subject; page numbers in brackets indicate that the appropriate section of the Education Act 1944 is listed in the Appendix, but not discussed.

More about Penguins and Pelicans

Deschooling Society

Ivan D. Illich

Is schooling the same thing as education? Obviously not. We all learn day by day, and most of us, to be honest, can find little in our lives which schooling has directly and profoundly influenced. Two questions emerge. What is it then that has given schooling such enormous and widespread prestige in all societies throughout the world? And what is it that schooling actually does if its educational function is in doubt?

Ivan Illich argues in this eloquent and persuasive book that school has the prestige it does because it is one of the major means by which the status quo is preserved. It is not only inefficient in terms of education, but also profoundly divisive. *Deschooling Society* has already become a classic statement of a new and disturbing view of the school as an institution. It is amply possible to disagree with Illich; it is hardly possible to ignore him.

'His assault on the school . . . demands to be considered seriously' – Peter Jenkins in the *Guardian*

'*Deschooling Society* is one of the most genuine subversive books in that it amounts to a radical re-interpretation of social reality' – David Gow in the *Scotsman*

Celebration of Awareness

Ivan D. Illich

'I and many others, known and unknown to me, call upon you:

To celebrate our joint power to provide all human beings with the food, clothing and shelter they need to delight in living.

To discover, together with us, what we must do to use mankind's power to create the humanity, the dignity and the joyfulness of each one of us.

To be responsibly aware of your personal ability to express your true feelings and to gather us together in their expression.'

This 'call to celebration' begins the first essay in this book, and sets the keynote for a series of essays, each of which, in Illich's words, record 'an effort of mine to question the nature of some certainty'. Pre-eminent among such questionable certainties is the value of institutions: charitable foundations, the Church, schools – all are subject to a remarkably fresh and radical insight.

'A deeply stimulating thinker' – *The Times Literary Supplement*

'Illich has the power of intellect, personality and life example to command serious attention as a subversive' – Peter Jenkins in the *Guardian*

'Illich and Reimer have asked some of the profoundest questions about education today' – Ian Lister in *The Times Educational Supplement*

Some Books on Education Published in Penguins

Some Books on Education
Published in Penguins

Some Books on Education
Published in Penguins

Some Books on Education
Published in Penguins